Dodging Diagnosis

Surekha Kandi
Shriwastav

Copyright © Surekha Kandi Shriwastav 2024
All Rights Reserved.

ISBN 979-8-89363-356-6

This book has been published with all efforts taken to make the material error-free after the consent of the author. However, the author and the publisher do not assume and hereby disclaim any liability to any party for any loss, damage, or disruption caused by errors or omissions, whether such errors or omissions result from negligence, accident, or any other cause.

While every effort has been made to avoid any mistake or omission, this publication is being sold on the condition and understanding that neither the author nor the publishers or printers would be liable in any manner to any person by reason of any mistake or omission in this publication or for any action taken or omitted to be taken or advice rendered or accepted on the basis of this work. For any defect in printing or binding the publishers will be liable only to replace the defective copy by another copy of this work then available.

To all the warriors battling their own storms,
may this story find you and remind you of your
unwavering strength.

Contents

❖ Contents ❖

Foreword

MORE THAN A MEMOIR

As a longtime family friend, I have had the privilege of knowing Surekha Shriwastav and her husband, Raj, for many years. Through our shared experiences and conversations, I have been a witness to Surekha's extraordinary journey – one that is marked by resilience, courage, and an unwavering zest for life. Her battle against cancer and multiple health issues, spanning over three decades, is a testament to her unbreakable will and determination.

"Dodging Diagnosis" is more than just a memoir; it is a powerful tribute to the strength of the human spirit. Surekha's honest and heartfelt account of her experiences serves as a guiding light for anyone navigating life's toughest challenges. Through her words, she provides an intimate look into the physical, emotional, and social hurdles that come with a life-changing diagnosis, while emphasizing the importance of compassion, understanding, and unwavering support from loved ones. I am deeply grateful to Surekha for sharing her story with the world, and I know that her words will continue to inspire and empower others for generations to come.

– Agnelorajesh Athaide
Chairman, Global St. Angelo's Group of Companies

LIVING BEYOND DIAGNOSIS

The world throws us curveballs. Some are minor inconveniences, while others threaten to derail our entire lives. In Surekha Aunty's case she's faced a series of health challenges that could easily have stolen her spirit. Yet, within these pages, you'll discover a testament to the indomitable human spirit.

This book isn't just a story of illness and survival. It's a celebration of life, a chronicle of unwavering optimism in the face of adversity. You will be inspired by her courage, her resilience, and her zest for life.

Her story will resonate with you. It's a reminder that life is precious and that every moment is a gift. It's a call to embrace challenges with a smile and to never give up on our dreams.

I hope you'll find Surekha Aunty's story as inspiring as I have.

-The kid neighbour who grew up;

– Sumona Chakravarti

Leading Indian Actress

"Growing up, I had the wonderful opportunity to spend time with Aunty Surekha, Uncle Raj, and their daughter, Shona who has been a dear friend of mine.

Whenever our families got together, her laughter would fill the room, and her energy was infectious. Even as a teenager, I admired Aunty Surekha's warmth, kindness, and infectious zest for life.

When I first heard about Surekha aunty's cancer diagnosis, it was a moment that shifted my perspective. But what truly struck me was how Aunty Surekha faced it all. There was no stopping her spirit. She battled on, her humor and determination never faltering.

Reading "Dodging Diagnosis" has been an eye-opener. It's a story of incredible strength, resilience, and the unwavering human spirit. It's a story that will inspire you, just like Aunty Surekha has inspired me."

With admiration,

– Aneri Vajani
Leading Indian Actress

Preface

One year into happily-ever-after, life swerved sharply. A diagnosis - thyroid cancer - became a seismic tremor, shaking my future apart. Thus began a thirty-three years odyssey, an unwelcome dance with illness that became the rhythm of my being.

Even when my future hung in the balance every time, I was wheeled into the Operation Theatre, one thing I was absolutely certain about - Life with all its imperfections is still worth every ounce of effort we put in.

Of course, If given another chance, I would likely do many things differently. Yet, I would not change how I confronted the torment—cancer.

No matter how excruciating it got, I faced it head on, refusing to give up or give in. The path was long and solitary, punctuated by peaks and valleys, light and darkness. Painful days bled into dreadful nights, yet I carved my path forward.

Along the way, my paths crossed with fellow warriors, each battling life-threatening adversaries. Their stories intertwined with mine, sometimes taking center stage. It was then that a seed was sown: could my tale offer strength and hope? If so, then baring my soul in this book, however vulnerable, would be a victory song.

Consider this memoir a warm embrace, a steaming cup of hope for those weathering similar storms. Scars mark my journey, each telling a story of battles fought and won. Within these imprints lie tales of resilience, unwavering hope, and a spirit that refuses to be extinguished.

For all the warriors out there, battling a formidable foe day after day, here's me wishing the same spirit of survival. Step into this journey with me, and together lets sail through.

Oceans will always be marred by thunders and storms, but as long as you and I are breathing, our journeys will continue, towards horizon and hope.

CHAPTER ONE

Twist of Fate

July 5th, 1966

For India, in some way, it was an auspicious day. After all, on this day, The Beatles came to India for the very first time. They had been touring Asia and on their way back, they chose to stop by in India. Perhaps, their fascination with the Indian sitar and spirituality was what drove them to the country. They landed in New Delhi.

But our story doesn't take place in the country's capital which was taking away all the spotlight at that time. Rather west central, in Aurangabad, Maharashtra, a city that holds both ancient echoes and modern aspirations. History whispers in the majestic Ellora Caves and the imposing Daulatabad fort, while the city itself hums with industrial growth. It has an eclectic aura with bustling bazaars, serene gardens, and the warmth of its people, offering a glimpse into the vibrant heart of Maharashtra.

It was a Tuesday, which in Sanskrit means "Mangalavara", literally translating as the "auspicious day". I chose to make my grand entrance on this day. Ideally, it should have been a smooth ride, given the fact that my parents were no longer amateurs. I was neither the first, nor the second, not even the third.

My parents had been through the roller-coaster journey five times already. My siblings Vijaya, Amarnath, Sujata, Sunanda, and Shivnath had graced the planet before me already. I was the sixth one. So, there were never supposed to be any surprises. But when do things ever go as planned?

So, on the fateful day, after the arduous process of childbirth, my mother Rukmini Bai Kandi, fondly known as Amma, gradually regained consciousness. She was gingerly wheeled out of the operating theater, having undergone a Tubectomy surgery.

A nurse entered the room, cradling a baby boy in her arms. Her eyes radiated warmth as she delicately placed the child beside Amma, who somehow got an inkling of the cosmic error. She looked at the child hard and keen before she decided - "No! This can't be mine!".

Amma wanted to inform the staff that she had birthed a girl child and not a boy child. Thankfully, the Head Nurse who came in to check on Amma figured out the mix-up and immediately rectified it.

On the other end of the hospital ward, while Amma was being offered a boy child, another family received a girl child. If not for my mother's instinct and the Head Nurse's vigilance, I would have easily ended up in someone else's family's home.

But perhaps, my home was preordained. I was to belong to the Kandi clan. And then, that is where I ended up. With my rightful owners - my Amma and Anna.

From the hospital, I was brought into a quaint Hindu household and introduced to a myriad of relatives, including the five siblings and cousins.

I am not sure how big the gathering was, but I have often been told by my parents that it was a full-day event. If I were to picture that day from the stories that made rounds in the family circle, I would say I was like a packaged product being passed around on a conveyor belt for final quality inspection.

The elders made a ritualistic circle around my mother while I was arm-hopping from one elder to another. Some held me up, some turned me around, some patted on my back. After a thorough Quality Inspection, I received my blessings by each and every one of them.

Though I am often referred to as "Rekha", my real name is "Surekha," which in Sanskrit means "beautifully drawn line on the palm". Ironically so, even my name implied - "a long, beautiful life".

Nevertheless, My journey began being raised in a joint Hindu family, loved by elders, teased by siblings, and cherished by everyone. That was my life. Within the boundaries of my abode, I got to see a spectrum of human nature.

The roles were pretty much set in stone. There was one head of the family. Contrary to popular opinion, the Hindu family is not always patriarchal. The head of the family could either be a man or a woman. It's just the revered person in the family who everyone respects and listens to. It just so happened that in my family, it was my father, Hanumantrao Kandi, fondly referred to as Anna.

Amma, was more of our friend and companion, while Anna played the role of the family guardian. The elders divided the responsibilities amongst themselves so the young ones could have all the fun. Being busy with their respective chores, they had little time to pay attention to what the kids were doing. As with any joint-family, the elders were always more concerned with maintaining the relationships than anything else. Getting involved with kids' issues could escalate and strain relationships with the grown-ups. So we young ones were left to resolve our issues by ourselves. It didn't quite work in my favour at that time.

Growing up in a joint family could be daunting at times, especially for the youngest child in the family. The fact that I would have been taken away by some unknown couple amused my siblings so much that one way or the other, they would bring that topic up during all our family gatherings. And then teasing would continue for weeks after the event. You would think shedding tears would warm the hearts of my siblings, but let me tell you, siblings could be harsh that way. And the more I got upset, the more it continued.

So, frequent were the claims and so elaborate were the conjectures about my hospital switch, that it got to me eventually. There were times, when even I wondered if the switch indeed happened. Unfortunately, DNA fingerprinting was still twenty years in the future. So, I had no way to deduce my biological connection to the Kandi family. Thankfully, for me who was drowning in self-doubt, Mother Nature had thrown a lifeboat. Sunanda predates me by a span of four years in terms of our respective birthdates. Initially, our personalities were distinctly individualistic; however, as destiny unfolded, we gradually evolved to exhibit an uncanny resemblance in our physical appearances. And so identical did we appear, that outside of the Kandi family, everyone would get mistaken. Yet, Nature's hard evidence was disregarded by my siblings. And the teasing continued all the way to my teen years.

And just when my siblings started feeling that the joke was getting old, another incident started making rounds which soon became yet another "favourite of Kandi family topic" to spice up the gossip sessions during festive occasions and every other family gathering.

And that incident was when I was just 18 months old. Being part of a joint family, the house was never out of buzz. Amidst one such flurry of activity surrounding our move to a new Bungalow, the entire Kandi clan had gathered at the house. In the midst of packing and rearranging, a small handful of tablets slipped from the grasps of my unsuspecting uncle, and found its way into my tiny, inquisitive hands. I, of course, unwittingly consumed those forbidden pills. The repercussions were swift and alarming. Foam bubbled forth from my mouth, signaling the intrusion of an unwelcome medication not intended for my fragile frame. News spread faster in the Kandi family. Soon, everyone in the close-knit family received the emergency bulletin. Panic ensued, and with urgency, I was whisked away to the sterile confines of a hospital room. Come to think of it, Hospital and me were somehow connected by the invisible red thread of fate.

As the hours stretched into days, my restless form exhibited an otherworldly energy, fueled by potent side effects of those ill-fated tablets. Obviously, I survived and my siblings found a new topic.

At times, I would get mad at them, but those silly battles, the teasing, and cribbing, all later became the fondest memories of my childhood. However, I may have reacted then, today I know I wouldn't trade those moments for anything. Those are the perks of being raised in a joint family. You get to experience a wholesome life of love, bonding, and support with a regular dosage of hazing. Yet, I brisked through life without much delving. After all, for some people one wake-up call is just not enough.

Whether you are spiritual or scientific in your outlook, you can't ignore the fact that being born is never an ordinary event. It's the inexplicable phenomena of the universe that can only be experienced. Yet, somewhere down the line, we tend to take this gift for granted. Like a mother, life becomes a permanent entity that doesn't need to be acknowledged or appreciated. Like mothers, we do not expect Life to go anywhere. Until she does.

It took me twenty-five years to come to this realization. I was born in 1966 and diagnosed with Cancer in 1991. That's one quarter of a century. Twenty-five great years just passed by, before I took Life seriously.

In retrospect, it seems that this near to death encounter with mortality at such a tender age served as a curious prelude to a lifelong tango with doom. Death had taken notice of my early triumph, and in its enigmatic wisdom, it spent its time meticulously preparing for an aggressive second attack. Its presence, ever elusive, recently materialized in a formidable foe—Cancer.

Yes! My eye-opener came in the disguise of Cancer. It was my first tryst with Cancerous cells.

Even after my Cancer surgery, my doctor would make sure to warn me about the impending threat - "Don't think you are free yet! Relapse can happen any time in your life".

I was detected with Thyroid Cancer. Thereafter, during each breast lymph node surgery and hysterectomy and other multiple surgeries, my doctor used to send my tissues for biopsy to confirm if the unwanted tissue growth is benign or malignant.

Those days, I felt like a fugitive on the run with a head-strong Jailor on my tail, obsessed to grab hold of me and put me back in the jail. But I have had enough imprisonments. I would rather be free, even if it means, the rest of my life is spent on the run.

CHAPTER TWO

Tracing the Roots

Those who have witnessed my journey since the Grand Revelation, have fondly labeled me as "Cancer Warrior". Guess it's the thing with outlaws to have nicknames. In a way I do feel like an outlaw who has violated the laws of fate. I don't know about being a warrior, but as far as this run is going to last, I will be a fugitive of fate.

Though, I don't take much to the name, I can understand why it may seem so to those around me. To many it has even come as a surprise, as to how I managed to fight this battle for so long. It had been over thirty-three years now, but this resilience didn't crop up all of a sudden. The seeds were sown in my earlier days. I strongly believe, an individual is a precipitate of the care and upbringing one experiences at home. So, perhaps it would make sense to delve a little into my lineage - my parents to be precise.

As you know by now, the Kandi clan love to get together which often leads to story sessions. While I was the popular genre of stories among siblings, the elders however preferred a different genre. Their stories revolved around my parents. Surprisingly, while my stories were of the coming-of-age genre, my parents' stories belonged to a different genre. As our elders would call it, theirs was a "match-made-in-heaven".

It was a time before India's Independence. Then, my paternal family lived in Hingoli, a quaint town in the Marathwada region of Maharashtra.

My grandfather and his elder brother had traveled to Nizamabad near Hyderabad, where a known relative of ours used to stay. Grandfather and his brother were considering the family's daughter as a prospective bride for Anna. However, the bride's parents didn't feel comfortable about sending their daughter to such a far-off place.

Hingoli is about 200 kilometers from Nizamabad. Around that time, it took five hours to travel by bus or train and days by bullock cart. Given that traveling was no easy feat in those days, the bride's parents respectfully declined the offer.

My grandfather respected their decision but was disappointed given that he and his brother had to wait a long time till the next opportune time for travel. To kill time, they lingered around the neighbourhood.

A young girl was playing with her neighbourhood friends. While she went about her merry cheerful way, my grandfather who was observing her from a distance, was taken in by her attitude and inclusiveness.

So, after a quick discussion between brothers, both ended up at the door of the girl's house the next day. The girl's parents were welcoming. The elders had a serious discussion, and the girl's fate was sealed. She was to become my Amma.

Anna was just 15 years old and Amma was 11 years old when they got married. However, Anna and Amma didn't get to stay together for too long. Anna, who was a brilliant student, was still pursuing his education. He had to leave for Hyderabad to pursue higher studies in Osmania University.

My great-uncle gave him whatever money he could manage, which was not enough at that time. Anna couldn't afford hostel accommodation. So, he had to stay at a distant relative's place. That meant, Amma had to stay behind with my paternal grandparents.

Away from home, Anna's path was far from easy, as he relied on the meager allowance. He would travel without a ticket in trains and walk twenty kilometers to reach the university, many times, barefoot. Yet, Anna never gave up on his dream. His journey stands as a testament to his sheer determination and resilience. A trailblazer in our family, he became the first to venture beyond the confines of our city, seeking education and becoming the first Engineer in the family.

On the other hand, Amma was fighting her own battle. She was hardly old enough to understand life when she got married. My great-aunt taught her everything. And soon, my Amma was busy running the household with her co-sisters, and enjoying their company. She would go to the Kayadhu river walking over two kilometers with heavy loads of clothes to wash them, fetch water from the well, and after all that, cook a meal for the great Indian joint family.

Anna believed in self-care and led by example, while Amma, with her simplistic and humble nature, often neglected her own needs. She would subsist on a mere cup of tea until late afternoon, never allowing herself to rest during the day, and tirelessly toiled in the kitchen until late at night. There were no set eating and sleeping hours for her, as she prioritized the well-being of others.

Anna, ever mindful of well-being, imparted valuable wisdom regarding the health benefits of various foods. Amma, given an insatiable thirst for knowledge, remained open to learning and embraced every opportunity for personal growth. Under Anna's direction, Amma dutifully incorporated the discipline into our lives.

After completing his Bachelors in Civil Engineering, Anna embarked on a remarkable journey that has left an indelible mark on the city's development. Anna, in his own way, ended up making a significant impact on the industrial landscape of Aurangabad.

His professional career began as an Executive Engineer in the State Public Works Department, where he served for approximately seven years. As a Civil Engineer, Anna's job took him places. He had to stay at different sites. Soon, Amma started accompanying him everywhere. And so began their own stories of adventure.

Once, Anna got an opportunity to lead the project of the Siddheshwar Dam construction, a local pool. Anna's contribution to the project led the villagers to name the pool as "Kandi Pool".

During one of their journeys, which happened before my grand entry, Amma and Anna got stuck in a jungle while on the way to attend an event along with my cousins and siblings. Their Jeep broke down, leaving them stranded in the middle of the forest. Anna immediately sent the driver to the nearby village in search of a mechanic and to get some meals for the kids.

The driver returned with the mechanic and some groceries and bare minimum utensils. Given that the vehicle would take hours to fix, Amma jumped into action. She used whatever utensils they had at that time to cook a meal on a makeshift chulha, made of stone from the jungle (Traditional Indian Stove). The same vessel was used in turn for rice, dal, and vegetables. Leaves from the forest trees were used as plates. Despite being trapped unexpectedly in the middle of the forest, Anna and Amma made the most out of it and ensured my siblings had a great time too.

Anna dedicated 7 years of his career to the government job. Eventually, he came to a realization that the prevailing office politics at the time would impede his progress. And one fine day, he decided to quit the job and start on his own.

It meant leaving the comfort of a stable income source and exploring the uncharted territory of entrepreneurship. Amma stood by every decision Anna made for himself and us. Despite being individuals with polarized personalities, somehow, they made the partnership work. For me and my siblings, they always came across as one entity.

Anna and Amma understood their respective roles in the family, they also rooted for each other behind the veils of cultural etiquette and social decorum.

With Amma's moral support, Anna went on to establish "Deogiri Cement Pipes", the first cement pipe factory in Aurangabad. This visionary move laid the foundation for his future success.

Over the course of fifty years, Anna's business ventures have flourished, and he has diversified his investments across multiple ventures. His astute foresight and strategic decision-making have propelled the growth of these enterprises and their associated properties. As a result, Anna earned a reputation as one of the first industrialists in Aurangabad.

The legacy of Anna's entrepreneurial spirit extended beyond his professional achievements. It became an integral part of our family's identity, with all siblings proudly carrying the mantle of belonging to an industrialist family. Anna's unwavering dedication and relentless pursuit of excellence only shaped his own success but also inspired future generations to dream big and strive for greatness.

Anna's generosity extended beyond us, silently aiding the underprivileged and empowering them to fulfill their dreams. Many individuals, who owed their education and subsequent employment to his financial support, often approached him to repay their debts, but he selflessly redirected them to help someone else in need.

Amma too effortlessly accommodated the needs of relatives, friends, and even strangers, epitomizing the spirit of selflessness. Our kitchen was always prepared with extra food, a testament to her belief that no one should go hungry and that there should always be enough to feed a hungry visitor.

Outside our bungalow gate, a half-cut cement pipe served as a makeshift drinking trough for thirsty animals, a small act of kindness that delighted us as we watched various creatures quench their thirst. She also made it a point to assist domestic helpers and their families, extending her compassion to those in need. Together, they extended their support to anyone in need, day or night.

Yet, it wasn't the case that Amma lived in Anna's shadows. She had her personality and quirks. Despite spending several years in a Marathi family locality, she couldn't get a hang of it. Occasionally, her conversation would spiral from Marathi to Telugu, leaving the people around her flabbergasted. Especially when she had to deal with local vendors, the conversation would become highly entertaining. A week after our return from the US in 2001 always brings a smile to my face. There she was, Amma, completely engrossed in the mundane yet charming act of buying vegetables. What made it unforgettable was her animated discussion about the prices—not in local currency, mind you, but in dollars.

Given that Anna's guests would often visit home seeking help and consultation from him, Amma had devised a secret language for the family, so the private conversation could happen smoothly in front of the outsiders, without any hitch.

"Uduku Nilu", which literally means hot water, was our code for whether to get tea for the guests. Since we were staying in a Brahmin locality, there was an unsaid rule forbidding the discussion or even mention of non-vegetarian meals. So, whenever we had to talk about it, we would use the term "Kura," the literal meaning is curry, this word is very commonly used in Telangana. Another one from her dictionary was "Nalli Bokka", which in Telugu, meant spicy gravy with mutton bones. Those were the fun days. We had so much fun having our own secret language which no one else understood.

Despite their polarizing personalities, both Anna and Amma always kept each other before themselves. From my earliest recollections, I witnessed the tireless dedication of my parents, each diligently fulfilling their roles. My mother toiled in the kitchen, nurturing us with her culinary skills, while my father navigated the realms of work, first as an employee and later as an entrepreneur.

Anna and Amma were true gems and it was only due to their unwavering determination and efforts that we siblings developed a strong bond and were united in everything we did. Their selflessness and dedication to the well-being of others served as constant reminders of the importance of empathy and kindness.

I believe a child's foundation about an ideal self is built with the bricks of role models. For me and my siblings, fortunately, Anna and Amma were the very first role models, whose beliefs and ideologies somehow seeped into our personalities. It's one thing to love your parents. It's entirely another thing to be in awe of them. We siblings considered ourselves fortunate to benefit from our parents' unwavering commitment to providing us with the best education and imparting essential values. Most importantly, Anna and Amma's progressive thinking gave us siblings a significant boost to open our minds and widen our horizons.

Feminism was not the word heard or advocated in that era, but Anna and Amma always practiced it, be it for our aunts, cousins or their daughters. Many of the parents gave their sons the best schooling. Convent were supposed to be the best then. But for daughters it was either no education or municipal schools. We however, were raised differently. Ever since I remember, I never felt we sisters were left behind in any of the activities, be it in education, extra-curricular activities, excursions, outings, everywhere we were present.

We grew up to be modern, not in our appearance but most importantly in our outlook. We can't tolerate it if girls are not treated equally and protest against it at every possible opportunity.

If I were to delve into my upbringing, I can confidently say that my Anna and Amma taught me to accept life's unexpected twists, to derive resilience from challenging situations, and to persistently pursue perfection in all my endeavours. This helped me later in my life, when I had to handle everything independently and to nurture my daughter, Shona to be a girl or woman of today.

In a way, I have survived long enough to pass on the legacy of my Anna and Amma, to my Shona. Perhaps that's been the purpose of my life.

Nevertheless, during my earlier years, I hadn't grown into an individual who could uphold the Kandi legacy. For that to happen, I had to endure the experiences life had in store for me.

CHAPTER THREE

Lessons Beyond the Textbooks

You know how they say having older siblings can be a blessing? Well, it is, but it's also a crash course in dealing with peer pressure. As the youngest among my siblings, I found myself growing up in the shadow of their achievements. They each pursued their own paths and found success.

I often felt timid and lacking in direction. Despite my siblings offering guidance and support to me, I still couldn't help feeling a bit self-conscious. Yet, somehow, in their company was where I felt most comfortable. At home, with siblings and parents, I had built my safe haven. Unfortunately, every little nestling has to someday leave the nest to explore the outside world. I came to that realization, only when it was my time to join school.

School was my first step into the real world, outside the huge joint family world that I was raised in until then. And at that time, I didn't like it much. Like I admitted already, my formative years were steeped in timidity, a tendency to withdraw rather than confront. Early on, I was well-acquainted with the art of surrender, a propensity that almost led me to relinquish my schooling aspirations.

Amma had limited education, so she let Anna oversee all matters related to our education. Anna, a strict disciplinarian, laid out rules that were never to be broken under any circumstances. Under those guidelines, we kids were expected to take ownership of our studies. We did abide by the rules, under Anna's regime. Yet, there's one rare occasion, when Anna bent his own rule.

During my Senior Kindergarten years, I fell ill at school once. My temperature soared alarmingly high. Worried, my teacher promptly informed Anna. I can still recall the rush of excitement I felt when he arrived at our school to pick me up. It meant the world to me that he had made the effort to be there for me during my time of need. Though it was a one-off incident, it still remained etched in my memory.

Both Anna and Amma were too occupied with their daily chores to assist us. Despite their limited availability, they chose to support us in the best way possible. This led to the introduction of Mr. Sable, a school teacher who became an integral part of our academic lives as our tuition teacher. His involvement commenced during my pre-primary years and extended well into my seventh grade. During my early school years, I didn't have to study much. Mr. Sable was always kind to me because I was the youngest in the family.

The bond between Mr. Sable and our family facilitated a well-earned respite for my mother. Her newfound free time was dedicated to crafting savoury Indian snacks, a temptation I couldn't resist. To savour these treats, I developed a crafty ruse, feigning drowsiness and seizing the opportunity when Mr. Sable sent me to my bedroom for a nap.

As I entered first grade, I went to school, simply because my family instructed me to do so. The fear of punishment from my teacher and the need to satiate my hunger motivated me to eat my lunch. In every sense, pre-primary felt like a fairy tale compared to the overwhelming academic load of first grade, which seemed akin to taking board exams for tenth grade.

My bench-mate turned out to be a notorious bully who tormented me throughout the day. As an introvert and not particularly confident child, I endured it as long as I could. But one fateful day, I couldn't bear it anymore, and I did what any brave kid my age would do.

I blurted out everything at home, making sure they knew the onus fell upon them to solve the problem. My family was shocked, as they had no idea what I was going through. I declared that I would no longer go to school. My mother tried to pacify me by preparing my favourite sweet dish for my lunch-box. She packed it, and I reluctantly headed to school with my uncle in our open Jeep.

Surprisingly, I was thrilled to be in the Jeep instead of the school bus. We started off from home with great zeal, but along the way, my courage faltered, and I confessed to Jagdish Kaka that I didn't want to go to school. He reassured me and took me to various places for some time before returning to the path that led to my school. It took me a while to realize this, and as my determination grew stronger, I started throwing tantrums.

Eventually, Jagdish Kaka gave in and took me back home. My siblings started teasingly referring to me as the "Ghar ki Sher, School mein Chuhiya" (a daring lion at home but a timid mouse at school). Despite all that, I was happy, somehow, I managed to bunk school that day.

The following morning, my elder sister, Sunanda, suggested that Anna write a letter to my class teacher. I agreed to the idea, but surprisingly, I kept the letter in my uniform pocket for two whole working days without mustering the courage to hand it over. On the third day, I had an epiphany. I realized that it was my battle to fight, and I summoned the strength to confront the bully. The way I stated my case, I believe there were subtle threats sandwiched between complaints. To my surprise, he immediately stopped his torment, perhaps sensing that he would face consequences if our teacher found out.

Amidst the challenges, there were also remarkable friendships that shaped my school days. I remember the day, quite distinctly even today. It was at the school bus stop where our paths first crossed. Seema had arrived with her mother, who approached me with a warm smile. "Will you show her everything she needs to know about the school?" her mother asked me. Without hesitation, I replied, "Sure, Aunty!" From that day forward, not a single day went by without our friendly encounters.

Seema and I faced another case of bullying, with another classmate of mine. There was a girl who exuded dominance and arrogance. She would often force some of us, including Seema and me, to eat the green chilies from her lunchbox. Despite the fiery and spicy sensation, we timidly obeyed her orders. And we would have continued to do so, if not for Seema. One day, she decided that enough was enough. She mustered the courage to stand up to the bully and refused to eat the green chilies. It was a small act of defiance, but it marked a turning point for us. From that day forward, we refused to be pushed around or bullied by anyone.

It also brought me and Seema closer. Our bond deepened over the years, and Seema became my rock. While I was a reserved child, she possessed strength and a protective nature that enveloped me. She was there for me through thick and thin, providing unwavering support during my toughest moments.

As I grew more assertive and resilient, I discovered a new sense of empowerment. The timid child who once contemplated quitting school had transformed into someone who was open to the myriad adventures of life. The support from my family, the guidance of Mr. Sable, and the unwavering friendship of Seema had played significant roles in shaping my resilience and determination.

I developed a particular fondness for history, mainly because of my favourite teacher, Mr. Sable. One of the memorable experiences from that time was our first school trip to Pune. We embarked on the journey in our school bus and stayed at a convent school during the trip. Part of the highlights of our trip was a visit to the magnificent Sinhagad Fort for sightseeing. Mr. Sable's enthusiasm was infectious as he passionately explained the fascinating history of the fort. He became so engrossed in his storytelling that he unintentionally exceeded the allotted time. Upon our descent, our principal reprimanded him for the delay. However, Mr. Sable responded proudly and respectfully, stating that it was his duty to ensure his students had a thorough understanding of the subject. His dedication to his profession and loyalty towards his students were evident in his response.

My academic performance improved, and I started participating in extracurricular activities over time. In fourth grade I had board examinations. So Sunanda took the responsibility of inculcating the study habit in me. She woke me up early in the morning and made me sit with her for studying. She explained the chapters in detail, that way I got the knack of how to study. Those experiences marked a turning point in my attitude towards learning and underscored the value of dedicated effort and support from both educators and family.

Through the school days, Seema and I remained steadfast friends. Her protective nature continued to shine through, often stepping in to address unwelcome comments towards me. Her loyalty and guidance were a source of comfort and strength. Happy recollections of my time at school with her, I can clearly recall taking part in a guiding camp where we did things like go camping, cook over fires, and raise saplings. Those were special experiences that we treasured at that time.

Seema and my kinship continued to flourish until we eventually parted ways in Junior College, when Seema had the opportunity to pursue sports studies in Haryana. Despite the physical distance that separated us, the strength of our connection remained intact, and she continues to be a pillar of support in my life to this day.

CHAPTER FOUR

Family Bonds and Unforgettable Adventures

In the summer following the completion of my second-grade, my eldest sister, Vijaya, entered the sacred bond of marriage. A mere seven days later, another joyous celebration unfolded as Jagdish Kaka tied the knot in the picturesque city of Gardens, famously known as Bangalore, or Bengaluru, and recognized as the Silicon Valley of India. Recognizing this as a unique opportunity, we transformed the occasion into a memorable family vacation, opting to explore the serene and architecturally captivating temples of South India.

Among the various temples we explored, the one that left an enduring impression was the Venkateshwara Temple situated in the Tirupati district of Andhra Pradesh. Steeped in history, the temple's roots traced back to the eleventh century when it was commissioned by King Krishnadevaraya of the Vijayanagara Empire. Spanning a vast complex, the temple houses numerous shrines, with the primary focus on Lord Venkateshwara's sacred abode.

This revered temple attracts millions of worshippers annually. An intriguing facet of devotion observed here is the act of tonsuring, wherein a substantial number of devotees ritually shave their heads as a symbolic sacrifice to Lord Venkateshwara.

Offering one's hair has been a longstanding tradition at the Venkateshwara Temple, serving as a profound expression of love and dedication to the deity.

Legend holds that Neela Devi, the mother of Lord Venkateshwara, accepts these hair offerings, further strengthening the believers' connection with the divine. Devotees believe that by presenting this symbolic gesture, Lord Venkateshwara bestows blessings upon them. Consequently, a considerable number of adherents, predominantly men but occasionally women as well, undertake the act of shaving their heads at the sacred precincts of the Tirumala temple.

Amma orchestrated a unique act of devotion by compelling Amarnath and Shivnath to sacrifice their locks. However, her fervour did not wane there; she turned her attention to my own tresses. Enthralled by her devotion to Lord Vishnu, she remained oblivious to the furrowed brows on my brothers' faces and the tears streaming down my cheeks.

If you think this was the pinnacle of our tribulations during the trip, brace yourself for the rest of the narrative. Throughout the journey, I observed Amma occasionally stealing glances in my direction. Unbeknownst to me, her experiment had rendered me bald, a fact she found endearing despite the evident discomfort on my part.

Amma's ingenious experiment bore fruit, as the subdued protest from my end resembled the feeble resistance of an amoeba. Convinced of my newfound cuteness with short hair and attired in a boy's dress, she adorned me in shorts and a t-shirt.

Despite these unexpected twists, our family vacation transformed into an unforgettable journey marked by love, laughter, and spiritual enlightenment. Returning home, we carried with us a profound appreciation for our rich cultural heritage and cherished memories destined to endure a lifetime.

Upon our return from the journey, an amusing incident unfolded during a bus ride from Hingoli to Aurangabad. True to our customary seating arrangements, we kids occupied our designated seats. However, a sudden interruption came from an elderly lady instructing me to move aside with a casual "Ae ladke sarak" (Move aside, boy). Finding humour in this, my siblings seized the opportunity to dub me "Ladka Ladka" for the duration of the bus ride, and the teasing persisted for a couple more years.

On another occasion, my elder brother, Amarnath's friend, visited our house. Catching me in playful antics, he remarked, "Tera chota bhai bohot accha dikhta hain" (Your younger brother looks cute). While I missed much of the subsequent conversation, the term "cute" was unmistakably etched in my memory. It marked the moment when the amoeba forgave its creators.

As the summer vacation concluded and school resumed, I attended with a scarf on my head. Some classmates found it amusing and attempted to pull it away, leading to playful pursuits where I, feigning irritation, chased after them.

During those days, I unwittingly became more effective than many stand-up comedians today. Stepping in front of a crowd resulted in resounding laughter, sustaining a streak that persisted long enough for me to entertain the notion that I was, indeed, a boy.

The "ladka" saga seamlessly transitioned into another unexpected chapter, catching us all off guard. It unfolded during our Diwali vacation when I was in fourth grade, on a chilly evening. The setting was our family gathering, with kids, including my younger brother Shivnath, cousins, and me, lying on the bed alongside our grandmother. Post-dinner, we eagerly listened to stories while my mother attended to her final chores.

In a corner of the room, my younger uncle, Prakash Kaka, had placed his air gun. Driven by curiosity, Shivnath inquired whether there were pellets in the gun. Absent-mindedly, Kaka responded that there weren't any, completely forgetting the fact that he had loaded them earlier to fend off a troublesome cat.

In a playful manner, Shivnath turned to me and asked, "Marru kya maru kya?" (Should I shoot you?!)

In my genetically-engineered amoebic mindset, a delusion took root, convincing me of a transformation into a stronger being accompanied by an irrationally courageous ego. Emboldened by this newfound bravado, I fearlessly challenged my brother with the words, "Maar mujhe kuch nahi hota" (Hit me, it won't hurt me). As history has often demonstrated, when one misguided ego challenges another, consequences unfold. Shivnath, enticed by the dare, playfully pressed the trigger. Much to his shock and my dismay, the pellet pierced through my sweater, embedding itself into the skin just below my left elbow.

In a display of unwavering confidence, I chuckled, "Dekh mujhe kuch nahi hua" (See, nothing happened to me), fully relying on Prakash Kaka's earlier assurance. However, reality swiftly dispatched pain signals through my neurons, and my brain erupted in a chorus of shrieks. The ensuing howls caught the attention of my family members, who rushed to the scene in response to my unforeseen predicament.

Amidst the ensuing chaos, Shivnath, gripped by terror at the prospect of facing our father's reprimand, hastily sought refuge behind the door. Meanwhile, Prakash Kaka, realizing the gravity of the situation, found beads of sweat forming on his forehead. Swift to act before Anna could intervene, Kaka scooped me into his arms, seized the car keys, and, accompanied by my elder brother Amarnath, hurried to Jagdish Kaka's place. Fortunately, Jagdish Kaka's residence was conveniently located in the medical quarters not far from our own.

Upon arrival at Jagdish Kaka's place, Prakash Kaka hastily divulged the predicament that had unfolded. Initially dismissing it as a potential prank, Jagdish Kaka and the nurse assisting him at the hospital was skeptical, considering Kaka's penchant for practical jokes. However, as the full narrative unfolded, both of them grasped the seriousness of the situation and promptly ushered me into the hospital's operating theater. The pellet was successfully extracted, and just as the nurse prepared to discard it, Kaka, in his characteristic teasing manner, requested her not to dispose of it. Instead, he suggested giving it to me, proposing that I show it to Amma as proof of their visit and the successful removal of the pellet. Teasing Amma was a customary facet of my Kaka's playful antics.

Until we returned home, a palpable tension hung in the air. However, as we unfolded the entire incident and presented the extracted pellet as evidence, a collective sigh of relief swept through the room. The atmosphere lightened, and unwittingly, I became the protagonist in yet another "favourite Kandi family story," destined to echo through family gatherings for years to come. Multiple versions of the tale emerged – one that my uncle shared with the elders, and another recounted by my brother to the siblings and cousins. In both renditions, I found myself at the epicenter of the narrative, enduring the brunt of all the jokes.

It's fair to say that, had it not been for me, my extended joint family might have been bereft of amusing stories. As the pellet incident gradually lost its comedic momentum, destiny seemingly intervened, paving the way for another memorable incident during our customary family get-together vacation.

Our extensive family, comprising around 40 individuals, including children, elders, and in-laws, gathered annually for a collective reunion at our native place, Hingoli. While the elders turned even the vacation into a structured affair, the children knew how to extract maximum enjoyment. For us, it was an extended celebration. The women collaborated in the kitchen, generating a lively ambiance filled with animated conversations and laughter. Simultaneously, the men formed a group, sharing tales of the family tree and intriguing anecdotes from their own childhoods. As for us kids, the entire vacation was an opportunity for relentless play and enjoyment. The Hingoli vacations held a truly special place in our hearts, leaving an indelible impression that lingered on in my memories.

In our native place in Hingoli, we had a deep well in the front yard of our house. I can distinctly recall the day when the children were informed that we would be taught swimming. That moment, the realization dawned upon me that I harboured a fear of drowning. Being an introvert, I chose not to express my apprehensions to anyone. Thus, I found myself standing in line with my siblings and cousins, on the brink of confronting the abyss of my fears.

A rope was secured around my waist, and I was gradually lowered into the well. Clutching onto the rope with determination, I resisted letting go, even as those outside encouraged me to release it and attempt moving my hands and legs to swim. After some coaxing, I reluctantly decided to give it a try and released the rope. However, my hands seemed to defy my intentions, remaining tightly clasped to the lifeline. A silent battle raged within me, while one of the aunts impatiently exclaimed, "Pull her up; she is wasting other's time."

Reflecting on it now, I wonder if a bit more patience from her might have allowed me to gain confidence, spurred on by the encouragement of others, and learn swimming at that very moment. Meanwhile, those outside continued their attempts to cheer me on. Whom were they rooting for? In the end, I reached a breaking point and erupted, yelling at them. For a brief moment, everyone was stunned – perhaps from witnessing the timid kitten roaring. Yet, as the shock subsided, they realized they had been handed yet another reason to tease me.

The teasing persisted throughout the rest of the vacation period, becoming a source of discomfort that led me to eagerly anticipate the resumption of school.

CHAPTER FIVE

From Adolescence to Independence

When I first stepped into the realm of formal education, there was a naive belief that school was merely a temporary space where parents sent their children while occupied with daily chores. I found solace in the thought that it was just a brief interlude, a compelled vacation, after which I could joyfully return to my safe haven. However, life has a way of defying such simplistic views.

As I matured, the realization dawned upon me that schooling was not a transient escape but a prelude to a lifelong journey of learning and evolution. Fortunately, my schooling experience was marked by exciting adventures. Transitioning from primary education to senior school brought a surge of excitement and anticipation about what was coming next.

My journey through adolescence was a time filled with a myriad of emotions and encounters with various individuals. Some intimidated me, while others became companions, but I also found a place among the academically inclined and socially adept. In the midst of this rollercoaster, I was fortunate to have Seema by my side. Her presence provided a reliable anchor when my easygoing nature occasionally led to discomforting experiences.

The new phase unfolded in a larger building, introducing me to a plethora of memorable incidents and interactions with teachers who would leave an indelible mark on my life. As my academic journey progressed, I actively engaged in various extracurricular activities alongside my studies.

Throughout those years, Hindi was a constant presence in the curriculum as the second language. Initially, my lack of interest in grasping its non-verbal intricacies led me to divert my attention to other subjects. However, a pivotal shift occurred when Sable sir, recognizing my shortcomings just before a Hindi class test, prompted a significant change in my approach.

Naturally, I was in bad form. That incident with Sable sir served as a turning point in my education, pulling me out of a phase of disinterest. After a tight slap, which was a common form of punishment then, he committed to teaching me Hindi from the basics. Anna, recognizing the need for diverse learning, subscribed to a Hindi magazine to expose me to the language through various mediums. Additionally, the well-equipped school library introduced me to a range of Hindi children's books, allowing me to fully immerse myself in the intricacies and literature of the language, a departure from my previous focus on English-language books.

Moving from reading to writing felt like a natural progression. I began contributing articles to the school magazine, expanding my writing repertoire to all three languages—English, Hindi, and Marathi—all of which were selected for publication.

In senior school, a pivotal moment unfolded when our basketball coach handpicked a group of friends, including me, to represent the school team. That marked the commencement of my involvement in basketball. Determined to excel, I devoted time to rigorous practice before and after classes, and even during lunch breaks. The routine became ingrained, and each practice session became an eagerly anticipated opportunity for enjoyment and comradeship.

In today's world, there seems to be a growing trend towards individualism, where people have become somewhat immune to sentiments. While modern generations engage in social interactions and make acquaintances, there often appears to be a lack of deep bonding. The attitude seems to be one of casual detachment – it's fine when friends are around, but equally acceptable when they are not.

Contrastingly, during those days, friendship held a special place akin to a religion, forming a familial bond beyond blood relations. The camaraderie I cultivated with my teammates instilled in me a profound love for being part of a team, working collectively towards a shared objective.

I made a conscious decision to pursue basketball more seriously, despite the inherent challenges, putting in the effort to enhance my skills. As time progressed, we engaged in a practice match with another school team in a different city. Although our seniors dominated the match, the exposure served as motivation to further elevate our skills. Basketball seamlessly integrated into my daily routine, becoming a healthy habit developed without external pressures.

As our senior players graduated, my friends and I assumed leadership roles within the team. While fostering our commitment to basketball, we emphasized the importance of balancing our studies with other activities.

Our school Principal, Reverend Father D.C. Kamath, played a pivotal role in shaping our all-around development through a myriad of activities and competitions. One particularly memorable instance occurred when I received a special mention during the morning assembly for my performance in a basketball match against Sunanda's team. Our principal, in his generous spirit, commended me for putting up a tough fight in the match, acknowledging and encouraging my efforts in front of the entire school community. That recognition not only boosted my confidence but also reinforced the idea that our achievements, big or small, were valued and celebrated in our school community.

While academic growth undeniably holds its significance, sports, often overlooked in the realm of schooling, possesses a unique power to shape one's character. For me, sports, particularly my involvement in basketball and the series of incidents that unfolded around it, laid the foundation for the person I am today.

Engaging in basketball allowed me to perceive and understand societal challenges faced by women. The rules, it seemed, were never the same for the female species. As teenage girls, we played basketball even during our menstrual cycles. In one particular intense moment of the game, a teammate leapt into the air, and her sanitary napkin fell on the court. This occurrence was not uncommon, given that sanitary products were still evolving and had not reached peak quality at that time. While menstruation is a natural biological process, societal taboos surrounding it led to an unfortunate incident where my teammate swiftly picked up the napkin and hurried inside the school building to avoid further embarrassment.

Post that incident, our approach to practice changed. Caution became the strongest player on our court, reflecting the societal challenges that young women often navigate with resilience and adaptability. Those experiences not only shaped our understanding of women's issues but also fostered a sense of camaraderie and support amongst us, transcending the boundaries of the basketball court.

As we entered the tenth grade, the focus shifted to preparing for the board examinations. Enrolling in special classes marked the beginning of independent city bus travels, a novel experience for us. During one of those journeys, our usual laughter at an internal joke caught the attention of an uncle of one of my acquaintances, who took it upon himself to reprimand me for what he perceived as shameful behaviour. The incident left me upset and tearful, prompting a deep reflection on the unspoken expectations thrust upon girls to conform to a certain public behaviour in order to safeguard their family's honour.

Upon reaching home, I shared the incident with Shivnath, my brother. In a commendable display of support, he took immediate action by visiting the uncle's place and confronting him. With clarity and respect, Shivnath made it explicitly clear that interference in his sisters' matters was unwarranted. I feel an immense pride in the solidarity and backing I received from my siblings during the time when our voices were often suppressed. Their unwavering support served as a testament to the strength of familial bonds in navigating societal expectations.

Shivnath's intervention provided a sense of ease during my bus travels with friends. However, a few days later, a boy started following me, eventually boarding the same bus we took to go home. Anxiety enveloped me, and Seema, my companion at that time, advised a swift exit as soon as the bus halted, urging me to reach home promptly. Overwhelmed by fear, I didn't wait for the bus to come to a complete stop and impulsively jumped off while it was still in motion. Landing on my stomach, I heard people around me shouting, "bacchi gir gayi, bacchi gir gayi" ("The girl fell down... The girl fell down"). In embarrassment, I hastily got up and ran home, a mere two minutes away from the bus stop. It wasn't until later that I noticed my injured knee, bleeding from the fall.

Reflecting on the incident, I questioned myself: "When I had done nothing wrong, why did I choose flight over fight in a fight-or-flight state?" The experience underscored the impact of fear and societal pressures on decision-making, revealing the complexities young women navigate in public spaces.

Just a few months after surviving a terrifying fall from a moving bus, I faced another horrifying ordeal. Returning from classes, I proudly wore a pendant of Saibaba, a revered saint in both Hindu and Muslim communities. Collecting these beautiful and meaningful ornaments had become a passion for me. On a dark night, the pendant sparkled in the streetlight as I was almost home. Suddenly, a cyclist raced behind me, ripping the chain off my neck. Frozen with fear and shock, I couldn't scream before he vanished into the darkness. Sprinting home, I tearfully recounted the incident to Amma.

The following day, Amma took measures to enhance our safety. She ensured that our servant put up more lights on the balcony to ward off potential intruders. That traumatic experience highlighted the vulnerability of young women in public spaces and the need for increased safety measures to protect against such incidents.

Reflecting on that incident today, I can't help but feel a profound sense of awe for Amma. In a society where mothers might have scolded or restricted their daughters after such traumatic experiences, Amma took a different approach. Rather than hindering my pursuits or imposing restrictions, she silently supported me. She not only facilitated my endeavours but also made sure I returned home safely. As I am a mother myself now, I can empathize with the worries that must have crossed her mind during those moments. Yet, she chose to set aside her personal concerns, ensuring that my path forward remained unblocked, unencumbered by societal expectations or limitations. Amma's quiet strength and unwavering support remain a testament to the resilience and empowerment she instilled in me.

As I navigated through my teenage years, I gradually learned to confront adverse events on my own. One memorable experience took place during a basketball tour to Nanded, where our team, dissatisfied with the initial accommodation, relocated to a charming old bungalow owned by a friend of our Team Manager. The architectural beauty of the place was complemented by the gracious hospitality of the host family, who treated us to delightful Marwari cuisine.

During that tour, our team's success in the matches drew the attention of local boys. Each time we left the stadium to return to our accommodation, a group of boys would follow us, ogling and making lewd comments. Their fascination with our modern outfits and confident demeanour created a strange and unsettling experience. Although we chose to ignore them to stay focused on our game, these encounters left a lasting impact on my character, shaping my response to challenges and reinforcing the value of friendship and dedication.

As our 10th-grade examinations approached, the looming State board exams cast a shadow over us like dark clouds. While not exceptional, our results were commendable.

In the midst of awaiting our results, the prospect of parting ways with dear friends enveloped me in melancholy. That juncture marked a divergence in our paths as various friends pursued different programs. Some of us, however, chose to embark on the same journey, finding solace in familiar company.

Yet, even in that togetherness, a realization hung heavy – things would never be the same again. We understood that we would grow apart, forge new friendships, confront fresh challenges. We knew we would miss each other, hold onto cherished memories, and endeavour to stay connected. Saying goodbye became an inevitable reality, one we didn't want to face. Thanks to social media, it became the thread that reconnected us with the same passion and eagerness as a child.

On the day of the results, we shared hugs and tears, laughter and jokes, promises and hopes. Gratitude filled the air as we thanked each other for being there, for being true to ourselves, for being friends. The bittersweet essence of that day encapsulated the profound bonds we had forged and the imminent changes that lay ahead.

These formative experiences, filled with basketball, travel, new people, and friendships, represent carefree days of fun and adventure. They evoke a sense of joy, hope, and dreams without fear or worry. Nostalgia creeps in when I reflect on those days, and there's an innate urge to relive those moments. The memories of that period have become etched in the corners of my mind, serving as a timeless reminder of who I was, who I am, and the endless possibilities of who I could have been.

CHAPTER SIX

Breaking the Silence

The journey into College Life brought with itself unforeseen experiences. Seema was no longer with me. She had left for Haryana to pursue a course in Sports Education in a Sports University. I remember the steps I was taking to the college premise on the first day. The anxiety around being hazed by the seniors was weighing on my spirit, slowing my pace. I realized we were both part of a different world now and will have to fight our own battles.

In Junior college too I pursued basketball. Given my earlier stints with the sport, I was selected for the college team. There a new cycle of life began. Meeting strangers, becoming friends, and then getting involved in each other's life stories. My tryst with Swati took place on the basketball court. By the time we finished our game, it was evident that I had found a new friend. Then came the season of sports in college and I received a letter stating that I was selected for the state-level basketball team. I had worked hard to earn it.

Gradually, my circle of friends expanded. During our college excursion, we got a chance to visit "Ellora Caves-Sita Nahani" (a scenic spot above a cave "the kailash temple"). Perhaps it's the setting that plays a role in bringing people together. In the confinements of a Classrooms, we were too caught up with the worries of examinations and grades. It was the travel to a far off place that solidified our bonds and made us friends for life. Those outings, brimming with enjoyment, became anticipated traditions, serving as fitting bookends to our collegiate experience.

Yet not every memory from the college days was carved in marble. Some were etched in the dark rocks of nightmares.

Once, I set out to meet my friend Swati. By then we had been visiting each other's homes frequently. So that fateful day in no way, felt out of ordinary. Swati was home alone, and our lively conversation lasted for about two hours. She treated me to some mouthwatering homemade dishes. It was her exceptional culinary skills that lured me to her home most of the time.

After bidding her farewell, I began my journey back home. Along the way, I passed by the home of another school friend I hadn't seen in ages. Intrigued by her recent move to a new bungalow, I decided to pay her a surprise visit and catch up.

As I pressed the doorbell, her maternal uncle greeted me and kindly offered a seat while he went to summon her. I waited in hopeful anticipation to surprise my friend. Meanwhile, her uncle sent his 10-year-old son to the terrace to fly kites.

After a few minutes, he returned, informing me that she was asleep but has been awakened and would join us shortly.

Perhaps it was the survival radar or just plain fear, I felt an uncomfortable vibe. Given that I was waiting for my friend to show up, I decided to fill the silence with noise. I asked the uncle about his wife. He told me she was out of town.

Then without any hesitation, He came and sat on the couch, engaging me in conversation on various topics.

As minutes passed, a sense of unease crept over me. I mustered the courage to inquire about my friend's whereabouts and suggested if I could go to her room. He assured me she would emerge soon and continued discussing my college life.

Minutes stretched into what felt like hours, and my patience wore thin. With growing discomfort, I pressed him once more, requesting an update on my friend's arrival. His response, evasive yet calm, only added to my unease. Despite his attempts to divert the conversation, my concern intensified.

Feeling increasingly uneasy, I made the decision to leave, politely informing him that I would catch up with her later. Despite his insistence that I wait a little longer, an unsettling sensation urged me to retreat. Yet, in an unexpected turn of events, he abruptly seized my hand, his grip tightening as he pulled me closer. Fear coursed through my veins, and my desperate pleas echoed in the air, "Mamaji, leave me! Mamaji, leave me!" But he refused to release his hold. Driven by sheer desperation, I summoned all my strength, and pushed him away, then hastily unlocking the latch, I raced out of there without once looking back. Even when I was out of the premise, I ran aimlessly, driven by an instinct to escape the sinister situation that had clawed on me. Disoriented and consumed by fear, I let my legs carry me, unaware of where I was heading.

I ended up at Swati's place hoping to meet with her again. She opened the door, her eyes widening at the sight of my agitated state. Without hesitation, she enveloped me in a comforting embrace and gently guided me inside. Sensing my shattered composure, she insisted I take a seat, urging me to collect myself.

Tears streamed uncontrollably down my face as I recounted the harrowing experience that had shattered my sense of security. Swati listened attentively, her shock mirroring my own.

It wasn't that I was seeking counsel. But friends never wait for cue or permission to advise each other. It's the natural instinct to protect one another that drives us to fix the problem the friend is facing. However, Swati was of the same age and maturity as me. So naturally, she suggested what she thought was the best course. She advised me to treat it as a dreadful nightmare and cautioned against divulging the incident to anyone, not even within the confines of my home.

Somewhere, I knew that was what I was inclined to do myself. It resonated with my own preferred course of action. Often the best course to avoid a traumatic incident is to ignore it. At least, then at that age, that seemed like the sensible thing to do.

For nights since the incident, I tried to fight a battle in my head as to who exactly was at fault. Given my gender conditioning at the time, I couldn't confidently point the finger at the other person and scream - "What You did was wrong!"

In Indian culture, while mother is referred as "Ma", Mother's brother (maternal uncle) is referred to as "MaMa" , which goes to say, someone can provide twice the motherly affection than the mother. I kept asking myself, how such an esteemed person could do such a condemned act.

In a joint family, it's not easy to hide your pain and sorrows. Every member of the family is quick to notice the slightest transformation in each other. Yet, I buried the memories of that incident so deep within me hoping to never share the incident with another soul ever, not even my family.

It was only after years had passed, that I mustered the courage to share the incident with my sisters - Sunanda, Sujata and Seema.

Naturally, my support system was offended, agitated and enraged at the perpetrator. But once the initial shock subsided, they supported me and wished I had reached out to them earlier. They would have taken some action on the matter. I am not sure; how many females have to go through such an experience in their lifetime. But I hope everyone finds a support system, such as mine. Without the support and understanding of my sisters and my friend, I would have never learnt to cope with that horrible incident.

Gradually, the scar from the old ugly wound on my soul began to fade away. I hoped I would never have to be in such a situation again.

Then one day, as a part of the basketball university team, I went to Anand in Gujarat for our inter university tournament. On day two after reaching Anand, we won a match in the morning session and the next one was scheduled in the second half of the day. As the room we were accommodating was quite far off, it was decided to go to the room after getting over with the second match.

Meanwhile we were sitting at one end of a big open ground, on the opposite end was a small garden and behind the garden was a hawker selling street food. One of our teammates got some samosas (fried triangle-shaped pastry) for all of us. We savoured them and felt tempted to go for a second round of Samosas. I took the initiative of getting them.

As I was crossing the garden to get to the hawker, I sensed a pair of eyes on me. As I instinctively turned, I froze in shock. A young man in his early twenties, who was working out in the garden, suddenly pulled down his track pants and exposed his genitals flashing it to me.

I may have shrieked in shock at the moment. My teammates felt something was amiss, and two of them came running.

My friends escorted me back, where I shared with my friends what had happened. My teammates who were medical students, used a new term and the "perverts" got introduced to my conditioning. On that day, I learnt how perverts are often on the lookout for such opportunities.

Years passed again, as I tried to ignore and overcome another scar on my soul. Then somewhere in May of 1990, we got the news that our maternal Uncle Mama was on his death bed. We siblings were traveling in a train to Nizamabad to see him. It was an overnight journey and we all were fast asleep.

It was Sujata's scream in the middle of the night, that woke up the members in the coach, including me.

As soon as I woke up, the passenger on the berth above me, who happened to be a boy, hastily jumped down and ran away.

It was still unclear to me what had transpired, but I could see my sister fuming in rage. Shivnath and Sunanda also woke up and joined us. Our sleep had gone for a toss. When I asked Sujata what had happened, She told me the boy was leaning out of his berth towards me in an attempt to kiss me. It was only then that my knees trembled. The horror of that incident had kept me apprehensive of sleeping in the train for years.

It didn't end there. Once Raj, Shona, and I were making our way through the bustling Andheri Railway station, a heartbeat of Mumbai. The chaos was palpable, people rushing past, all absorbed in their own urgent missions. As Raj, Shona, and I pressed through the bustling crowds lining Mumbai's busiest platforms, Shona unknowingly fell behind our hurried pace. Her sudden cry pierced the din - turning back in alarm, we caught sight of Shona swinging fiercely at a man now beating a hasty retreat. Raj bolted after the fleeing figure, but he soon disappeared into the endless sea of commuters.

As Shona reoriented herself, the sordid details emerged - the anonymity of the crowded station had empowered a deviant to violate her, subjecting her to demeaning contact she neither asked for nor deserved. Shona simmered with impotent fury in the following minutes. It was a dismaying reminder that despite progress in other spheres, for all the gains society trumpets, female indignities at the hands of emboldened miscreants continue unabated. The bitter taste of that day lingered long for each of us.

Today, when I look back at it, I can understand how misguided we were in that age. Honestly, I don't think blaming the world, society or the family makes sense for our flawed conditioning. However, the fact is somewhere the female of the species has learnt to see any act related to lust as their fault. Yes, No doubt, the world is doing its best to convince the female species of the same, but that's never a justification for the women to accept it. The sad reality of our world is that even a victim of theft is seen as a victim, however a victim of sexual assault is considered as party to the crime. And while, the intellectuals condemn such thought processes, the prevalent mindset of the masses remains unperturbed by the influence of progressive thinking on this particular matter.

CHAPTER SEVEN

Forging Unbreakable Bonds

Towards the end of junior college, life took another unexpected turn. Sujata, my elder sister, now assumed the role of someone's wife. Simultaneously, Sunanda immersed herself in her aspirations, spending long hours secluded in her room, softly humming as she delved into vast medical encyclopedias to prepare for her Medical Degree.

With both sisters engrossed in their respective pursuits, the unexpected onus of household responsibilities suddenly shifted to my shoulders. In hindsight, I should have seen the signs, but at the time, I felt far from womanhood. Being the youngest among my siblings, I was accustomed to being cared for and not yet equipped to care for others. Nevertheless, the responsibility fell upon me to assist Amma with household chores—a role unfamiliar to me as the youngest sibling.

My new routine consisted of helping Amma in the early morning, attending college, returning home to assist her again with lunch preparations, studying, going for basketball practice, and helping her once more in the evening with dinner. At that time, I didn't harbour any ambitious goals for myself, but I aimed to contribute as much as possible to support Amma in managing the household. That period of responsibility marked a significant chapter in my life, shaping my understanding of commitment and the importance of familial bonds.

What initially seemed like an extra-curricular activity had transformed into a passion, and I was thrilled at the prospect of playing for the State level Basket Ball Tournament in Junior College.

In Senior College, participating in the inter-university basketball tournaments provided me with an exclusive experience, allowing me to compete against exceptional teams that were already active at the national level.

Around the same time, I also found myself selected for the university hockey team. While I wasn't particularly keen on hockey and had initially enrolled for it as one of the various sports options, I tried to balance my presence on both courts. However, on the fourth day of the 10-day hockey training, I received the news of being shortlisted for the university basketball team. Faced with a decision at the crossroads, I chose to focus on basketball and returned home from the hockey training camp. That marked a crucial moment where my dedication to basketball took precedence, further solidifying my commitment to the sport.

On October 31, 1984, my chosen path led me to participate in the inter-university matches hosted by Madras University in Chennai (erstwhile Madras). The tournament brought together several teams, and we were provided accommodation in a university hostel dormitory alongside three other teams. Each team had its designated section in the dormitory, fostering an environment of shared anticipation and excitement.

Upon our arrival at the destination, I took a moment to freshen up while my teammates continued with their activities. I was experiencing some discomfort, so I decided to lie down for a short while. Eventually, when the rest of the girls and our manager were ready, we headed down for breakfast. However, my discomfort persisted, and I chose to skip the meal, hoping to alleviate my unease through rest.

As my teammates and our manager enjoyed their breakfast, a sense of normalcy prevailed. Yet, amidst the meal, a subtle undercurrent of whispers began to circulate around the restaurant. Initially, those whispers didn't raise suspicion, and the girls carried on with their meal uninterrupted. It wasn't until later that a sudden shift occurred – the owner of the restaurant abruptly closed the iron entrance gate and made an announcement that caught us all off guard.

The reason for this sudden imposition of restrictions became chillingly apparent—India's Prime Minister, Mrs. Indira Gandhi, had been assassinated. The news sent shockwaves through the nation, triggering riots in Delhi and various other regions.

The country found itself in the throes of political and social turmoil, and the repercussions were felt deeply. The ensuing riots claimed thousands of lives, left many injured, and caused widespread damage to property. The aftermath of the assassination fueled political instability and social unrest.

In an effort to quell the escalating violence, the government took measures such as closing roads, railways, and even canceling flights. Security checks were heightened at all transportation hubs, making travel more time-consuming and challenging. The atmosphere of fear and uncertainty discouraged people from venturing out, wary of potential targeting based on their religion or ethnicity.

As events unfolded, the repercussions of this tragic incident cast a long shadow over the country, affecting the dynamics between different communities and leaving an indelible mark on the social fabric. The period that followed was characterized by a deep sense of mistrust and tension between Hindus and Sikhs in certain areas. The impact of these events extended beyond the immediate aftermath, shaping the course of the nation's socio-political landscape.

Amidst the unsettling turn of events, our team manager's stern advice compelled me to order some food, despite the lingering discomfort. The realization of the escalating volatility prompted a decision to pack some food for the uncertain times ahead. Unfortunately, the owner's acknowledgment of potential closure dashed our hopes of securing additional provisions.

As the situation outside grew more precarious, we grappled with the shifting reality. The world beyond the hostel gates had transformed in ways we could hardly have foreseen. In response, we pooled whatever homemade snacks we had brought with us, rationing them among ourselves to sustain through the uncertain period.

In an unexpected twist, the initial unspoken rivalry with rival teams dissolved in the face of shared adversity. An incident miles away had a profound impact on our perspectives, forging a strong bond among the once-competitive teammates. The unity that emerged became a testament to the human spirit's ability to connect, even in the midst of challenging circumstances.

As the evening descended, a piece of invaluable information circulated among us: a shopkeeper was discreetly selling bread, jam, and butter from a back door. That clandestine opportunity sparked a renewed sense of energy amongst us, and we swiftly joined the forming queue. The shopkeeper, managing limited stock for each team, ensured that we each obtained our share, providing a temporary reprieve for breakfast, lunch, and dinner.

That arrangement sustained us for an additional day, but after about two days, the authorities caught wind of the unauthorized sales, forcing the shopkeeper to cease the practice. The uncertain prospect of our next meal added to the already palpable concerns during those tumultuous times.

Amidst the challenges, a ray of hope emerged from an unexpected source. The male students from the university recognized the dire situation we were facing and took it upon themselves to be part of the solution. They decided to prepare meals for the entire group, gathering basic ingredients like wheat, rice, potatoes, onions, tomatoes, and various spices. That initiative, communicated to all team managers, aimed to provide essential food items at a minimum cost, alleviating some of the immediate concerns we faced. The gesture underscored the resilience of collective efforts in the face of adversity.

Upon reaching the campus, we found ourselves in the midst of a community kitchen where various activities were underway. Some were engrossed in preparing a hearty potato and tomato curry, while others were dedicated to the art of making chapatis (Indian bread). To streamline the distribution of meals, two volunteers were tasked with selling coupons for each team. Eagerly, we purchased our coupons and joined the queue, anticipating our turn with a mix of hunger and gratitude.

However, our relief was short-lived as we encountered yet another unforeseen challenge. Not all the volunteers were well-versed in the intricacies of making chapatis. Their sincere willingness to contribute was overshadowed by their lack of experience in the culinary arts. In that moment of need, the girls decided to step in. Amidst the looming clouds of tragedy, we managed to create pockets of camaraderie. Meals were generously shared with fellow students, irrespective of the jersey one was wearing. The distinct colours of our contrasting jerseys began to fade, leaving behind the colour of peace and compassion.

After a couple of days, a semblance of normalcy returned. The canteen facilities were fully reinstated, tournament dates were confirmed, matches were conducted, and our team even secured a victory. However, the subsequent day posed a challenge as we faced the second runner-up team from the previous year. Despite our best efforts, we suffered a defeat, marking the end of our time in Madras.

On the following day, we embarked on our journey to the train station, bound for Hyderabad, where we were to change trains to return home to Aurangabad. With anticipation, we boarded the train, and our manager promptly dispatched two of us to procure some food. Unfortunately, the station lacked food stalls as the atmosphere had not yet fully normalized.

After some time had passed, a fellow passenger, dressed in traditional South Indian attire, joined us on the train. She settled into her seat and proceeded to unpack two packets of Upma (a popular South Indian dish made of semolina) and began to enjoy her meal. Our own hunger became increasingly pronounced, and we found ourselves engaging in a conversation in Marathi, discussing the ironic situation we found ourselves in. Here was a fellow traveler relishing a hearty meal while we had nothing to eat.

Amidst our predicament, one of our group members had the foresight to bring along some saunf (fennel seeds). In a gesture of solidarity, she shared the saunf with each one of us. Though a modest offering, we accepted the gesture gracefully. Sipping on water and fatigued from the events, we eventually succumbed to sleep, using slumber as a means to temporarily escape the pangs of hunger that accompanied us on our journey.

By the time we reached Hyderabad, the tiny pangs of hunger within us had grown into a giant pest that could no longer be ignored. Fortunately, at Hyderabad Station we spotted food stalls. With hunger finally satiated, we spent a few hours meandering around the train station, waiting for our scheduled train to Aurangabad. As the day progressed, our journey continued smoothly, the wheels of the train bearing us towards our destination. By the following morning, we were back in Aurangabad.

While we returned safe from our Madras expedition, our Hockey team who had traveled to Srinagar for their matches, had to bear the brunt of harrowing circumstances. Departing earlier than us to begin their tournament, they reached Srinagar on schedule. Taking a day of respite, they readied themselves for a match the subsequent day, only to suffer a loss. In an attempt to salvage some enjoyment from their trip, they decided to indulge in sightseeing, embracing the scenic beauty of Kashmir, often referred to as "The Paradise on Earth." These few days of solace were a welcome respite from the challenges that lay ahead.

The following morning, they boarded the train, heading towards Delhi, which had by then lost its leader. There was anarchy and horror all around, as angry mobs unleashed their fury on the innocent. Their Team Manager disembarked to gain more information about the unfolding situation. Yet, as he stepped onto the platform, he noticed the curious and wary gazes directed his way. Perceiving the danger that hung in the air, he decided to consult the Station Master, who hastily rose from his seat and uttered a warning in a concerned tone. "Sardarji, why are you out here? It's a significant risk to your life." By then the Prime Minister's assassins were identified as Sikhs, and it had incited a wave of violence against those of the same ethnicity.

On returning back to the train, the Sikh manager earnestly conveyed the encounter to his team members. The prevailing anxiety was further heightened by the presence of their manager's ten-year-old son and his wife, who had accompanied him on this ill-fated journey. Displaying remarkable unity, the Hockey Team promptly convened to strategize and collaborated to shield their manager and his family from potential danger, opting to conceal them beneath their seats.

Demonstrating collective determination, they strategically scattered luggage to obscure any indication of their presence. Anticipating possible inquiries, the team devised a meticulous strategy: in the event of questioning, the female members would respond in Marathi, while their Madam refrained from uttering anything, a calculated effort to deflect attention and avoid unnecessary risks.

Gratefully, their collaborative efforts bore fruit as they managed to reach Aurangabad and return home safely. That incident not only showcased their camaraderie but also highlighted their quick thinking and ability to navigate unforeseen challenges with resilience and unity.

While both teams successfully navigated the incident, the experience left an indelible mark on our memories, becoming an integral part of our shared stories.

Despite the Madras incident, I persevered and continued to participate in inter-university tournaments over the years. Those journeys afforded me the opportunity to visit Anand in Gujarat, Jaipur in Rajasthan, and Banasthali University in Rajasthan, where my final inter-university matches were held in the autumn of 1989.

Renowned as one of the world's largest fully residential women's universities, Banasthali is nestled within the picturesque Tonk district of Rajasthan. Reflecting on my experiences, even in its earlier state, Banasthali remained a beacon of hope for Rajasthani women. It provided them with a platform to pursue higher education and aspire to greater heights. It was a place where women could nurture lofty dreams and accomplish their objectives, effectively becoming a crucible where women could change the world.

My time at Banasthali left an indelible mark, characterized by a profound appreciation for the serene surroundings, the camaraderie shared with fellow students, and the captivating allure of the institution itself. It stands as a testament to the transformative power of education and the role institutions like Banasthali play in empowering individuals to shape their destinies.

As the matches unfolded, our team embraced the competitive spirit with a blend of enthusiasm and determination. The cool breeze and agreeable climate only served to heighten our sense of excitement. Each passing day saw us fully immersed not only in the heat of the competition but also in the unique atmosphere of the university.

The initial two matches resulted in victories, a testament to our unwavering dedication and collective effort. The cheers of triumph reverberated amidst the university's grounds, forming memories that would forever be etched in our minds. However, the third match presented a formidable challenge as we faced off against Annamalai University. Despite our best efforts, that encounter ended in defeat, reminding us of the unpredictable nature of sports and the valuable lessons that come with both victory and loss.

As the sun set on our inter-university matches, we departed Banasthali with a myriad of emotions. Gratitude permeated our thoughts for the invaluable experiences gained and the enduring friendships forged. Yet, there was a bittersweet realization. Somehow, we knew that trip marked the end of an era. The matches may have concluded, but the memories crafted during those days of spirited competition and camaraderie would forever remain a cherished chapter in our lives, a testament to the transformative power of sport and the lasting impact of shared experiences.

To truly comprehend the strength of any meaningful relationship, one must recognize that bonds are forged in the crucible of adversity, akin to steel being strengthened in the raging heat. For us, it took the unforeseen aftermath of a national tragedy to bring us together and transform us from mere teammates and opponents into genuine companions. That incident revealed the resilience of our good fellowship and the profound connections that can emerge from shared challenges and experiences.

Upon my return from Rajasthan, while hanging out with my sisters, I learnt about Sunanda's plan for her future. She had decided to pursue her aspirations and went on to get a Diploma in Child Health (DCH), after which, she set her eyes on postgraduate entrance exams. Through her determination and hard work, she achieved her goal, earning the prestigious degree of Doctor of Medicine. Before heading to the US, she worked around several hospitals in India. Then meticulously prepared for all the mandatory tests and other requirements to fulfill the criteria to migrate and work in the US. She built a career as a neonatologist, leveraging her affinity for nurturing fragile newborns to become a seasoned specialist trusted by hospitals to care for even the most delicate premature infants.

Obviously, the Kandi Family was on top of her VIP list. With her expertise and compassion, she always took care of the health and well-being of all the children in the Kandi family. She eventually became the primary source of guidance, whenever any of us in the entire extended family needed timely advice before consulting a specialist doctor or a second opinion of our own trusted one.

In a way, when it comes to anything related to health and wellness, the Kandi family was fortunate to have too many professionals in the field. My sister-in-law, Dr. Supriya Kandi, a seasoned practitioner, who was available be it night or day for everyone in the family, extended the same VIP privilege to us just like Sunanda.

Then there was Sujata, who has been a motherly figure to me and other young ones in the extended family.

Family is the nest that nurtures the younglings till they get their wings. It's the launch pad that pushes them away when they are ready to soar in the sky, and then again, it's the safety net to catch them if they ever fall from the sky. Dysfunctional may have become a fad in today's family dictionary, but thanks to Amma and Anna, it was not the term we ever had to learn. The principles and the ideologies they instilled in each of us, lives in us as their legacy, giving us strength to be our own individuals, while being inseparable part of a one whole unit.

Unfortunately, that realization dawned on me quite later in my life. At that time, shock overwhelmed me when Anna decided it was time for me to leave the nest and soar into the vast expanse of the world. Sunanda was preparing to embark on her journey to the US. Naturally, Anna was relieved that her career was on the right path.

Now free of yet another responsibility of his, he looked around in his bid to see whose life he could fix next. And his gaze stopped at me. So, he initiated the search for potential suitors on my behalf. As with an Indian family, once the pandora's box of matrimony is opened, it can never be shut. Then, there's only one outcome - you get sucked into the box and end up getting married.

Unfortunately, I had already flapped my wings during my pursuit of basketball. Therefore, I found myself unable to argue that I had no wings to leave the nest.

CHAPTER EIGHT

From Stranger to Soulmate

Women often regard their homes as their private sanctuaries, a safe haven where they can escape the judgment and prejudices of the outside world. Within the confines of home, there is no pressure to dress up or maintain a presentable appearance. There are no concerns about how one stands, sits, or leisurely lounges on the couch. It is only in the presence of parents that a girl can find the comfort and assurance to be herself, free from any apprehensions. Home becomes a space where authenticity is valued, and the unconditional support of family fosters a sense of security and acceptance.

So naturally, when a distant Uncle paid us a surprise visit, I wasn't prepared for it. It was a Sunday. I was lazing around in the house, lounging in the living room, watching the "Discovery of India" show on television.

I heard the knock on the door, which was instantly followed by the voice of my uncle. So, I didn't bother to compose myself. After all, uncle is family. However, much to my shock, this very family member had brought with him a perfect stranger.

Naturally, I did the bravest thing, an introvert like me would do in such a situation. I ducked my head and fled the scene. I erased the episode from my memory with a shrug.

Uncle made another appearance a few days later. Uncharacteristically, he sent me away under the pretext of fetching water. I was astute enough to recognize that I was being purposefully shooed away, still, I complied. However, in hindsight, it became apparent that Uncle's actions were not unintentional; rather, they were diabolical in nature.

During my absence, he broached the topic of my marriage with Anna, proposing the stranger as a prospective match. The stranger happened to be his sister-in-law's son, employed as a Medical Representative for a pharmaceutical company. Anna, however, was not enthusiastic about the proposal and promptly turned it down. The plot thickened, revealing the intricate dance of familial dynamics and the complexities of marriage negotiations.

Despite my uncle's initial setback, he proved to be persistent. Days later, he managed to corner my elder brother, Amarnath, during a family gathering, slipping in new information that the stranger got selected as a Police Officer. Amarnath, swift in his actions, wasted no time in conveying this revelation to Anna.

At that point, I found myself silently thanking my stars for Anna's initial rejection of the proposal. However, the news took an unexpected turn for the worse. Anna began to harbour second thoughts, and the unsettling prospect of that change in perspective started to worry me. Sensing the shifting tides, Amarnath took it upon himself to visit my uncle and express an interest in pursuing the proposal for my marriage with the stranger who had dropped in unannounced.

A date was announced when the Stranger would visit again. At that time with his family. So, there I was sitting all decked up in the living room in front of a man, who had already seen me in my worst condition. And to make the situation worse, both families sat around us, with their gazes fixed on me. Given that the Stranger had already conveyed his interest to both families, now all eyes were pinned on me in anticipation of my response.

I was determined not to rush into decisions without careful consideration. Recognizing the importance of choosing a life partner, I sought to be diligent in my decision-making process.

When I expressed my desire for a one-on-one conversation, momentarily there was a dead silence in the living room. My family however recovered faster than the Stranger's family and backed my decision. But Uncle spoke opposing the idea. Anna however, made it clear that any further discussion would happen after I got my private conversation. Unfortunately, the private chat didn't take place on that day.

Later that year, during the Diwali festival, the Stranger was on his way to his hometown, in Nanded. He chose to make a detour and visited my hometown, in Aurangabad. And that's how I first met Rajkumar Shriwastav a.k.a "Raj".

Raj and I ended up spending half an hour. I had sought to find a life partner who was open in communication, ambitious, and confident. The little time we got to spend with each other, provided me with a profound sense of comfort. Later, I conveyed my decision to my parents.

Anna, wasting no time, swiftly organized the engagement ceremony. The date was set for November 1, 1989. At that time, Raj was on his way to complete his remaining training. His family visited us, and the engagement ceremony took place on our bungalow terrace in the evening, attended by a small group including the two families, Raj's childhood friend Prakash, and his police buddies. Following the engagement ceremony, Raj had to depart to resume his training.

Six months later, on 4th June 1990, our union was sealed in matrimony, with both families radiating joy and graciously hosting the attending guests. As I stood beside Raj, receiving greetings from family and relatives, I couldn't help but reflect on how, in a matter of hours, my entire life would undergo a profound transformation. Similar to Anna and Amma, Raj and I were individuals crafted from different wood.

I hoped for Raj to be more forthcoming with reassurances. After all, I was leaving behind all the familiar comforts, embarking on a journey and sailing off with him into the unpredictable mist of the future.

On the other hand, Raj was a man driven by a strong moral compass but grappling with the complexities of human connection. His personality had been forged by the demands of his profession, resulting in an intimidating, reserved, yet composed demeanour. He was disciplined, methodical and committed in his thoughts and actions. Every facet of his life was characterized by a deep ingrained sense of order and structure. He was a man, dedicated to following protocols and adhering to the rules. When it came to communication, Raj predictably took the direct and to-the-point approach. He took pride in conveying information with authority and clarity. And he struggled with situations that demanded spontaneity or needed him to deviate from an established routine. While those features worked wonders in his professional role, for me, at first, he came across as blunt and lacking empathy. It took me months to truly see the person he was, underneath his stern exterior.

Immediately after our honeymoon, Raj's probation period commenced. Following a pattern reminiscent of Anna and Amma's relationship, Raj, too, left me in the company of strangers as he returned to resume his job in Ahmedpur.

My mother-in-law, understanding the nuances of this transition, exercised utmost patience, allowing me ample time to acclimate to my new life and its routines. Raj's brothers, Sunil and Anil, made sincere efforts to keep me entertained in his absence. Despite the warmth and support I received from my in-laws; the adjustment proved to be challenging initially. I found myself feeling isolated from my family and detached from my new in-laws.

Having grown up in a family that championed openness, empowerment, and equality, I was accustomed to voicing my opinions and pursuing my dreams without impediments. However, in that new setting, I encountered expectations and obligations as a daughter-in-law, creating a contrast to the familial dynamics I had known. It was a phase of adaptation and understanding between the familiar and the unfamiliar.

It was on June 4, 1990, Raj and I tied the knots, one that kept us together till date through all the storms in the ocean that we sailed into. Somehow, in some inexplicable way, Raj and my relationship found its way into the mold of Anna and Amma's enduring bond. Raj brought the constant to the equation, where I was always happy being a variable.

CHAPTER NINE

Coping with the Fragility of Life

In this new chapter of my life, I found myself compelled to embrace the overarching theme of "Adapting to a Changing World." The dynamics of my surroundings and relationships underwent shifts, prompting me to navigate the challenges and transformations with resilience and openness.

At my maternal place, the concept of limitation was foreign to us. Everything existed in abundance. My father had constructed a palatial bungalow ensuring that everyone had their own space. While Amma faced challenges with limited resources in her early married life, Anna's flourishing business eventually changed everything. Financial concerns became a thing of the past, and I can confidently say that I was born with a proverbial golden spoon.

Amma always prioritized our well-being, ensuring that we had access to the best and healthiest nutrition. Abundance of fruits, vegetables, and dry fruits was the norm. As mentioned earlier, she habitually prepared extra food in anticipation of unexpected guests, as our house frequently welcomed them with open arms. The contrast in lifestyle and abundance became more evident as I transitioned into a new phase of life with Raj's family.

After marriage, I relocated to Raj's hometown, Nanded, where we resided in a small rented place, partially surrounded by slums, equipped with basic facilities. In this setting, discipline permeated through everyone's daily routines. Due to limited income sources, everyone in the family practiced moderation in consuming meals and snacks.

My mother-in-law, whom I eventually started referring to as "Mummy," served as the Headmistress of a Telugu-medium school. Remarkably, she walked four kilometers every day from her school to save four to five rupees, which she would use to buy vegetables on her way back. This selfless sacrifice of hers amounted to providing one meal for the entire family. Witnessing such sacrifices, I gradually learned to adjust and curb my own accustomed habits in this new environment. The contrast in lifestyle and the value of frugality became evident, emphasizing the importance of adaptability in the face of changing circumstances.

Similar to Anna during his tenure as a government servant, Raj, a few months after our marriage, requested me to join him at his posting in Ahmedpur.

Ahmedpur, being a small town, lacked proper accommodation for us initially. We had to reside in a Government Guest House for a while before securing a place in the Government Quarters. Life in Ahmedpur was distinctly different and more constrained, but it did come with some conveniences. I was relieved from the duties of cooking and cleaning, as we had a Khansama (a male cook and housekeeper) to take care of those tasks. After a couple of weeks, we shifted to a government quarters, which consisted of a room barely 200 square feet in size, with a kitchen, a toilet, and a bathroom all crammed together. This adjustment marked another phase of adaptation to a changing environment and lifestyle.

The transition from the comforts of a luxurious and vibrant maternal bungalow in Aurangabad to a small and isolated apartment in Ahmedpur was quite stark.

The first night in Ahmedpur proved to be a nightmare. Raj had to go for his night rounds, leaving me alone in the dark. The window panes in the washroom were broken, and I had only flimsy covers to block them. The fear of someone breaking in through the washroom was overwhelming. I locked the door tightly and anxiously awaited Raj's return. The phobia lingered, and throughout my stay in that government quarter, using the washroom became a persistent source of anxiety.

Everything in that new town felt unfamiliar and strange. I was like a fish out of water. Despite Raj's presence, he was often on duty, leaving me lonely and isolated in a house surrounded by neighbours with a different culture and lifestyle. Those days were undoubtedly the most challenging of my life. The only solace came from the kindness of Raj's sister, Shailaja's in-laws, who were the only relatives we had in town. I visited them every day, finding comfort in their company. Their warm welcome, along with the presence of other women and children in the family, helped alleviate some of the isolation and loneliness I felt.

Gradually, I found a sense of purpose and joy in my new life by teaching the kids of Shailaja's co-sisters, and their friends from the neighbourhood. The involvement in education brought meaning to my days in Ahmedpur.

A couple of months later, on my birthday, as I was becoming more accustomed to the town, Raj and I were driving through the city, returning from the temple. Suddenly, Raj developed a craving for some roadside Dhaba food. We pulled over at one that appeared suitable. However, the moment we stepped inside, it felt like entering a parallel universe. I was the only woman in sight, and everyone else stared at us as if we were aliens who had lost their way. The realization hit us instantly — couples openly mingling were taboo in these small villages. We decided to hastily leave before our presence sparked any controversy. It turned out to be the most unforgettable birthday, but for all the wrong reasons.

The next day, Raj approached me with a troubled look on his face. He shared that some of his colleagues had questioned him about our visit to the dhaba. According to them, it was deemed improper to take women to such places in small towns. They imparted lectures on the importance of respecting the local culture and traditions, emphasizing how one should dress and behave accordingly. Raj found himself constantly bombarded with unsolicited advice from his co-workers, who attempted to impose their narrow-minded views on him.

A few months after the birthday fiasco, I began to notice that my periods were overdue, and I experienced persistent nausea throughout the day. With a vague idea that I might be pregnant, I felt clueless and alone, unsure of whom to contact. During those days, I visited Shailaja's family. Her mother-in-law took one look at me and confirmed what I suspected. It was then that I realized education alone might not be enough to solve every problem, and experience could be invaluable in such matters. I couldn't help but feel a grudging admiration for this woman who accurately diagnosed my situation.

Raj and I were overjoyed, but also bewildered. Raj was engrossed in his work, and I had no one to look after me. We faced challenges in reaching out to my family in Aurangabad since phones were not readily available. Moreover, I was unaware that the first trimester of pregnancy demanded extra care and nutrition. Before long, I found myself unable to bear the heat and smell of the kitchen.

Two months later, Raj's uncle and aunt came to visit us from Mumbai. In an attempt to make the most lavish lunch I could manage; I prepared a hearty meal for them. After lunch, Uncle suggested that we join them for a day trip to Nanded. Both Raj and I readily agreed to accompany them.

On the way to Nanded, I began to feel a strange pain in my stomach. Despite my discomfort, I kept quiet, not wanting to spoil everyone's mood. However, as we reached Nanded at night, my anxiety heightened when I noticed blood on my clothes.

While everyone else was asleep, Mummy, who woke up to receive us, was the only one aware of my situation. I confided in her about the bleeding, and she reassured me, urging me to go to sleep. Despite my nagging fear, Mummy's words provided some comfort, and I eventually drifted off to sleep. The next morning, I shared the news with Shailaja, who expressed concern that we should have gone to the doctor during the night.

Feeling the urgency in Shailaja's tone, I became increasingly anxious. I decided to go to the hospital and was about to leave when my brother-in-law, Sunil, dropped a bombshell. We learned that Sunil had eloped and married a neighborhood girl, Purnima, two weeks ago. That revelation added another layer of complexity to an already emotionally charged situation.

Facing the tumultuous turn of events, I turned to Raj immediately, grappling with the decision of which news to break to him first. As I shared the news of Sunil's elopement, Raj was left stunned.

Simultaneously, Mummy's fury erupted, and she began to yell at Sunil. The house became chaotic as emotions ran high, leading to Sunil having no choice but to leave.

Amidst that upheaval, we rushed to the hospital, clinging to the hope for a miracle. However, our hopes were shattered when the gynecologist delivered the devastating news. There was no fetal movement, and we were informed that we had to terminate the pregnancy, as there was nothing else that could be done. The weight of that tragic loss left us feeling numb and broken as we mourned the precious child we had lost. The news was undeniably devastating.

In a desperate attempt to cling to a feeble strand of hope, we consulted another doctor for a second opinion. Sadly, the diagnosis remained unchanged. Raj and I were faced with the painful decision to terminate the pregnancy. The procedure took some time, and I was kept in the hospital for a few hours.

Throughout this ordeal, Raj, as was his usual approach, kept his emotions bottled up, not wanting to worry me further. He tried his best to maintain a calm exterior despite the emotional turmoil that engulfed us.

I, however, wanted to shriek, curse and even rant uncontrollably. The abrupt and heart-wrenching end to our journey into parenthood left me in disbelief. While I have never adhered to any orthodox views on womanhood, recognizing the biological aspect of the power to give birth made me ponder the significance of this innate ability. I firmly believe that Nature never does anything without a plan. If women are engineered to give birth, there must be a purpose behind it in the grand design of nature. On a personal level, I have always cherished the idea of having children, yearning to have someone to call my own. Becoming a mother was, for me, a significant and meaningful part of my life journey. Yet, the painful termination of the pregnancy had brought that part of my journey to an unexpected and heartbreaking halt, leaving me to grapple with the weight of unfulfilled dreams and aspirations. Unfortunately, that journey had led me to a dead end.

CHAPTER TEN

From Grief to Hope

The journey back home from the hospital was the most dreadful. The silence between Raj and me, though understandable, was unnerving. Both of us were emotionally shattered. In that grief-stricken quietude, we found solace in the shared belief that everything happens for a reason.

The heaviness in my knees, a familiar sensation from when I left my mother's home, returned as I entered Raj's home once again. Once again, I was feeling the same ache in my knees, as I was entering Raj's home.

I tried to muster the courage to stand firm, with my head straight through all the barrage of questions from my in-laws. Raj stood beside me, calm as a rock, so I could lean on if there was ever a need for it. I held my tears till we reached home. But the moment I stepped in, I burst into tears. After the initial shock and grief, the in-laws put aside their personal pain, and tried to nurse mine.

Mummy came over to me and sat me down. She looked into my eyes and calmly uttered - "Kyun, ro rahe ho ek maas ke gole ke liye, mera to pachhis saal ka beta ghar se chala gaya" ("Why are you weeping for a two-month-old embryo? My twenty-five-year-old son left me"). Her way of reassuring me, made me realize her pain but at the same time it hurt me a lot,as Mummy did not understand my pain in that heart wrenching moment.

Fate took an ironic turn when Raj was called in for duty the very next day, leaving me alone as I was advised to avoid exertion. In his absence, I received a letter from Sunanda, filled with detailed instructions on how I should take care of myself during the pregnancy. Ironically, around the same time, she received my letter informing the family about the heartbreaking news of my miscarriage. The exchange of letters mirrored the complexities and challenges life had thrown our way.

Later, I discovered that when Amma learned of the news, she retreated to the staircase and mourned for hours. She insisted on meeting me at once, believing it was necessary for her peace of mind.

Setbacks in life often bring self-doubt in their wake. That was the first significant health-related setback in my life, prompting questions about my well-being, my future, and my fate. Negative thoughts inundated my mind, and tears flowed freely. The tragedy had left me utterly shattered. For a week, I secluded myself in my room, reflecting on my life and questioning whether joy or pain had dominated my journey so far.

Already grappling with the challenges to my mental health, I found myself unfairly becoming the scapegoat for Sunil and Purnima's marriage. Due to my association with both of them and our shared outings, everyone laid blame on me for their runaway romance. This unjust accusation persisted until I could no longer bear it. Eventually, I decided to confront Mummy with the truth, dispelling all misunderstandings and proving my innocence.

In those difficult times, my pillar of strength emerged in the form of Karuna, Prakash's soulmate and my best friend. The bond between Prakash and Raj, forged since their junior kindergarten days, extended to the entire family. Prakash was regarded as Mummy's fourth son by all the kids in the family until they grew up and learned the truth. Their family became more than just a family to me; it became a source of support and solace.

Karuna and I shared the same school and college in Aurangabad, but our paths didn't cross during those years. Interestingly, the first time I met her was on the day of my wedding. Our chance encounter took place at a beauty salon, where Karuna was working as a trainee at that time. Little did we realize that our lives would become intertwined later on. After our weddings, we met again and quickly became inseparable friends. It seemed like destiny had brought us together, providing the emotional support I so desperately needed in life.

What added to the serendipity was the similar story of our husbands. Raj and Prakash were childhood friends from Nanded who had studied in the same school and college. The discovery that they had both married girls from the same city and school delighted them. This connection further deepened the bond between our families.

After days of rest in Nanded, I gathered my belongings and joined Raj in Ahmedpur, hoping that this change of scenery would be a chance for healing and a fresh start. Raj made efforts to distract me by taking me to various places to create new memories. During one trip, we came across trees bearing raw mangoes. I expressed a desire to pluck them myself, and without hesitation, Raj stopped the bike, helped me climb the tree, and fulfilled my wish. Such small gestures and moments of joy held immense significance for me.

Meanwhile, back in Nanded, Mummy's fury over Sunil's elopement with Purnima lingered, even though two months had passed since they ran away. She had disowned Sunil and vowed never to see him again. In a family gathering, Anna attempted to persuade Mummy to reconsider and welcome Sunil back home. He argued that Sunil and Purnima deserved a chance to live happily with the family. Mummy, shocked and offended by Anna's suggestion, resisted the idea vehemently.

Together, Raj and I faced challenging times, not just in our personal lives but also in those of our families. There was a common trait between us – we couldn't stay down for long. We were the kind of people who would bounce back sooner rather than later. If life brought us down, so be it, but we were determined to rise up stronger. Raj and I had resolved to put the past behind us and move forward. I came to realize that good times don't reveal character; rather, it's during challenging times that one's true character is illuminated. Navigating through that difficult phase of life, I found solace in the fact that I had stumbled upon a partner for life.

In due time, Raj completed his probation in Ahmedpur and was ready for his first assignment. Raj's ambition compelled him to aim for a city where he could gain hands-on experience in solving cases and maintaining law and order. However, fate had other plans for him. His posting was at the airport security in Mumbai.

Raj always looked at the bright side of things. He told me that this was an opportunity for him to spend some time with me in the city of dreams.

For Raj, Mumbai was truly a city of dreams. He had completed his graduation in Mumbai and had family connections through his uncle's family in the city. Naturally, he eased into the urban rhythm comfortably.

On the other hand, for me, it was a huge transition just a year after our marriage. We had moved from Nanded to Ahmedpur, a small town, and now to Mumbai, a thronged metropolis. I felt overwhelmed and disoriented by the change in pace and lifestyle. Although I had visited Mumbai before, it was more as a tourist, captivated by the city's glamour. I vividly recall feeling like a stranger in my own country when I first stepped out of our house.

Upon our move to Mumbai, our accommodation arrangement was seamlessly facilitated by the gracious support of Shailaja and her husband, Mr. Chandrashekhar. Their generosity allowed us to establish a stable foundation during that transitional period. As we settled into our temporary residence, I gradually warmed up to Shailaja and her family. She became a comforting companion during Raj's work hours, and the presence of her two daughters, Parinita and Namrata, added a delightful touch of entertainment.

Thus began our immersion into the vibrant heartbeat of this bustling metropolis, where the relentless rhythms of life echoed ceaselessly.

CHAPTER ELEVEN

The Abyss of Illness

During my stay in Mumbai, my responsibilities and ties continued to keep me connected to Nanded. As the eldest daughter-in-law, I found myself being present for the rituals that Mummy, despite her religious competence, was forbidden from performing due to societal norms associated with widowhood. That discrepancy never made sense to me, as Mummy was fully capable of handling such responsibilities on her own.

The conservative society we lived in imposed restrictions on widows, preventing them from performing sacred pujas (worship). It seemed as though there was an unfounded belief that God would take offense if a widow engaged in prayer rituals. My limited understanding of God led me to question the emotional sensitivities attributed to the Almighty. Despite my passive rebellion against orthodox social norms, I couldn't bear to let Mummy miss out on her traditions. Raj's busy work schedule left me as the representative of the family during those occasions. I often pondered who had the authority to interpret God's will for the rest of mankind and whether those individuals were truly qualified for such a responsibility.

During one of my trips to Nanded, I participated in a family Puja that, as a daughter-in-law, only I could perform. Before returning to Mumbai, I decided to visit Karuna and engage in a heartfelt conversation, sharing our joys and sorrows. As these conversations tend to be endless, it became dark, and I had to pack my bags. So I told Karuna goodbye and headed to the door. That's when I noticed a lump on the right side of my neck, a peculiar and unsettling discovery. Concerned, I checked the left side and found nothing. Feeling worried and scared, I discussed it with Karuna and her mother-in-law, who suggested seeing a doctor. I agreed to their advice.

The next morning, as I headed to Aurangabad, where I planned to stop over on my way to Mumbai, the lump slipped out of my mind. I convinced myself that it was nothing serious, a minor oversight.

While in bed at night, I confided in Sunanda about the lump on my neck. She listened with concern and assured me that she would get some medicine for me in the morning. However, instead of waiting, she promptly consulted Jagdish kaka over the phone at the break of dawn. After the consultation, she approached me with a serious expression, informing me that I needed an urgent ten-day antibiotic course. Although she didn't specify the reason, I could sense that something was gravely wrong.

Sunanda recommended antibiotics and advised me to postpone my journey, suggesting that I observe any changes. Unbeknownst to me, my stay would unexpectedly extend as days turned into weeks. Playfully, Sunanda hinted at additional tests, and I, oblivious to the seriousness of the situation, agreed, unaware of the storm brewing on the horizon. Eventually, a biopsy was performed—an unfamiliar term to my ears at the time—and we awaited the results that would unravel the mystery behind that enigmatic lump.

Anticipation filled the air as Sunanda and I went to collect the reports, but our excitement soon turned to confusion. To our surprise, the report we received did not belong to me; it was for someone else. Naively, I trusted Sunanda's reassurances, unaware of the concealed truth.

As days passed, hushed conversations and whispered exchanges became more prevalent around me. Initially, I dismissed them as trivial matters, but gradually, I started sensing that something was amiss. It became apparent that everyone around me had suddenly started walking on eggshells, being extremely cautious about what was spoken. I became intrigued and played along as much as I could. However, every time I overheard the family discussing something, I couldn't help but stay back and listen in. The mention of Tata Hospital caught my attention, but its connection to my own life remained elusive.

One day, I observed Amma in tears, and when I inquired with Sujata about the reason, she downplayed it as a trivial matter. Naively, I believed her explanation.

The revelation of the truth came to me during a solitary bathing ritual. The scattered pieces of the puzzle— the erroneous biopsy report, Amma's tears, the mention of Tata Hospital, and the hushed whispers that enveloped me—all coalesced into a devastating realization. The truth struck with a force that rendered me immobile. It was about me. Cancer had cast its ominous shadow upon my life.

In that suspended moment, the weighty words "Cancer? Cancer in me?" reverberated through my consciousness, shattering the illusion of invincibility that had shielded me until now.

Betrayed by fate, I found myself yearning to assign blame, to pinpoint a culprit responsible for that cruel twist of misfortune. A torrent of questions inundated my mind, demanding answers that could never fully quell the depths of my concern.

That harsh reality collided with disbelief and fear, tearing through the fragile fabric of my existence. Mortality, once a distant concept, now stared back at me with unyielding eyes. Uncertainty cloaked the path ahead, obscuring the once-clear road of possibilities.

Isolation descended, casting me to the edge of an abyss. The fear of the unknown clawed at my consciousness, threatening to consume me. Vulnerability seeped into every crevice of my being, leaving me adrift in a sea of apprehension. The comforting illusions of invincibility shattered, leaving behind a chilling void that taunted me relentlessly. The nefarious villain had dramatically stormed into the pages of my fairytale existence.

Witnessing the devastating toll cancer had taken on my maternal family, the memory of my uncle's battle against leukemia loomed large in my mind. Within a mere two years, he was snatched away, leaving a void that forever marked the hearts of those who loved him. My Granny was not the same after his demise. Countless stories of others who succumbed to the disease echoed in my ears, amplifying the weight of my own diagnosis.

Why had I become the chosen recipient of this malevolent fate? Society's misconceptions had whispered fallacies of immunity in the ears of the young, yet at the tender age of twenty-four, married for a fleeting year, I found myself ensnared in this somber reality. Cancer, it seemed, spared no one. In the midst of my swirling emotions, a realization emerged—a beacon of hope amidst the darkness.

Medical advancements had flourished since my uncle's battle, and my family, blessed with a lineage of medical professionals, would rally behind me, ensuring that I received the best care possible. Their unwavering commitment to my well-being offered a glimmer of solace in this tumultuous storm.

Contemplating the deep love I held for my Amma, Anna, and Raj, their existence forming the very foundation of my world, I summoned the strength to conceal the weight of this knowledge from their unsuspecting hearts. I understood that shielding them from the harsh reality would be my burden to bear.

In Indian culture, a woman is considered Goddess Laxmi. Even when she's born, her parents fondly refer to her as "Laxmi ghar aayi hain!" meaning Goddess Laxmi has arrived home. It is considered a blessing. Goddess Laxmi is a symbol of wealth and prosperity for the family. On the flip side of the coin, any ill omen that occurs in the family is also attributed to the woman. Especially among the in-laws, if after marriage, some unfortunate incident happens, then the blame falls upon the newlywed woman. So prevalent is this belief that even in 2024, TV shows would depict in-laws cursing the newlywed bride for their ill fortunes.

I was, however, fortunate; I did not have to bear the brunt of their anger. I had the support of my husband, my in-laws, and my maternal family.

Yet, my mind couldn't help but think about "Karma." Indian spirituality is woven around the concept of Karma, which suggests one always has to pay for one's deeds. I began ravaging the memory lanes of my past, wondering if I had ever done anything wrong with anyone, consciously or unintentionally.

The diagnosis of cancer intensified the emotional turmoil. The revelation plunged me into a deep well of fear, uncertainty, and vulnerability. Facing a life-threatening illness after experiencing a recent miscarriage added layers of complexity to my emotional state. The fear of the unknown, coupled with the uncertainty of life and health, became paralyzing.

When the miscarriage happened, I had begun to worry if it was a prelude to a lifelong battle with health issues. Cancer just confirmed those fears for me. It was the second blow that knocked me out, hitting so hard that it shook me to the core.

I realized the journey was not just a physical battle but a profound emotional one. The ordeal had just begun. The fragility of life became glaringly apparent, and the journey towards healing was daunting.

As I stood on the precipice of this harrowing journey, I recognized the gravity of the battle that lay ahead. It demanded every ounce of strength, resilience, and courage I could muster. In the face of uncertainty and fear, I made a silent vow to confront this formidable adversary head-on, to defy the odds, and to emerge from the shadows of illness stronger and wiser.

CHAPTER TWELVE

Battling the Beast Within

In cinematic portrayals, when the threat of an asteroid looming over Earth is imminent, global leaders convene to strategize on averting the crisis. The gravity of impending danger unites humanity's leaders in a collective pursuit of a singular objective – the preservation of their cherished planet.

A similar scenario unfolded within the confines of my maternal home. Family members assembled, their countenances grave, engaging in earnest discussions that mirrored the gravity of a global crisis. Ideas and suggestions flowed freely, each one scrutinized, pondered upon, and either discarded or earmarked for subsequent deliberation.

What struck me profoundly was the genesis of the serious discourse, rooted in the revelation that within the recesses of my own physical being lurked insidious cancerous cells. Amidst this macabre moment, a stark realization dawned – a multitude of souls had congregated beneath one roof, not to salvage a planet, but to safeguard a cherished individual soul.

Ultimately, the jury reached a consensus, and it was decided that I would be transported to Mumbai for consultation with Dr. Rao, the esteemed Dean of Tata Memorial Hospital and a close associate of Jagdish Kaka.

The following night, Sunanda, a steadfast companion, accompanied me as I embarked on my journey to Mumbai. Trains required advanced booking. So, we opted to travel by bus, which was a nine hours journey. Raj was supposed to be there to receive me. After having spent time with my family, I was eager to meet Raj. It was the first time, since the discovery of the torment, that I would be coming face to face with my husband. In my heart I knew, Raj stood by me, but I couldn't help questioning if anything about that was fair. Out of all the possible pairings, he was paired with me, a woman who just after a year of marriage, was doomed with cancer. I wondered, if he had ever weighed the pros and cons of his decision. A wave of similar thoughts flooded my mind, given that I had hours to kill.

When the bus reached Dadar Station, my heart slowed down, in its attempt to brace for a shock. As I alighted from the bus, I scanned the crowd for that one familiar face, that would bring answers to all the questions I had brewed enroute. And then the answer came to me.

Raj maneuvered through the crowd as he spotted and approached us. I stood there wondering what would be his first response. And then Raj came over and stared at me. I could see he was searching for words. Minutes later, we both realized he was never going to find them. For a cop, he was good at finding criminals who fit the crime, but never the words to fit the situation. Then Raj realized, action speaks louder than words and gave me a hug. In his silence, Raj spoke volumes. And in that warm, comforting embrace of my life partner, I found my answers.

Later that day, we encountered Dr. Rao, who had already received a briefing from Jagdish Kaka. Dr. Rao granted me the green light to undergo my surgery in Aurangabad. He was familiar with Dr. Bhagwat, designated as my surgeon, while my uncle would take on the role of an Anesthesiologist, top most Anesthesiologist in Aurangabad. According to the outlined plan, following the surgery, I was scheduled to return to Mumbai for consultations and subsequent treatments under the guidance of Dr. Rao.

Papillary carcinoma of the thyroid is a slowly progressing form of thyroid cancer, typically responsive to treatment when detected in its early stages. However, receiving a diagnosis can be an overwhelming experience, given the nature of the ailment - Cancer, which inherently carries a sense of fear.

Similar to other forms of cancer, it brings forth numerous unknowns and uncertainties. When I questioned the doctors about the likelihood of a complete cure and the possibility of relapse, their response was not reassuring. They conveyed an inability to guarantee complete eradication of the cancer and offered no assurance against a potential relapse. This lingering uncertainty in the doctors' statement continues to weigh on my mind even to this day.

Nevertheless, my doctor conveyed that had I not discovered the cancer when I did, my journey might have taken a different, more somber path, leading to my heavenly abode within six months.

The impact of that revelation extended beyond my personal concerns; it deeply affected my in-laws. None of us had envisioned that, within a year of our marriage, our lives would undergo such a profound and unexpected transformation.

That day passed as Raj and I bore the burden of an uncertain future on our shoulders. As we returned home, our conversation stretched into the late hours of the night. It was one of those days, when the conversations between two people lasted longer than the tides governed by the sun and moon.

The following day, Raj and I resumed our conversation, seamlessly picking up from where we left off the night before. However, our exchange took an unexpected turn when Raj suddenly halted, overcame by a wave of emotions that led him to tears. It was my first time seeing him in that state. In that instant, all I could offer was a comforting embrace, accompanied by reassurances that together, we would navigate the challenges looming on our path. Placing my trust in the medical expertise within our family, I sought to instill confidence in Raj. For my sake, Raj gathered himself, summoning the strength to brave a smile that concealed the turmoil within.

Sunanda accompanied us as we embarked on the journey to attend my doctor's appointment for the scheduled checkup. From the hospital, we roamed around the city for a while and enjoyed a meal at the restaurant, before returning home.

Later that night, Sunanda and I returned to Dadar Station to catch our bus for the journey back to Aurangabad. Raj accompanied us to the bus station, even though he couldn't travel with us. Despite his inability to join us immediately, he opted to be present during my recovery period.

Upon my return to Aurangabad, I found solace in the embrace of my maternal family. It became evident that the preparation for the impending surgery wasn't an individual endeavour; rather, my entire family stood united in support.

The necessary preoperative tests commenced, leading to my admission to KamalNayan Bajaj Hospital at Aurangabad a day prior to the surgery. As I underwent a comprehensive full-body scan, I grappled with the appropriate demeanour. Striving to embody the ideal patient, I remained perfectly still, not even batting an eye. When Dr. Bhagwat visited to check on my condition, he humorously inquired if I had already been administered anesthesia. That night, Sunanda steadfastly stayed by my bedside.

In October 1991, merely fifteen months into my life journey with Raj, I underwent the surgeon's scalpel for the first time, without the realization that more such procedures lay ahead.

Under the skilled hands of Dr. Bhagwat, assisted by Jagdish Kaka, a total thyroidectomy was performed, marking a transformative moment in my anatomy. Thyroidectomy is basically removal of the entire thyroid gland. The prospect of such a surgery stirred fear and anxiety within me, yet Jagdish Kaka's reassuring presence and expertise provided the courage needed to proceed. He ensured my comfort throughout the procedure.

Following the surgery, my voice became hoarse, and I encountered challenges in eating, swallowing, and experienced some bleeding. Mummy, accompanied by her co-sister, visited the hospital. Unable to witness my condition, Raj's uncle delegated the responsibility to his wife.

My hospital stay extended to three days, during which my siblings took turns being by my side, lifting my spirits. They became my unwavering pillars of strength and support during this trying period. Rama, my brother Amarnath's wife, and my sister-in-law also extended her care.

Surprisingly, many maternal relatives, who hadn't been particularly vocal in the past, came forward to visit me, showering an overwhelming amount of love and care. Their affectionate gestures left me deeply grateful and humbled.

Upon discharge on the third day, I returned home to recuperate for a couple of weeks. Gradually, my symptoms subsided. Despite the rollercoaster of emotions, this experience fortified me, instilling a deeper sense of gratitude for the incredible people in my life who had shown unwavering love and support.

The medical advice prescribed three weeks of complete rest—a novel experience for me, as daytime rests were seldom part of my routine since childhood. It felt unusual to find myself in a position of repose while other family members attended to my needs.

In the midst of the stress and trauma of the recent days, Sunanda strongly advocated for a much-needed break, insisting that we embark on a vacation. Our destination of choice was the Pal-Yawal Wildlife Sanctuary in the Jalgaon district of Maharashtra State. Raj's friend, late Sopan Potulwar, a Range Forest Officer stationed there, had extended several invitations for us to spend time with him.

Despite the impromptu nature of the plan, Raj expressed a willingness to accompany us. Sujata, her three sons, Sunanda, Raj, and I—all eagerly embarked on a three-day journey to immerse ourselves in the natural and historical splendors of the sanctuary. Sopan orchestrated our accommodations within a log house, a guest residence administered by the Forest Department nestled amidst the verdant expanse of the forest. That sojourn marked my first encounter with the distinctive ambiance of a log house.

Encompassing 168 square kilometers, the sanctuary boasted a diverse array of wildlife, including various predatory mammals. Adding to its allure, the sanctuary housed ancient temples and historical landmarks, providing a unique dimension to our getaway.

During our visit, we explored a deer breeding farm, where Sujata's sons Vishal, Kunal, and Varun delighted in feeding baby deer with milk bottles. The post-surgery excursion proved to be a beautiful experience and a much-needed stress buster.

Sopan, a kind and generous host, guided us through the wonders of the jungle. He led us on a thrilling ride through the dense forest, imparting knowledge about the remarkable plants and animals that inhabited the area. His profound understanding enriched our experience, allowing us to appreciate the beauty and mystery of the forest. Sopan truly proved to be a gem of a person.

Upon our return from Pal, we consulted Dr. Rao over the phone. He recommended a second round of treatment at the Radiation Medicine Center (RMC) located behind Tata Memorial Hospital in Mumbai.

During that round of treatment at the Radiation Medicine Center (RMC) in Mumbai, I was accompanied by Vijaya, Sujata, Sujata's sons, and Amma. However, due to safety concerns, particularly the potential exposure to radiation, infections, or diseases that could impact their health, Sujata had to return to

Aurangabad with her sons. The medical advice prompted the precaution, emphasizing the well-being of the children.

At the RMC Center, I embarked on a course of radiation therapy, prompted by the unfortunate metastasis of my papillary carcinoma of the thyroid to the lymph nodes. The primary objective of that treatment was to eliminate any residual malignancy.

While the therapy proved to be rigorous, it was considered a pivotal step in my journey toward recovery. The medical team provided a comprehensive briefing, emphasizing that radiation therapy involves the targeted use of high-energy beams to eradicate cancer cells.

During my stay at RMC, I resided in an isolation room, separated from my loved ones by a glass barrier. During this period, Raj, accompanied by Amma and Vijaya, visited to bring lunch. Amma spoke from the other side of the transparent glass door, unaware that the sound wasn't transmitting through. Sensing her distress, I responded, but she couldn't hear me. Misinterpreting the situation, she assumed I had lost my voice, leading to her tears. Raj clarified the issue, explaining that the sound was hindered by the glass barrier.

While my family members were a constant presence, there were moments, especially after visiting hours, when I found myself alone.

In the isolation room, I shared space with an elderly woman, approximately 75 years old, who spent her time in tears. As she lacked formal education, her husband requested me to explain the treatment procedure. Attempting to bridge the gap proved challenging due to our language differences. She spoke a regional dialect that I struggled to understand, and vice versa.

After I was moved out of the isolation room and back into a ward with eight other women. Those women hailed from different parts of India, each with unique problems and concerns. Language barriers had become a common theme at the RMC. I found myself in the role of a mediator, interpreter and translator relaying their issues to the hospital staff. Somehow, the spirit of leading the eight fellow patients had instilled in me the seed of taking control over my life. I developed a routine of rising early, making my bed, and freshening up by 6 A.M. before the nurse's rounds and breakfast. I was always ready to face the day.

The nurses were noticing this. Eventually, they began encouraging fellow patients to follow my example.

When the day came for my discharge, I felt more overwhelmed than overjoyed. The patients who had become pals and the nurses who cared beyond the call of duty all contributed to building a sense of leaving behind close ones. On my way out, I wondered If I should give tips to the hospital's maids and sweepers. I even attempted it, but the staff politely declined, stating that they were well compensated. When I shared that with Raj later, he humorously remarked that their salaries exceeded his.

From the Hospital, Raj led me to the renowned Mahim Dargah, a revered mosque in Mumbai, where believers from all faiths and religions would come to get their wishes fulfilled. Amma and Vijaya also accompanied us. At the Dargah, Raj, the otherwise idealistic cop, bribed the Almighty to have mercy on my soul. From there, we proceeded to a restaurant to share a meal together.

Perhaps, Amma found her reassurance in Raj's unwavering determination to stand by my side. Despite their concerns, they departed for Aurangabad that night. They had to take care of their families respectively. It was a difficult parting for me, torn between my desire to stay by their side and the consideration for Raj.

CHAPTER THIRTEEN

Radiation, Resilience, and Rumors

While Amma made efforts to be physically present whenever possible, Anna played a pivotal role behind the scenes. He generously covered the expenses for the surgery and my aftercare during a challenging period in my life. Facing such an ordeal at a young age, Raj initially wanted to bear the financial burden himself. However, recognizing Anna's emotional turmoil, he yielded to Anna's wish to shoulder the financial responsibility.

It wasn't easy for Raj to accept this. The very society that burdens women with it's prejudices, doesn't spare the men either. Men are supposed to be the guardians. And with it comes the honour of not taking aid of any kind from anyone. The father of the bride if and when he visits his married daughter's in-laws, is not supposed to even drink water at his daughter's in-law's house. Similarly, the husband is not supposed to take aid from the wife's father. Yet, Raj was a progressive man. He had a choice to make. Whether to fight his own battle for society-imposed code of honour, or care for me and my family during the crisis. He relinquished his personal battle, to join my fight against cancer.

Later on, Raj repaid the money, and Anna graciously accepted it. Raj and I had prepared for such contingencies, drawing on a valuable lesson from my maternal family—wise investing.

Anna, being a forward-thinking individual, had meticulously planned his finances, contributing to the establishment of his empire. As his daughter, I recognized the importance of planning for the future. Shortly after marrying Raj, I understood that we had yet to embark on the path of financial planning and savings. Together, we were determined to shape a different future. Taking the initiative, I assumed the responsibility of planning our financial endeavours.

In our pursuit of financial stability, we invested in a comprehensive life insurance policy. During those years, government department salaries were disbursed in cash, prompting me to open a bank account to manage the incoming funds and meticulously plan our monthly budget. Though the journey was not without its challenges, we navigated through.

Fortuitously, we had the foresight to acquire a Mediclaim policy, a decision that proved crucial in coping with the exorbitant expenses that accompanied my health challenges. The support system became indispensable, and I shudder to think how we would have coped without it. The future, at that point, loomed larger than we could have ever imagined, and this prudent planning became a lifeline for us.

Radiation therapy, while targeting cancer cells, inevitably affects both healthy and cancerous cells, leading to certain aftermaths. Common side effects include fatigue and dry skin. However, in the subsequent days, additional challenges surfaced, encompassing issues like depression, anxiety, weight loss, hyperactive metabolism, diminished quality of life, and insomnia. The cumulative impact left me irritable for an extended period, underscoring the toll that such treatments can take on both the physical and mental well-being.

Amidst the challenges, the unwavering presence of my parents, in-laws, siblings, Sunanda, Sujata, and Raj, became a source of solace. Their constant support and encouragement served as a pillar of strength, providing much-needed comfort throughout the journey.

In my case, I even observed a peculiar aspect of the radiation therapy – a temporary darkening of my ornaments. This served as a visual reminder of the unique journey I was undertaking, becoming a tangible symbol of the battle against cancer that I was actively fighting. Those transformed ornaments stood as a powerful symbol of the resilience and strength exhibited during the challenging period in my life. They became a tangible representation of the courage and determination required to face and overcome the hurdles presented by cancer and its treatments.

While grappling with cancer and its aftermath, an unusual piece of news surfaced from Ahmedpur. Gossipmongers seemed to be in abundance, spreading the unfounded rumour that I had already passed away and that Raj was considering remarriage. The news of my surgery provided fodder for speculation, leading people to entertain various thoughts.

As the rumour reached our doorstep, I looked into Raj's eyes and uttered, "You don't have to stay with me. You can find someone else."

To that, he responded with a hearty laugh, embracing me tightly. "Don't be silly," he reassured, "You are the only one I want. I'm not going anywhere." His words conveyed a steadfast commitment, providing comfort and dispelling any doubts that may have surfaced amid the baseless rumours.

Another story that reached my ears purported that a certain relative asserted a pre-marital diagnosis of cancer on my part, a disclosure ostensibly concealed by my family from Raj and his kin. Raj and my in-laws vehemently refuted these speculations. Had I been apprised of such information beforehand; I would have refrained from entering into the matrimonial alliance with Raj.

Following the conclusion of radiation therapy, I visited Dr. Rao's assistant, Dr. Deepak Parikh, who later became my lifelong doctor. Dr. Parikh supervised my recovery and outlined a comprehensive treatment plan, including large-dose scans, medication, and regular tests scheduled quarterly, bi-yearly, and annually.

Despite the physical weakness that plagued me, I embarked on a journey of self-improvement, seeking guidance from books about thyroid cancer patients. Realizing that I was not alone in my emotions and challenges, I resolved to overcome them as soon as possible and embraced a holistic lifestyle, incorporating a regular fitness regime and healthy habits.

Over time, the fear of cancer recurrence diminished, but I remained vigilant about my health, attending regular check-ups and adhering to the recommendations of my doctors.

Life after cancer marked an unexpected journey with a new addition: My Pillbox. I became meticulous about my medications, never missing a dosage. Over time, my commitment to medication became a routine. I got so meticulous and programmed to take the right pills at the right time, that it had become a usual sight for the family. Everyone, including myself, learned to accept that my pillbox was now an extension of me.

With every check-up, relief surged through me as the reports confirmed my good health, and the doctors reassured me of my well-being.

Once, during a visit from Mummy, she witnessed me taking pills regularly and remarked, "Rekha, Davai aaise khati hai, jaise khana!" ('Rekha, you eat your medicines as if you are eating food!') Her words made me reflect on how I treated medication almost casually, akin to consuming candy. My pillbox has become an integral part of my routine.

Although I quickly adjusted to the new life post-cancer, accepting that cancer was a struggle and its treatment would bring emotional challenges.

Living with cancer allowed despair to sneak into my psyche periodically. Feeling bored at home, boredom sought the company of dread. Determined not to let cancer define me, I turned to various activities to find happiness and keep myself occupied. Cancer, instead of deterring me, made me more determined. I even took up tutoring for school children during this period.

Once, I surprised Raj at the airport where he was stationed. Raj proudly introduced me to his colleagues, surprising them with my appearance. Female co-workers expressed shock, unable to reconcile my youthful appearance with the fact that I had battled cancer.

My fight, hidden from the outer world, continued to shape my journey. After the Radiation Therapy, my doctor had advised me to wait for two years before considering having a baby, a stark reality that none of us had foreseen. The memory of losing my unborn baby lingered, and I found it difficult to process that pain and sorrow. The desire to become a mother weighed heavily on me, a burden I bore in silence. The unspoken weight of unfulfilled maternal aspirations, intertwined with the haunting memory of the child I lost, casted a profound shadow over my inner world.

CHAPTER FOURTEEN

Rebuilding Life through Resilience

After months since my surgery, life gradually returned to a state of normalcy. Once again, our home was filled with joy and happiness as Anil, my younger brother-in-law, prepared for his wedding. The atmosphere buzzed with mixed emotions—an orchestra of laughter, tears, and heartfelt moments.

Taking on the responsibilities as the eldest daughter-in-law, I eagerly dove into the preparations. In India, weddings are lavish events, aptly known as the Great Indian Wedding. However, we don't settle for ordinary challenges; we up the ante by embracing the grand carnival of life.

Arriving early, I was determined to assist my widowed Mummy in pulling off the wedding. Relatives gathered for the pre-wedding rituals. Our home became a whirlwind of colours, fragrances, and excited voices. Sarees of every hue adorned the rooms, bangles clinked merrily and the glow of designer henna, highlighted our joys. The aroma of freshly prepared sweets and savory dishes wafted through the air. The house echoed with laughter as we discussed intricate details and made meticulous plans. From weeks before the wedding, every day we slogged tirelessly, ensuring that every aspect of the wedding was perfect.

When I got married to Raj, I was too caught up in the whirlwind of my own emotions to notice anything else. But this time, I was not on the grand stage. Rather, I was the one pulling the strings from the backstage. It was exciting to witness a new set of customs besides what I had grown into. The pre-wedding rituals, the ceremonies, and the family customs were all steeped in tradition, each carrying its own significance and symbolism.

Surprisingly, despite it being a wedding ceremony, I found myself at the center of most conversations. Relatives inquired about my health, to which I politely responded. Basic social etiquettes had not become second nature to me, but I realized this was a new normal. Even after years, conversations and phone calls often began with inquiries about my well-being.

As the days passed and the excitement continued to build, the stress of ensuring that everything ran smoothly began to weigh on me. I juggled responsibilities, managing the needs of both the bride's and groom's families, ensuring that traditions were upheld and making certain that the wedding day would be a memorable one for everyone. I enjoyed being in the forefront of all the celebrations. It was of course taking a toll on me; I got tired fast but did not stop any stone unturned.

As the festivities eventually settled down, and we welcomed Rohini, Anil's wife home, we returned to Mumbai, our hearts full of cherished memories and a sense of fulfillment that only a great Indian wedding can bring.

Back in Mumbai, Raj and I found ourselves relocating once again. We moved into temporary accommodation in a private building until we secured our designated police quarter in Marol, Andheri.

Raj's senior, the late Mr. D. N. Jadhav, the then Additional Commissioner - Administration, Mumbai, displayed remarkable kindness. Upon learning about my battle with cancer, he showed great compassion and generosity. Going out of his way to assist us, he allocated us quarters out of turn. Once again, I found myself in a new place, far from the familiar comforts of being around my loved ones.

Being inherently introverted, socializing didn't come naturally to me. Essentially, it was just me, surrounded by four walls, feeling suffocated and bored. As the days grew longer and quieter, I often found myself shedding tears in moments of solitude.

Shailaja dropped by frequently with her charming daughters. I always enjoyed their company. However, when they left for their home, I would often cry in their absence. On a couple of occasions when they came to spend the weekend with us, their departure on Sunday evening triggered tears that I couldn't hold back. Raj would console me during those emotional moments.

Eventually, I realized that dwelling in sadness would only prolong the gloom in our home. Catching myself before slipping into a depressive zone, I decided to channelize my emotions elsewhere. I needed something to occupy my thoughts and time. Determined not to let cancer define me, I turned to various activities to find happiness and kept myself occupied—something that could not only help me pass the hours but also be meaningful in some way.

After considering numerous options, I found myself drawn to a distance Montessori teacher training course. Many who knew me were taken aback by my choice, but I felt an inexplicable pull towards it. Enrolling in the course required me to embark on a journey, both physically and emotionally. I would travel from our residence in Andheri to Dadar, which amounted to an hour of commuting by local train, navigating through the draining Mumbai crowd.

The course comprised several modules, and I was expected to come and collect course materials for each module one at a time. Although I could study at home, I had to visit to submit my papers for the module and collect course materials for the next one. It had become a ritual of sorts. With each completed module, I felt a sense of accomplishment that went beyond the academic—it was as if I was rebuilding my life module by module, piece by piece.

As I immersed myself in the pages of the course, memories of the dark chapters of my life began to fade away. Delving deeper into the content, I couldn't help but notice the subtle ways in which it helped me cope with my own losses. The Montessori philosophy, emphasizing the nurturing of each child's unique potential, resonated with my own journey of self-discovery and healing. In the act of guiding and educating young minds, I found a way to heal my own.

A year passed by, marked not just by the completion of my course but also by my transformation. I emerged from the experience with newfound strength.

As life settled back into its familiar routine during the course, one day, I realized there had been subtle yet persistent transformations within me. My body seemed to have its own agenda, often leaving me fatigued and weakened. The cramps in my fingers and toes became an annoying addition to my daily existence. Then, one day, my fingers stiffened. The sudden loss of mobility in my hands pushed me to the brink of despair.

Sunanda suggested something so simple, yet so powerful: calcium supplements. They transformed my life for a while. Vijaya also called and jogged my memory that the doctor had advised me to take calcium supplements when I left RMC. However, even after taking them faithfully, along with vitamin D3, I still experience these cramps now and then.

Regret coursed through me like a relentless tide as I grappled with the weight of my own ignorance. The echoes of my cramps were merely the surface ripples of a much deeper sea of consequences brought on by cancer.

I delved into the realm of knowledge, devouring books and articles that laid bare the experiences of thyroid cancer patients. Each word became a lifeline, connecting me to a community of individuals who, like me, bore the indelible mark of this relentless adversary.

Understanding the causes of my inner conflict, a spark of self-care ignited within me. From then on, I vowed to myself to handle health issues by myself as much as I could. As I took charge of my health, it was a quiet but resounding declaration that I would not be defined solely by the battles I faced, but by the determined steps I took toward reclaiming my sense of self.

CHAPTER FIFTEEN

Navigating the Labyrinth Alone

Once the fitness bug strikes, one just cannot help getting addicted to the health regime. There are even individuals who opt for intense three-times-daily workouts. Meaning three times a day, they would put their life on hold and head to the gym. It's their way of life.

I, however, was turning into a different kind of fitness-savvy. I had to make three separate trips to the hospital for a single investigation, which involved a rigorous cycle of blood tests, scans, and doctor consultations.

The journey was full of fear and doubt, but I did not give up. Like any gym session, often my sessions would leave me feeling parched. First, I had to visit RMC for a blood test, based on the appointment I had booked in my previous consultation. Second, I had to collect the report of the blood test and meet my Doctor in RMC. Then, I had to book an appointment with Dr Parikh in the main Tata hospital building. Third, I had to visit Dr Parikh, my oncologist with the reports, whose consultation area was always crowded with patients from all over the world. Finally, I had to book another appointment for a blood test a few months later, at RMC, as there was no phone booking facility at that time.

From my home in Andheri to the Tata Hospital in Parel, commuting became a challenge in itself. Raj's frantic work schedule kept him away at odd hours. So, I couldn't wait for him to be available. That meant carrying a huge and heavy pile of reports with me, every time I had to go for the follow-up treatments and various medical tests at the hospitals. From Marol Police Quarter to Marol Maroshi Road Bus Stop, it was a long tiring walk. Then I would take the City Bus to reach Andheri Station, from where I would travel by train to reach Elphinstone Road and finally walk for around 1.5 KMs to reach my destination - Tata Hospital.

I would start with booking my appointments in advance. Then visit RMC for a blood test. Then collect the report of the blood test and go over to meet Dr. Venkatesh in RMC. That would follow with booking an appointment with my oncologist, Dr. Parikh in the main Tata Hospital building, during an extremely busy time of the day. Dr. Parikh's consultant area would usually be crowded with patients from all over the world. Dr. Parikh would also review my reports and plan the next course of action. The day would conclude with me fixing another appointment a few months later, as there was no phone booking facility at that time.

And then journey all the way back home. More than the bus and the train commute, it was the walk that truly shook me. A silent walk often triggers an explosion of thoughts in the mind. Whether I was heading to the hospital or returning from there, my thoughts could escape the influence of dread. Like a lone survivor caught in the desert of life, with a storm chasing behind. Parched, and exhausted, and with no strength to even stand on my feet, all I could do was look back at the storm and wonder, if I could make a run for it. Even if I tried, would I succeed? And if nothing I do can change my fate, was it even worth trying. It took every ounce of will to keep doing it day after day. And I would be lying, if I ever claimed the thought of quitting had never crossed my mind. Often, I would oscillate between hope and despair, but eventually I would catch myself swinging on the hope's end. Yet, I didn't quit on myself. The visit to the Tata Hospital and RMC had become my way of life.

Even though the sessions would take place every few months, the day's stress would linger in my psyche for weeks to come. On most days, I would worry about myself. However, my thoughts would often slip away from me and focus on those fellow patients who sat beside me in the waiting room. During my regular visits to consult Dr. Parikh, I had crossed paths with individuals not only from India but also from Pakistan, Kenya, Bangladesh, and other countries.

Amidst the prolonged wait, a peculiar phenomenon caught my attention. The passage of time was marked by an unspoken detachment, a collective reluctance to engage or meet the gaze of fellow patients. Lost in their thoughts, others emerged from their contemplative trance only to fixate on the reports in their hands, as if anticipating a miraculous metamorphosis that would herald good news.

Unable to bear the weight of the silent sorrow that pervaded the room, I decided to break the somber silence. As I intervened, a subtle transformation occurred, and the barriers of isolation crumbled. Gradually, we embarked on a collective journey of sharing our stories.

I got acquainted with a resilient Pakistani woman who underwent surgery every six months to address breast cysts, a Sheik from the Middle East, and a young African man.

Our conversations revealed a common thread—profound gratitude and appreciation for both Tata Hospital and the nation of India.

In foreign land, these institutions transcended their conventional roles as providers of medical care. They became symbols of hope, offering the promise of healing amidst the arduous battle against cancer. The unspoken camaraderie among us, born from shared adversity, illuminated the transformative power of compassion and shared stories in the face of life's most daunting challenges.

During one of my RMC staycations, I struck up a friendship with a 22-year-old young mother hailing from Madhya Pradesh, who happened to share the room with me. Waiting back home was a toddler eagerly anticipating the mother's return. However, here she lay on the bed, gazing at the ceiling, contemplating whether fortune would favour her enough to reunite with her child.

Sharing our temporary abode were other patients as well. We were accompanied by a resilient 70-year-old woman from Kerala. Despite grappling with recurring cancer, she had managed to raise eleven children. Alongside her, there was a 72-year-old woman from Bihar.

It was truly heart-wrenching to witness the presence of young souls under the same roof as us. Among them, there was a 17-year-old girl from South India and a 24-year-old boy from Meghalaya. Despite the challenges they faced, the girl carried an infectious smile, sacrificing her college attendance for a crucial appointment. The boy, an equally cheerful individual, radiated happiness consistently. His mother shared with me the uplifting news that the doctor had given her son the green light for his marriage plans.

What brought us together, regardless of age or background, was a shared yearning to connect, listen, and offer unwavering support to one another. In our exchanges, we traded stories and valuable tips on how to navigate the daunting side effects of radiation, forming a unique bond in our collective journey to overcome cancer.

With time, the routine of navigating the hospital alone and enduring prolonged, exhausting waiting hours in my weakened state began to weigh heavily on me. Frustration gradually seeped in, casting a shadow over the resilience we had collectively fostered.

In the midst of my cancer battle, another front opened up—the realm of education. My Montessori course persisted, demanding my attention while I grappled with the responsibilities at home and the ongoing duel with cancer.

Upon completion of the Montessori course, I found myself at a crossroads, contemplating the pursuit of employment. The eagerness to embark on a new professional journey and progress in life was palpable. However, destiny intervened, throwing obstacles in my path. Managing the effects of weakness, fatigue, and deficiencies, I found myself unable to actively pursue job opportunities.

After months of contemplating securing employment, I found myself back at square one. Alone in the house, my husband ventured out to confront criminals while I navigated the challenges life presented, both on the health and professional fronts.

Raj was astutely aware of my state of mind, recognizing the potential trouble looming if the circumstances persisted. He understood that he would soon be a second-time offender if things did not change. Displaying the instincts of a seasoned individual, he sought ways to navigate the intricacies of the homemaker law.

Taking a proactive approach, Raj decided to introduce a Doberman puppy into our lives, hoping that the canine companion would alleviate the absence he couldn't entirely fill. I acquiesced to the addition of the new family member but made it explicitly clear that he wouldn't get off the hook so easily. I christened our canine companion "Brainy," a welcomed addition to our household.

Brainy played his role admirably, filling my days with his amusing antics and providing a welcome distraction. He became a silent companion, a confidant capable of bearing the weight of my secrets. Whatever I shared with him remained secure, a commitment I expected and appreciated.

The routine of our conversations would commence the moment Raj left for work. Brainy, a loyal companion, would trail me from room to room, and I would share my thoughts on a myriad of topics with him. Whether it was discussing what to cook, the fluctuating prices of groceries, Raj's busy schedule, or my longing for my maternal family, our conversations covered everything. It was an unrestricted dialogue each time, with Brainy sitting there and nodding occasionally, providing me with the right cues to keep the conversation flowing. In a surprisingly short period, Brainy had absorbed so much about me that even Raj and my siblings combined couldn't surpass his understanding.

Yet, even Brainy had his moments of opting for beauty sleep, leaving me to navigate the labyrinth of my existential nihilistic thoughts alone. In those silent and isolated moments, I grappled with my own thoughts and fears, yearning for Raj's reassuring presence. Within the confines of solitude, I concentrated on mustering every ounce of strength, acknowledging that each passing day marked a victorious battle against cancer. From the clutches of mortality, I had successfully snatched yet another day of existence.

CHAPTER SIXTEEN

Echoes of Chaos

In December of 1992, India found itself engulfed once again in the flames of communal violence. The Last time I had witnessed it was when the Prime Minister was assassinated. This time, it was the demolition of Babri Masjid that acted as a catalyst, unleashing a cascade of bloodshed across the nation, where more than 2,000 lives were lost in interfaith clashes.

That time, however, I found myself right in the midst of the turmoil. Fate had guided me to Mumbai, the very city that became a focal point for the chaos stemming from the communal discord that had gripped the entire nation.

Mumbai descended into unprecedented turmoil as Hindu and Muslim mobs clashed, resulting in over 900 casualties and countless injuries. The violence inflicted extensive damages to the properties, with businesses looted and set ablaze, homes destroyed, and the city's infrastructure severely impaired.

Those adversities hindered the efforts of aid workers to reach the affected areas and provide timely assistance. The echoes of this tumultuous period left an indelible mark on the social fabric of the nation.

On December 6, 1992, Raj, then posted at Mahim Police Station like many of his colleagues at that time, found himself assigned to patrolling duties to check and control the escalating situation. His duty kept him away from home for extended periods, and with no mode of communication, as our police quarter lacked a phone connection. Shortly after his departure for the police station, the doorbell rang, catching me by surprise. Peering through the peephole, I observed a man in his twenties on the other side, holding a dozen bananas as if on a delivery mission. Oddly, Raj had not informed me about this, and he was typically meticulous about such details. If he anticipated someone's visit or had arranged for something to be sent home, he would give me a heads up.

"Sahab sent me, Madam, to give these to you!" the voice from the other side of the door echoed, leaving me in contemplation about whether to open it or not. My mind raced with questions. Why would Raj send me bananas when I could easily procure them from the local hawkers in the neighbourhood?

In that tense moment, Brainy took charge. He surged towards the door, barking ferociously, and the intruder, after a brief struggle, hastily retreated. Brainy, with a vigilant sniff under the door, then directed his gaze at me. I mustered the strength to approach the door and checked through the peephole, finding no sign of any accomplices. In that critical juncture, Brainy's protective demeanor offered a reassuring sense of security amid the turbulent environment.

After the riots subsided a few weeks later, Raj returned home and noticed my distress. He attempted to lighten the mood by assuring me that he would exercise more tact in dealing with such situations in the future. His humorous suggestion involved a transformation where, if he encountered a culprit, he would politely bow, fold his hands, and request them to accompany him to the station. The image of Raj's imagined transformation brought a hearty laugh to our faces. However, the echoes of our joy were swiftly swallowed by the cacophony of the city outside, where cries and turmoil drowned out any possibility of hearing anything else.

Months passed, and the city regained a semblance of normalcy. However, on March 12, 1993, Mumbai was once again thrust into turmoil as 13 coordinated bomb blasts rocked the city, claiming 257 lives and injuring over 700. The targets included major landmarks such as the Bombay Stock Exchange, the Air India building, and the Taj Mahal Palace Hotel. The following day, the Maharashtra government imposed a city-wide curfew and initiated a manhunt for the perpetrators, plunging the city into chaos with a pervasive sense of fear and insecurity. The police made numerous arrests, and trials were conducted, yet the masterminds behind the attacks remained elusive.

Raj's responsibilities heightened, and he found himself unable to return home for many days. It was later revealed that the masterminds of the serial blasts were residing within the jurisdiction of Mahim Police Station, where Raj was stationed. The absence of landlines in the police quarters added another layer of challenge, leaving me in a state of uncertainty and anxiety, unsure of how to reach him during these critical times.

In the midst of the prevailing uncertainty, I made the decision to seek refuge at Shailaja's place, accompanied by Brainy. Navigating through the city's tense atmosphere, we commuted in an auto-rickshaw. Even Brainy, usually exuberant, seemed to sense the unusual eeriness that had descended upon the city, a sight unfamiliar to both of us. Armed police personnel were stationed at every corner, underscoring the gravity of the situation. At a checkpoint situated along the highway in the vicinity of Behrampada, an area marked by heightened tension, a police officer intercepted the auto-rickshaw, seeking information about my intended destination. Upon learning my plans, he cautioned that the situation remained volatile, deeming it unsafe for me to proceed.

With a change of plans, I redirected towards Borivali police station, I managed to contact Raj's police station, but he was still in the field. I informed his colleague about my presence in Borivali. Unfortunately, due to his demanding responsibilities, Raj could only return home after about a week.

During that time, I stayed in Borivali for a few days with Raj's uncle before relocating to my sister-in-law's place. As the situation gradually improved, Raj finally returned, bringing me back home. Life resumed amidst these unexpected events; challenges I had never envisioned facing.

Reflecting on these incidents, I came to realize that they were not isolated events but rather reflections of the inherent risks associated with being part of a policeman's family. The constant unpredictability of their duties meant that we had to be prepared for the unexpected at all times.

During those tumultuous times, I bore witness to the unwavering determination of police personnel like Raj. They exemplified the true meaning of resilience and sacrifice. It is through their steadfast dedication that they protect society, while we, as their families, stand by their side, confronting our own internal struggles.

As things began to settle down, we found ourselves at a nearby hospital for a medical issue. To our surprise, my regular doctor was on leave, and another doctor was assigned to examine me.

However, during the examination, I felt uncomfortable due to his inappropriate behaviour. I glanced at Raj, and it was evident that he, too, recognized the situation and felt uneasy. Without hesitation, he asked me to get up, and we left the hospital immediately. Both of us remained silent on the way home, grappling with the disconcerting realization that if doctors couldn't be trusted, then who could be. I was grateful that Raj had accompanied me during that specific incident, reinforcing his determination to be present for all my medical visits.

CHAPTER SEVENTEEN

Pregnancy Amidst Shadows

In one of my many moments of introspection, the idea of pursuing a Bachelor of Education (B.ed) spontaneously surfaced in my mind. The prospect of embarking on a new educational adventure ignited a sense of excitement within me. The mere thought of returning to the classroom, surrounded by eager fellow students, passionately exchanging knowledge, brought a comforting sense of solace.

Teaching was a noble profession, offering the opportunity to make a significant impact on the lives of future generations. The idea briefly filled my heart with hope, but then reality set in. How could I dream of guiding future generations when my own future seemed to be drowning in the abyss of darkness?

As I pondered over this decision, Raj returned from work. Sensing that something was on my mind, he settled in and came over to sit beside me.

"I am thinking of pursuing B.ed," I muttered calmly. Raj didn't flinch before responding, "That's a great idea!"

With determination and anticipation, I started exploring the possibilities that lay ahead. Once again, I was filling the dark corners of my uncertain future with little bright stars of achievable plans. Now, I knew where I was heading, the path I was taking, and everything seemed just right. Only briefly, though.

Not long after, I was compelled to put my B.ed dreams on hold. Something more important than my personal dream had cropped up — I discovered that I was pregnant again. Raj and I were ecstatic and nervous at the same time.

That night, before I shut my eyes, I was filled to the brim with joy, hoping my dreams would lead me to the glimpse of my motherhood. However, as the lights got turned off and fear crept in, the scars of my past tragedy and my current predicament with the nefarious cancer seized my spirit in a blink, and darkness took over. I was haunted by a silent dread. What if the pills I took hurt my baby? But I didn't let it show to anyone. I smiled through my uncertainty and fears.

Pregnancy made me more diligent; I started taking extra precautions about my health, always being particular about my medications. I even initiated morning walks, both hoping and praying that history wouldn't repeat itself.

It was a time when I needed all the support I could get. Poor health conditions and the pregnancy made it difficult for me to handle Brainy. Raj was gone for long shifts, and we did not have the resources to hire full-time domestic help. I found myself unable to care for Brainy by myself like before. In desperation, Raj and I reached out to friends and relatives, asking if they could house Brainy temporarily. Understandably, it was a significant commitment to ask from anyone, but for Brainy's sake, we were desperate.

Unfortunately, none of our family and friends had the bandwidth to take him in temporarily either. Left with no other choice, we were compelled to make one of the hardest decisions we ever had to face. It felt like losing not just a pet but a cherished companion and confidante. Brainy, my vigilant canine guardian, exhibited an intense protective instinct towards me. Even seemingly playful gestures from Raj, such as a jesting raised hand, particularly in the presence of family or friends, would incite a steadfast defense from Brainy. His response transcended mere barks, manifesting in bites that unequivocally emphasized his unwavering loyalty. On numerous occasions, his teeth served as a steadfast warning that my safety stood as his foremost priority.

The void left by Brainy's absence weighed heavily on my heart. For days, I felt guilty and selfish. We still repent and shed tears for him, unable to forgive ourselves for our decision. Deep down, though, I knew that giving him away to a loving home was the best decision for all of us. The day we parted ways with him was incredibly emotional. I couldn't hold back my tears as I watched him go, tail wagging, into his new life.

The house felt emptier without Brainy's energetic presence. Loneliness once again crept in, but this time it was different.

I began experiencing constant morning sickness, the aftereffects of which lingered throughout the day, making it challenging for me to cook or eat properly. I resorted to the simplicity of fruits, and Raj, in his unwavering support, would bring me assortments of fruits, coconut water, and other nutritious foods.

Despite his tangible support, Raj seemed to miss the emotional support I needed at times. Consumed by his work, he often appeared serious and irritable, leaving me disheartened. Fortunately, my perceptive Mummy stepped in and decided to guide him. In her typical motherly way, she wrapped necessary wisdom and crucial instructions in light conversations, helping Raj understand that while his old job required him to roll up his sleeves, his new job required him to pull up his socks.

After the conversation with his mother, Raj approached me, attempting to steer the conversation in the right direction. However, it was evident that Mummy's subtle hints didn't quite land on the target. Thus, the onus fell upon me to hit the bullseye. In my attempt to salvage Mummy's efforts, I proclaimed with a straight face, "I am going to my Amma's place."

Around the same time, Raj was called away again for outstation duties. A complex and controversial issue had erupted elsewhere in Maharashtra, specifically in Marathwada. Before Raj embarked on the outstation duty, he decided to accompany me to Aurangabad.

I was elated to be back in Aurangabad and reunite with my parents. Amma took exceptional care of me, relieving me from the burden of cooking. Given my previous battle with cancer, I took extra precautions to safeguard my well-being. When the time came to return to Mumbai, Amma accompanied me for a comfortable arrangement that allowed us to spend quality time together.

Soon after, Raj's outstation duties called him away again, this time to Nanded. With a heavy heart, I bid farewell to Amma, understanding that she needed to be with our other family members. Our stay in Nanded lasted a couple of weeks, during which I began experiencing unsettling white discharge.

Memories of my previous miscarriage in Ahmedpur resurfaced, fueling my determination to prevent history from repeating itself.

As Raj was engrossed in his responsibilities, I mustered the courage to visit the gynecologist alone. She attentively examined me, noted my symptoms, and strongly advised complete bed rest.

In a peculiar twist, she even prescribed medications and emphasized the importance of bed rest in bold letters. Understanding the prevailing cultural norms in India, she encouraged me to show the prescription to my in-laws. I assured her that my case differed; they were all very caring, but she insisted, shedding light on the complex dynamics within Indian families. Thankfully, I responded well to the prescribed medicines and experienced a smooth recovery.

Back in Mumbai, the familiar challenge of struggling to eat pre-cooked meals resurfaced. Nevertheless, I found solace in indulging in an abundance of fruits, refreshing vegetable salads, and discovered a newfound fondness for cheese.

Around that time, Shivnath's wedding was planned. The date was set for Shivnath to wed Supriya. All the siblings jumped into wedding preparations. Sunanda had planned to join me in Mumbai for shopping. However, the family, worried about my health struggles, canceled the trip and invited me to Aurangabad instead.

Back home with my family, I got the much-needed rest for a couple of days before setting off again to Goa. A family trip was planned because Supriya hailed from Shiroda, a picturesque beach town close to Goa. It was a memorable family outing, after which we all returned to Aurangabad for the joyous Wedding Reception.

Jagdish Kaka's wife, Shanta Aunty, was my gynecologist this time around. She had prescribed medication to alleviate my nausea during my earlier visit to Aurangabad, ensuring a smoother journey through the next few months.

After the wedding, Raj and I returned to Mumbai. After our session with Shanta Aunty, Raj had become self-aware of his responsibility and had chosen to shower me with care by bringing a variety of foods every now and then. However, Anna was the one who did not let Raj get ahead in scoring points with his daughter. During my stay in Aurangabad, he started coming home from the cement pipes factory sooner, with loads of fruits for me to relish. It was a sweet gesture that brightened my day.

In a way, Raj and Anna were alike. While at work, their vocabulary and tone would be as vast as an Oxford dictionary, but the moment they stepped into the house, it would shrink to the size of a nursery book. Besides repeating a few rhymes, neither could do much. Yet, every once in a while, there would be cracks in their stern exterior, and their affection would ooze out. Nevertheless, I was going through a phase where all forms of love were accepted. Those small gestures brought immense happiness, reminding me of their unwavering support for me.

As the due date approached, it was time to return to Aurangabad for the delivery. I was surrounded by immense love and care from my mom, sisters-in-law, and sisters. However, my restless nature urged me to find something to occupy my time. It was then that my sister-in-law, Supriya, introduced me to the art of thread-work, which captivated my interest. Additionally, as an avid reader, I delved into a variety of fiction, non-fiction, and autobiographies, immersing myself in captivating stories.

On 4th June 1994, I overcame my fears and anxieties and delivered a healthy baby girl, our little Shona. She was a beam of hope in our dark times. I was terrified when Sunanda took her blood sample for a test right after her birth. The test was to check if she had any complications from my ailments. Thankfully, it was negative. God was kind to us.

Ironically, Shona's birth could not be conveyed to Raj directly. As in earlier postings, at the Airport Security Office, Mahim Police Station, and now at a special branch known as Airport Immigration branch, he had gone out for some official assignment. So, it was again through his colleague that he got the joyous news. Raj sounded elated when he called back.

Shivnath threw a lavish party for our siblings and relatives the next day. Everyone in my family was happy and relieved. We were grateful that everything turned out well for us.

Raj's happiness was radiant as he arrived in Aurangabad with our family friend Mohini, his colleague, and his colleague's wife, along with Shailaja and her family. He had transformed into a new person since the last time I saw him. The only other time he was happy was on our wedding day. He surprised me with a gold choker, a precious gift for gifting him his princess. He cherished every moment with Shona before returning to his job. His team at the airport was very supportive and had witnessed our ups and downs through the years. They all rejoiced in our bliss.

Shanta Aunty was a blessing in my pregnancy and post-pregnancy journey. She cared for me with love and ensured my safety at every step. She made the whole process of carrying and delivering Shona a joyous experience for me. We will always be thankful to her for bringing our angel into this world.

Shona became the vessel through which we poured out the love and affection that had accumulated within us. Each day unfolded as a new adventure with Shona, and her innocence and laughter served as a remedy for any lingering sorrow. We witnessed her inaugural steps, listened to her utter her first words, and marveled at her boundless curiosity about the world. In her presence, we discovered fresh reasons to smile, new hopes for the future, and an unbreakable bond that filled the void left by Brainy's absence. Shona stood as a living testament to this miracle, a constant reminder that even in the darkest times, moments of pure happiness and love could emerge.

Then, just as I was settling into the bounties offered by fate, post-partum depression stealthily crept into my life. The transformation was profound, shifting me from a calm and serene person to one who was moody and snappy.

The overwhelming combination of sleep deprivation, the challenges of post-partum adjustments, and the high dosage of thyroid medication left both my physical and mental health in disarray. Raj, seemingly clueless and impatient, added to the sense of loneliness and helplessness that engulfed me during those months. Amidst the turbulent phase, Shona's inquisitive and playful eyes emerged as my source of strength.

Shona brought significant changes to my life, including altering my routine visits to the Radiation Medicine Center (RMC). When the time arrived for another scheduled therapy session, I had to leave her behind to shield her from the potential harmful effects of radiation.

The day prior to leaving for RMC, I was to be given a dose, I was reluctant to leave Shona alone and was continuously hugging and kissing her. I was overwhelmed yet I held my tears lest my inquisitive baby got a clue that something was amiss.

Thankfully, Shivnath and Supriya had moved to Mumbai by then. They insisted on keeping Shona with them. She could feel at home, with their son, Shreeshail. It was the best thing for Shona as opposed to being unattended at home. We took her to Shivnath's place, left her in my family's custody, and with a heavy heart, I left for the hospital.

The usual solitary walk I took to the RMC was now accompanied by a different set of questions. At barely a year old, how could I leave my daughter alone? How could I deprive her of my breast milk? How could I subject her to the separation? Would she miss me as much as I would miss her?

For eight to ten long days, I would be deprived of her smiles, her laughter, and the comforting warmth of her presence. Shona, being the good baby she was, adapted quickly to formula and cow's milk, sparing me the added concern of her distress during my absence.

Post-iodine dosage, I had to stay away from Shona until the doctors said it was safe for her. I moved in with Shailaja, who lived close to Shivnath's place. I tried to keep myself busy by helping her with household chores. One day, Raj brought Shona to Shailaja's place, where she played happily with her cousins in the ground below. Shailaja asked me to look out of the window and see her. As soon as I saw her, I broke down in tears. I couldn't stop crying for hours together, feeling a surge of emotions that drained me completely.

After a few days, the RMC doctor gave me a go-ahead to see Shona again. I rushed to her, and she ran into my arms, holding me tight. Raj said that, she had been missing me all this time, looking for me everywhere. That memory still makes me cry whenever I think of it. I am teary eyed even when I am inking these lines.

The bond shared by Shona, Raj, and me is truly special. During Shona's early years, Raj's absence didn't register much with her. However, as she matured, the void left by his work-related commitments became more apparent, and she yearned for his presence whenever he was away.

One significant instance was when Raj had to travel to Nanded for his law exams, a journey we couldn't undertake due to Shona's school schedule. Recognizing her longing for Raj, I made earnest attempts to lift her spirits with various games. We delved into the realm of imagination, taking on roles as circus performers, alternating between jesters and trapeze artists. Our adventures extended to treasure hunts with unique twists, concealing not only her favourite treats but also craft materials that brought her joy. I went the extra mile, treating her to street food and indulging in occasional junk food, rare in our usual dietary choices. Yet, despite all the efforts, one night, she sought solace in Raj's T-shirt, adorning it over her dress, enveloping it in affectionate kisses and warm hugs.

As Raj's return neared, I proposed that Shona prepare a special snack for him, to be served in her miniature toy dishes. The excitement in her eyes was palpable. With my guidance, she crafted Sabudana vada (sago snack) and presented it to Raj. His joy was uncontainable. Over time, as Shona matured, she came to terms with Raj's workaholic nature, finding ways to navigate his limited involvement in her school events. This journey of understanding and acceptance became an integral part of our shared narrative.

Life with cancer is undeniably a challenging journey, marked by its tumultuous terrain of highs and lows, twists, and turns. The adversities that accompany this formidable adversary test one's courage and endurance. Amidst the trials, if joys manifest, they do so in modest installments, akin to unexpected drizzles after the sweet monsoon of life has subsided.

Despite the inherent hardships, enduring this ordeal offers a unique vantage point from which to view life. It compels a shift in perspective, encouraging a profound reflection on the value of the precious gift of life and the significance of cherishing every moment shared with our loved ones. In these challenging times, life's true essence emerges, emphasizing that perhaps, the love accumulated from our cherished ones throughout a lifetime encapsulates the essence of our existence.

Bearing the Weight of Solitude

From the moment of our birth, an inexorable countdown towards death commences. As we traverse the journey of life, the specter of death manifests all around us. Strangely, we often delude ourselves into perceiving it as a distant reality. Oblivious to the capricious nature of life, we immerse ourselves in its pursuits, heedless of the fact that death is an uninvited guest capable of arriving unannounced at any moment.

This psychological phenomenon finds its apt descriptor in "Repression," a defense mechanism that consigns undesirable thoughts, feelings, or memories into the recesses of the subconscious mind.

For nearly a decade, the memory of my initial harrowing surgery had been buried deep within the recesses of my consciousness. Life unfolded seamlessly, punctuated by its share of highs and lows, as I cherished the various phases of Shona's growth. Yet, the passage of time couldn't erase the underlying truth—that life, with its ephemeral nature, is a delicate balance between embracing the present and acknowledging the inevitability of our mortality.

In the year 2001, my life commenced on an unexpected trajectory. We transitioned into a modest private apartment, a significant milestone after navigating through various rented accommodations and even police quarters. Finally, our dream of owning a humble abode materialized. The excitement was palpable, and I eagerly took it upon myself to shape the simple but sweet interior according to my vision.

Engaging with contractors to orchestrate the remodeling, I remained blissfully unaware of the constant swirl of dust and debris around me. Like a silent infiltrator, allergens seized the opportunity to enter unnoticed, much like a Trojan horse.

Soon after settling into the charm of our newly designed apartment, the revelation struck— I had developed a dust allergy. Seeking professional counsel, a doctor confirmed that bronchial asthma had become an unwelcome companion in my life. Initially hesitant to embrace medication, I opted for a holistic approach and introduced yoga into my daily routine. This decision marked the commencement of my journey towards managing and mitigating the challenges posed by this newfound health condition.

When Shona was a mere seven years old, and with no one else at home to tend to her, I made the decision to bring her along with me to my yoga classes. Surprisingly, she embraced the experience, finding joy in sitting through the sessions, relishing some delightful snacks discreetly tucked away at the back of the room, and immersing herself in her colouring books. What began as a practical solution evolved into a delightful field trip for her. As I observed her enjoying this time, memories of my own snack parties in the kitchen during Mr. Sable's tuition sessions came flooding back.

The practice of yoga played a pivotal role in enhancing both my physical and mental well-being. It proved to be an effective tool in managing my asthma, providing a semblance of control over the condition. However, it was not a foolproof solution. When asthma attacks did manifest, they were intense, with bouts that could persist for days, challenging the equilibrium I had sought through yoga and underscoring the unpredictability of my health journey.

Night after night, the ordeal of being unable to recline in peace unfolded. Unwilling to disturb the undisturbed slumber of Shona and Raj with my restless tossing and turning, I opted to suffer in silence. Stealthily, I exited the bedroom, seeking solace in the living room. There, I meticulously arranged pillows, fashioning a makeshift support for my head as I sat upright on the couch for hours on end. Through the window, I gazed at their serene sleeping faces, yearning for the elusive embrace of sweet sleep.

Despite the nocturnal challenges, yoga persevered as a steadfast companion in my life. To this day, I dedicate five to six days a week to its practice, a discipline that has fortified me against a spectrum of challenges, offering a reservoir of strength to navigate the unpredictable contours of my health journey.

As part of my routine, and in a proactive effort to preempt any potential health concerns, I adhered to a biannual pilgrimage to the RMC for a comprehensive blood test. Back then, the facility did not entertain phone appointments. Post-test, the RMC card provided me with a scheduled date for the report. Given the accumulation of years of tests, the card necessitated frequent renewal. Additionally, I consulted with Dr. Parikh, who meticulously adjusted my medication based on the Thyroid-stimulating Hormone (TSH) levels and conducted thorough examinations of my neck and breast. Thankfully, all indicators consistently reflected normalcy.

Those routine check-ups often entailed scans, some of which mandated a temporary cessation of my medication to ensure the accuracy of the results. Therefore, during the particular incident, I had temporarily halted both my medication and iodine intake as per the protocol associated with the diagnostic procedures. This meticulous approach to health management aimed at maintaining vigilance over my well-being, ensuring a proactive response to any potential deviations from the norm.

Life has bestowed its blessings upon us, allowing us to accumulate enough savings to fulfill a cherished dream – the purchase of a car. On a seemingly routine day, Raj and I were navigating the roads when an unforeseen incident unfolded. An elderly man, perilously placed due to the recklessness of another four-wheeler driver, caught our attention. In a split-second decision, Raj skillfully swerved our vehicle to shield the elderly gentleman from harm. However, our noble act of intervention resulted in a collision with the side rails along the road, leaving both of us injured.

Upon returning home, in the aftermath of the ordeal, I unwittingly applied Iodex to alleviate the aches and pains that had ensued. For those unfamiliar, Iodex is an externally applied pain-relieving balm with a substantial iodine content. Recognizing the inadvertent error, I promptly sought guidance from my doctor. Graciously, the doctor extended the duration without medication, understanding the unique circumstances surrounding the incident. Consequently, in the aftermath of this incident, I had temporarily halted both my regular medication and iodine intake.

Usually, I would endure a medication hiatus for a month, but this particular episode stretched to an extended period of 45 days. As a consequence, my body experienced swelling attributed to hormonal imbalances. Recognizing the rarity of this occurrence, my family and I decided to immortalize the moment in our memories by capturing it in a photograph. Embracing a lighthearted approach to the situation, akin to a celebrity, I posed alongside my niece for the photo, acknowledging the uniqueness of the moment amidst the challenges posed by the prolonged break from medication.

During a subsequent routine examination with Dr. Parikh, an unexpected and severe pain in my left breast caught my attention. Swiftly addressing the concern, Dr. Parikh conducted a thorough examination and recommended a series of tests, including a Mammogram—a diagnostic method employing x-ray imaging for the early detection of breast cancer and other related diseases—and Sonography. The experience of undergoing a Mammogram, as a first-timer, proved to be excruciating. Dr. Parikh clarified that the discomfort was primarily attributed to a lymph node formation in my breast. Following those diagnostic procedures and a subsequent consultation, the verdict was delivered – surgery was deemed necessary to remove the lymph node causing the pain. Dr. Parikh emphasized that neglecting this issue could lead to two significant problems: the possibility of it turning malignant (cancerous) and an escalation of the pain as it continued to grow.

That revelation was startling, shattering the semblance of assurance we had harboured, as we believed that cancer and its malignant manifestations were no longer a looming threat in my life. The news propelled us into a renewed confrontation with the challenges of my health journey, prompting contemplation on the uncertain path that lay ahead.

Seeking clarification about the potential reasons behind the unexpected pain in my left breast, I inquired with Dr. Parikh. He pointed towards hormonal imbalances as a possible factor affecting some females. This revelation left me perplexed, and for a moment, I questioned whether my own lapses in health management had played a role. Dr. Parikh, however, reassured me, emphasizing that it wasn't a consequence of negligence on my part. He advised us to return home and contemplate the situation.

That revelation marked a significant development for our family and friends, especially given the extended period of respite from cancer concerns. It was a stark reminder that, despite our best efforts, health challenges could emerge unexpectedly, compelling us to accept them as part of a greater plan, perhaps ordained by a higher power.

In a span of a year, I encountered two distinct medical setbacks — the onset of Bronchial Asthma and a second surgery.

Confronted with the imminent need for yet another surgery, our contemplation deepened, casting a shadow of reflection over our family. At the forefront of our concerns was the impact on our beloved Shona, still tender in age and highly impressionable. As parents, the realization that she might be exposed to the stress and uncertainties accompanying my upcoming surgery weighed heavily on our hearts.

In the delicate juncture, we grappled with the intricate balance between attending to my medical needs and safeguarding Shona's innocence and emotional well-being. Our fervent desire was to shield her from any distresses, ensuring that she continued to revel in the simple joys of childhood, unburdened by the weight of our worries. The impending surgery became not just a personal challenge but a familial one, demanding a nuanced approach that prioritized not only my health but also the tranquility of our family dynamics.

Acknowledging the swift approach of Shona's Christmas vacation, we found ourselves faced with a profound decision that required careful consideration of her well-being. After extensive deliberation and weighing various options, we collectively arrived at a choice that we believed would be in Shona's best interest. The decision was made: during the period, she would temporarily relocate to Aurangabad with Shailaja and her daughters. This arrangement aligned with their existing plans to spend the Christmas holidays with cousins in Aurangabad.

While not an easy decision, the temporary separation felt like a necessary sacrifice for the greater good. It was a testament to our commitment as parents to prioritize Shona's emotional stability and shield her from the potential stresses associated with my impending surgery.

The night before Shona's departure was charged with a myriad of emotions that enveloped our home. Shona, still too young to grasp the full complexity of the situation, was understandably apprehensive about leaving her parents. Her tears, poignant and sincere, tugged at our hearts. It required every ounce of our strength to reassure her that this separation was temporary, and that we would soon be reunited.

The following evening, we accompanied Shona to Shailaja's home, where her journey to Aurangabad would commence. Despite the presence of her cousins, to provide comfort and companionship, Shona's visage mirrored the melancholy of parting from us, her parents.

As they began their journey by bus, we accompanied them to the station. Shona, tearful and reluctant to part, expressed a heartfelt desire for me to join her. Witnessing her distress, my emotions welled up. Once Shona's bus vanished from view, I sat in the taxi and couldn't hold back my tears. I poured out my concerns to Raj, grappling with the worry of how Shona would manage in Aurangabad without us.

Upon returning home, the house felt noticeably emptier, the silence more pronounced, and our thoughts were invariably tethered to our daughter. That night was a restless one for me, with sleep proving elusive. The awareness of impending pre-surgery tests the following morning only added to the weight on my mind. The emotional turbulence of parting with Shona and the impending medical journey created a profound sense of unease that lingered throughout the night.

After concluding the assessments, the next morning, I promptly dialed Aurangabad. The response I received indicated that Shona had shed tears for a brief duration during the journey, yet succumbed to sleep amidst the traces of those tears. Vishal, her maternal cousin and my nephew, had graciously welcomed her upon her arrival. With the knowledge that Shona was in the comforting company of her relatives, I turned my attention to the practicalities, gearing up for my hospitalization.

The prospect of being admitted to a hospital in Mumbai, especially one as renowned and sizable as the Tata Memorial Hospital, introduced a unique set of concerns during the unfamiliar juncture. Mumbai, a vast metropolis, with its hustle and bustle, raised questions about the efficiency of healthcare, particularly in an institution known for being the largest cancer hospital in India, often grappling with crowds and overbookings. The uncertainty lingered, prompting me to contemplate whether I would indeed receive the thorough and proper treatment one hopes for, in such circumstances.

Upon our arrival at the hospital, Raj and I navigated through the necessary procedures, including registration, payment for a private room, and other formalities. Grateful for the foresight of having invested in a medical insurance policy during our early years of marriage, we were afforded the luxury of a private room. The decision proved to be a pleasant surprise, as the room exceeded expectations — exceptionally well-maintained and equipped with all the comforts one could desire.

As we settled in, the evening had already descended, and the doctor's rounds for the day had concluded. After a nourishing dinner, I dutifully took my medication and retired early for the night. The serene environment of the private room provided a comforting backdrop, setting the tone for the upcoming surgical journey. Gratitude for the privileges afforded by the insurance policy mingled with a sense of readiness for the challenges that awaited in the days to come.

The following day unfolded with an early wake-up call, ushering in a series of tests and doctor's rounds that spanned the entirety of the day. Amidst this medical routine, Raj received an unexpected call from his senior in the Police department, presenting an assignment that required his attention. Raj, however, promptly clarified that he was on leave due to my hospitalization. Concerned about my health and the impending surgery, his senior inquired about the timing of the procedure.

Upon learning that the surgery was scheduled for the following day, a suggestion was made that Raj contribute a couple of hours to work.

Reluctantly, Raj agreed, promising to return within a two-hour timeframe. Following Raj's departure, the room witnessed a revolving door of staff – first the cleaning crew, expressing surprise at my solitude. I reassured them of Raj's imminent return. As the day unfolded, the technician for some tests echoed the same surprise. The administrative staff, bearing the surgery consent form, made multiple attempts for our signatures, only to be met with the request to return later.

The doctors, during their rounds, light-heartedly inquired about the absence of a day off for policemen during family emergencies. Although their tone was jovial, the underlying sentiment brought me close to tears. Despite the attempts to maintain composure, the solitude in the hospital room underscored the poignant reality of navigating a critical medical journey without the constant presence of a loved one.

Loneliness became my unwelcome companion throughout that day. As I lay in the hospital room, the weight of Raj's absence lingered heavily. In moments of vulnerability, the comforting presence of a loved one can serve as a soothing balm, and his prolonged absence added an additional layer to the burden of anxiety I carried. The emotional landscape felt particularly challenging during those solitary hours.

When Raj finally returned that evening, the floodgates of emotion burst open. I couldn't contain my feelings, and I sobbed uncontrollably for about an hour. Raj, attempting to offer an explanation, shared that an unforeseen exigency had kept him from leaving earlier. However, instead of alleviating my distress, this revelation left me even more upset.

The night cast a looming shadow over me, akin to a heavy, ominous cloud. In the sterile confines of that hospital room, my mind became a battleground of swirling emotions and uncertainties. The impending prospect of surgery, laden with its inherent risks and unknowns, bore down on me with a weightiness that seemed to penetrate to my very core. Despite the dedicated support and care provided by the hospital staff, I found myself unable to dispel the fear that had taken root in my heart.

Anxiety wrapped itself around me, and a palpable heaviness settled in my chest.

Maybe it's the uncertainty, the vulnerability that comes with lying on that operating table, or perhaps it's the simple acknowledgment that, despite the routine of it all, there's an element of the unknown. Whatever it is, that pre-surgery unease seems to have a permanent reservation in my emotional rollercoaster.

It was a facet of my emotions that I had kept hidden, a secret burden that I had never shared with anyone. The hours passed at an agonizingly slow pace, and sleep remained elusive. I tossed and turned, my thoughts oscillating between the impending surgery and the severe ache of missing my Shona.

Memories

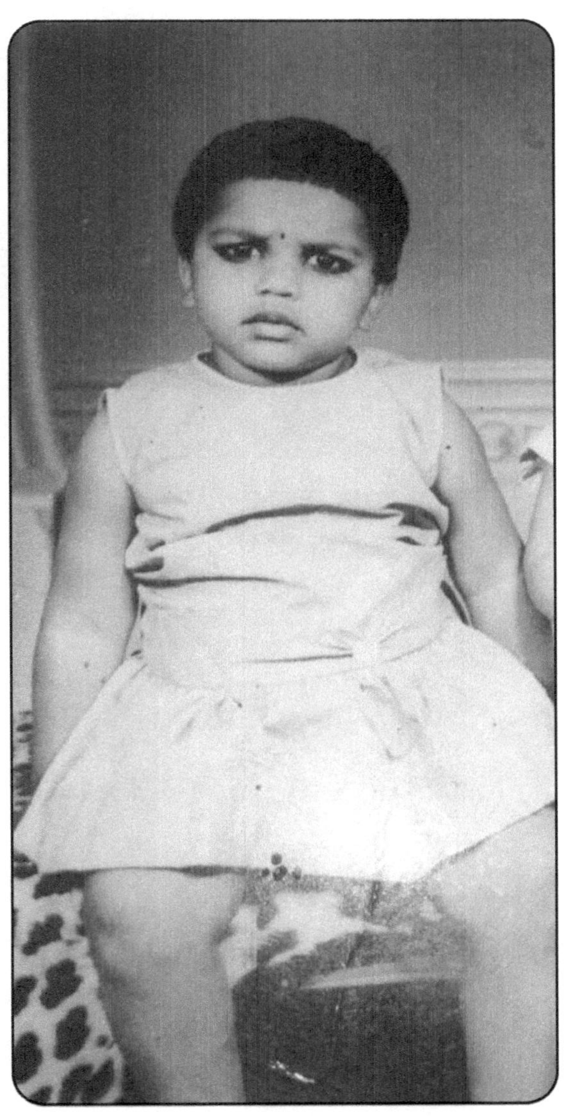

My Childhood Picture

Receiving a trophy as the
School Basketball Captain

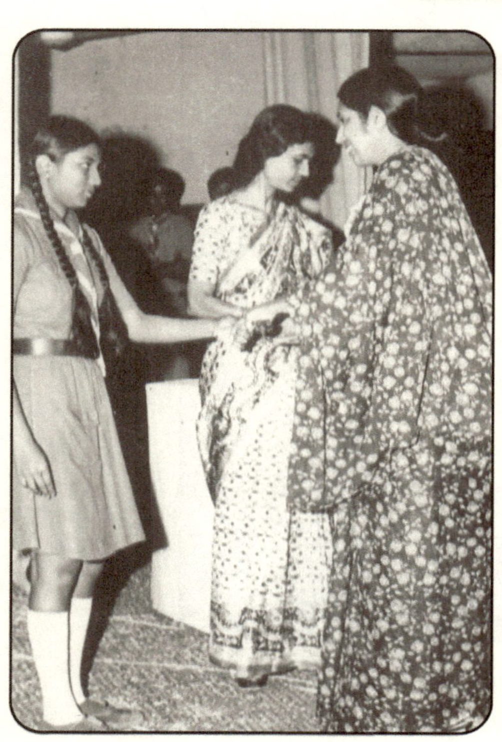

Receiving Prize for
Best Girl Guide

Elected as the Vice President of School Student Association

Receiving University Basketball
Captain Trophy at the Hands of
Noted Actor Mr. Parikshit Sahni

Our Wedding Reception

After the Cancer Surgery

Sonika's First US Trip

Sonika's Birthday Celebrations

Our Thailand trip after
Sonika's Grade 10 Exams

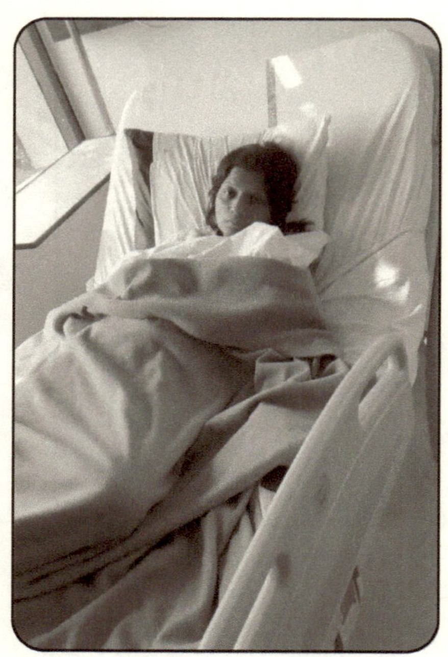

My Surgery at Somaiya Hospital

Housewarming Ceremony at
my Brother-in-Law's House
in Nanded

Our Italy Trip in March 2016

US Trip in July 2016

A US Trip for Roma's Birth in 2016

Our US Trip in July 2017

Berry's First Birthday in March 2017

CHAPTER NINETEEN

Surgeries, Scars, and Healing with Family

The day of the surgery dawned, demanding an even earlier awakening than usual. Rooted in a childhood tradition, our family had long embraced the practice of entrusting our medical care to our own trusted physicians, seldom seeking the counsel of others. However, this time around, the nature of the surgery altered the familiar landscape. It loomed as a daunting prospect, and the realization that I had to place my trust in a doctor outside our family circle added an additional layer of stress to the already charged atmosphere.

The fear of the operating theater, an unsettling specter that haunted my thoughts, was something I couldn't easily dispel. Each time, the nagging question persisted: would I emerge alive? This fear, entrenched within me, has persisted until the present day, serving as a constant companion on the precipice of each surgical journey.

The experience of being under general anesthesia presented a novel sensation. In my previous encounter with surgery, during the cancer procedure, I had felt as though I was in a trance, oblivious to the events transpiring around me. However, this time proved to be different. As I was wheeled into the operating theater, my senses heightened, and I took note of the array of medical equipment, machines intricately connected to my body, and the doctors scrutinizing my test results and vital parameters.

Dr. Parikh entered the room with a palpable sense of urgency. To his surprise, he found me wide awake, attentively observing everything in my surroundings. With a swift instruction to his assistant, who administered a likely prick of anesthesia, Dr. Parikh engaged in a brief conversation with me. In those fleeting moments, he inquired about Shona and her well-being. As the anesthesia gradually took effect, I drifted into unconsciousness, blissfully unaware of the surgical proceedings unfolding around me.

The aftermath of the surgery required several days of recuperation in the hospital. This time around, a surgical drain was affixed to my breast, serving the purpose of collecting the fluid that emanated post-procedure. The doctor, adopting an unconventional approach, encouraged me to engage in intermittent walks, even with the drain bag in tow. Despite the initial surprise, I dutifully adhered to the instructions.

Upon reaching the point where the fluid discharge had completely ceased, I was deemed fit for discharge. The very next day, I found myself at the airport, comfortably seated in a wheelchair, eagerly anticipating a flight to Aurangabad. The prospect of reuniting with Shona and indulging in some much-needed rest propelled me forward, marking the beginning of the post-surgery recovery journey.

Returning home, the reunion with Shona was a heartwarming experience, her excitement and love palpable as she ran towards me. The embrace of her affection marked a moment of profound gratitude, and I cherished the warmth of being back with my daughter.

As the family gathered, Shona had become the central figure, each member harbouring their own "Shona stories" to share. Sujata recounted a particular incident involving a sticker book that Shona had brought along. In a moment of confusion, a different sticker was torn, prompting an unexpected reaction from Shona—she pulled Sujata's hair. It became a humorous anecdote, with Sujata jokingly expressing that if not for my surgery and absence in Aurangabad, she might have considered giving Shona a light spanking.

During my recovery period, an unexpected turn of events led me to become a de facto brand ambassador for Yoga. This newfound role sparked interest among my sisters, nieces, and nephews, inspiring us to gather early in the mornings at Sujata's place. There, I took on the role of a guide, imparting knowledge about various Asanas. What began as a therapeutic practice evolved into a joyous and bonding experience, akin to a trainer teaching her eager disciples.

The time spent with Shona and the rest of the family during my recovery was truly cherished. It became a period of reconnection, love, and the sharing of stories. My elder sister, Vijaya, even extended the generous offer to come and assist me during my recuperation. We deliberated on how her younger son, Sunil, and my brother-in-law, Mr. Kishan, would manage in her absence. With unwavering assurance, she conveyed that it was just a matter of a few days, and they would find a way to cope. And so, the three of us — Vijaya, Shona, and I —united in Mumbai, finding solace and strength in each other's presence.

As we established our daily rhythm, Vijaya seamlessly integrated into our lives. Temporarily shouldering the responsibilities of a caregiver, she not only helped with household chores but also played a crucial role in Shona's life. Vijaya shared mythological stories and imparted shlokas to Shona, creating a bond enriched with love and wisdom. Shona, in response, cherished every moment of this special time with her aunt, absorbing both the teachings and affection extended to her.

The familial warmth extended further with the presence of Vijaya's elder son, Anil, who also worked in Mumbai. Together, our family gathering during those days became a harmonious blend of shared responsibilities, meaningful teachings, and the comforting embrace of each other's company.

For 33 years, I've navigated the shadow of cancer, a journey that commenced with the first surgery, altering the course of my life irrevocably. However, the relentless tide of medical interventions did not cease there. I've weathered fifteen more operations since that pivotal moment. Each surgery seemed like a coin offered by fate, presenting a dual perspective. On one side, there lay surgeries and pain, and on the flip side, there stood loved ones and their unwavering support. It was almost as if fate intended to engage me in a cruel game, a continuous flip between heads and tails.

This enduring journey seemed to impart a profound lesson – life, akin to a coin, perpetually oscillates between the dichotomy of heads and tails. No matter the desire for consistency, the reality persists that life's trajectory is an unalterable dance between contrasting experiences. In the face of this unyielding reality, the enduring love and support of my cherished ones emerged as a constant, a source of solace and strength that remained unwavering even in the tumultuous dance of life's coin toss.

CHAPTER TWENTY

Beyond Surgical Challenges

Until 2002, my annual mammography had become a customary ritual. The doctors had expressed their concerns about the presence of fibroids after my second surgery. In 2003, their apprehensions were validated as a fibroid resurfaced.

As the impending hospital stay loomed, preparing the house became a top priority. Gathering the essentials and packing for my time away, I found myself akin to those constant vagabonds or enthusiastic travelers who possess a go-to travel bag, ready to embark on a new journey at a moment's notice. However, in my case, the destination was always the hospital, and the capricious nature of this journey belonged to Cancer.

Once again, apprehensions for Shona occupied my thoughts. Both Mummy and Sujata, who were educators by profession, found it necessary to take a hiatus from their respective vocations to attend to Shona's needs. Sujata, despite having three sons of her own in Aurangabad, chose to be present for me during those challenging period. Amma, too, extended her support by joining Sujata, notwithstanding the health concerns of her diabetic condition and the challenges of a compromised cardiac health, with only one functioning kidney. Despite her own ailments, she consistently demonstrated a selfless dedication, rushing to stand by my side whenever the need arose. Shona, perceptive beyond her years, comprehended the temporary necessity of my absence, thereby facilitating a more manageable acceptance of our separation.

Shona, at her tender age, comprehended the necessity for me to be away for a while, and the separation became more manageable for her to accept. To ensure a smooth transition and minimize disruptions, I meticulously planned everything. Shona's upcoming quarterly tests were on the horizon, so I assisted her in completing her revisions and organized everything for her and Raj.

For this particular surgery, I found myself admitted to S. L. Raheja Hospital in Mahim, Mumbai. It was noteworthy that my doctor, Dr. Parikh from Tata Memorial Hospital, had relocated to this new medical facility. My hospital bed was strategically positioned near a large glass window, offering a captivating view of the Arabian sea, providing a source of solace that kept me engaged and content during my hospital stay.

Taking advantage of the serene view, I meticulously arranged our personal belongings to create a semblance of order in the hospital room. Once everything was in place, I delved into reading a book—a therapeutic escape that momentarily allowed me to forget the hospital environment. Interestingly, my reading preferences evolved over the years, spanning from romantic to fiction, cookery, history, healthcare, and finally settling on motivational genres. In recent times, the influence of social media has grown, but I make a conscious effort to maintain a balance.

Reflecting on my days in Ahmedpur, I vividly recall the joy I felt when I started receiving books from the government library, which surprisingly had an impressive collection in such a small place. The solace found in literature, whether physical books or digital content, has remained a consistent companion throughout my journey.

By the next evening, I had finished the book. Meanwhile, a battery of tests was underway throughout the day, laying the groundwork for the surgery scheduled for the following morning. The brief respite that the book provided became a much-needed break and a moment of rest, offering solace after an extended period marked by challenges and uncertainties.

Interestingly, I found that I often got better rest in hospitals than at home, where relaxation was a luxury rarely afforded.

On the day of the surgery, I rose at the crack of dawn, prepared to be transported to the operating theater. The moments leading up to the surgery were consistently nerve-wracking, heightening my anxiety. Seeking solace, I turned to prayer and meditation, attempting to center myself amidst the swirl of emotions.

Subsequently, they wheeled me into the operating theater. Following a few reassuring words, I was administered anesthesia. When consciousness returned, Dr. Parikh, my surgeon, had already completed the procedure, although his absence felt peculiar. At times, I found myself wondering who operated on me, only to realize that, with their myriad responsibilities, surgeons are exceptionally busy and primarily focused on their crucial role in the surgery. The anesthesiologist, in turn, plays a pivotal part in the procedure.

A couple of hours later, I was back in my room. Despite the persistent hunger, eating was postponed until evening.

As twilight descended, fatigue set in, prompting a light dinner followed by an early night.

The next morning, my doctor made his rounds, advising me not to adhere to the stereotypical patient behaviour and to incorporate some physical activity, like taking a stroll. Despite my weakness, I heeded his counsel and embarked on a short walk. However, fatigue caught up with me quickly, prompting a decision to rest.

A few days later, I was discharged from the hospital. Without wasting any time, I delved into helping Shona prepare for her upcoming test the next day. Amma, Sujata, and Mummy found amusement in my diligence. However, they acknowledged and appreciated my efforts, with Mummy expressing, "You are a responsible person. You take care of the house, Shona, and Raj well. No nonsense, no fuss, no delay."

Sunil and Anil, my brothers-in-law, were initially regular visitors to Mumbai for my initial surgeries. However, as the frequency of these medical procedures escalated, the demands of their hectic schedules rendered it impractical for them to sustain frequent trips to the city due to their busy schedule.

Prakash, Karuna, Sunil, and Purnima came from Nanded to pay me a visit during the recovery period. After a few days of post-surgery, Amma and Sujata returned to Aurangabad. Given Amma's own health concerns, she did not want to burden Raj with additional responsibilities. Mummy, on the other hand, extended her stay with me for some more time. She provided valuable assistance with household tasks for a few days before eventually departing for Nanded.

Over the years, I have explored various avenues for wellness, including consultations with multiple homeopathic practitioners, engagement with naturopathic approaches, and the adoption of home remedies.

In 2005, prompted by a recommendation from one of Raj's seniors, we decided to explore alternative therapy for my condition. He suggested consulting a prominent Ayurvedacharya in Pune, known for successfully treating numerous cancer patients. By this time, it was widely known within our circle that I was seeking alternative treatment options due to the toll that repeated surgeries had taken on my body.

Raj and I conducted thorough research on the Ayurvedacharya, who had garnered recognition in the media and received accolades for her work. Convinced by the positive reviews, we decided to give it a chance. Furthermore, Raj, having adopted the Kandi family tradition of never traveling alone, insisted on company. Alongside Shona, we invited some of her cousins, transforming what would have been a regular commute into a delightful travel experience filled with friendship and adventure.

During my visit to the Ayurvedacharya's clinic, I underwent an extensive session of questions related to my medical history. Upon completion, I was given a promising assurance that I would be free of surgeries within six months. The Ayurvedacharya provided me with four bottles of the prescribed Kada (herbal concoction) along with detailed instructions.

After leaving the clinic, we turned the day into a memorable experience for the kids by taking them on a field trip. We relished a delightful meal at a popular Pune restaurant and then commenced our journey back to Mumbai.

The very next day after acquiring the Kada bottles, I integrated them into my cancer pill-box, foreseeing a harmonious companionship between the two. These bottles became my ammunition against the various ailments attempting to subdue me. With unwavering commitment, I began the regular consumption of the Kada, receiving a monthly supply via courier from Pune.

However, around the fourth month, I observed a drastic and concerning weight loss. I appeared bony and malnourished, prompting immediate consultation with the Ayurvedacharya. She explained that the weight loss was expected as the Kada was effectively purging the body of toxins. Despite the Ayurvedacharya's reassurance, Raj found the explanation vague and unsettling. Concerned for my well-being, he advised me to cease the Kada immediately, a decision I willingly followed.

Commencing on the Ayurvedic adventure, I harboured hopeful expectations, unsure of what the journey might entail. Unfortunately, the alternative therapy did not yield the desired results for me. Nevertheless, I remained open to the possibilities of other alternative treatments, recognizing that not all experiments lead to anticipated outcomes. Living with cancer felt akin to solving an intricate puzzle, and my determination to conquer the seemingly unconquerable persisted.

In 2007, I began seeing a naturopath doctor who made a real impact. She tailored her holistic treatments to fit my needs, and I soon felt and looked better - with even friends and family commenting on the positive changes. More vital was my own sense of improvement. At last, I enjoyed renewed energy and optimism. Sadly, when my naturopath fell ill herself, our productive work together reached an abrupt end, leaving me disappointed yet thankful for the lasting benefits our time brought.

During my annual ritual of mammography in 2009, a sense of unease crept in. Intuition hinted that something might be amiss. Dr. Parikh confirmed my worst fears when he contacted me. Another surgery was required, this time for breast Fibroadenoma. With a resilient mindset, my motto became "Go Rekha Go," as I began the process of planning and facing yet another surgical challenge.

As Shona transitioned to the 10th grade and engaged in preparations for her Board Examinations, her busy daytime schedule prompted me to hire a cook to assist her. However, the nights remained a lonely period for her. A kind-hearted aunty from our neighbourhood extended her support, staying with Shona to give her company during those solitary hours. I was deeply touched by her generosity. Additionally, my gratitude extends to other neighbours — Tasneem, Vijaya, Lavanya, and Ritika — who offered unwavering support throughout the challenging ordeals.

Facing surgery for the fourth time brought forth numerous questions from those around me — family, neighbours, maids, and friends — all wondering how I could cope with it. Although I remained silent, a serene smile adorned my face. I had made peace with my destiny, finding joy in every challenge that life presented.

Returning to the familiar room at S. L. Raheja Hospital in Mahim felt like a repetition of my previous surgery in 2003. The soothing view of the sealink outside provided a relaxing backdrop. That recent addition became a stroke of fortune for me, adding a positive turn to my circumstances. To distract myself, I reached for a book, seeking solace in literature. Diabetes had now joined the array of health issues, a genetic trait in the Kandi family. Adhering to a diabetic diet and embracing positive lifestyle changes became imperative. By the grace of God, my sugar levels remained under control, except during the surgeries. I remained vigilant, meditating daily to calm both my mind and body, recognizing that stress could potentially spike sugar levels.

The irony struck me as I navigated through a liquid diet with the consistency of water during my recovery, limited to a piece of watermelon and a slice of bread. I couldn't help but recall Raj's uncle jokingly remarking every time we invited him for lunch at home, "Why do you eat like patients?" His words seemed perfectly fitting for this situation.

After a smooth week-long stay, I returned home with a new prescription, now requiring insulin for a week. In need of assistance, I reached out to a friend—a general practitioner in the neighbourhood. She readily agreed to help, a gesture that highlighted the positive outcomes of my willingness to assist others, I had taught her daughters, a value that has consistently enriched my life in unexpected ways.

In 2011, during my routine mammography, it unveiled not just one but two lumps, each in one of my breasts. The spots, resembling like stones in hardness and size, signaled a "Double Whammy", as I thought to myself.

As those masses increased in size, so too did the accompanying discomfort, reaching a level of excruciating intensity. Subsequent consultations with medical professionals led to the decision to undergo surgical intervention once more. It was during this period that I had whimsically coined my recurrent hospital visits as "Picnics." As the surgery date approached, I underwent the necessary pre-surgery tests. Meanwhile, on the home front, I began making arrangements for the days I would spend in the hospital. The impending challenge of managing the aftercare, particularly due to the limitations on using my hands after the double surgeries, added an extra layer of apprehension to the process.

As the surgery approached, Shona, now more independent and grown-up, expressed a strong desire to visit me at the hospital after the procedure. Despite my initial reluctance to expose her to the challenges of the hospital environment, Shona insisted on being by my side.

After the surgery, Shona, rushing from her new school where she had moved for Eleventh grade, visited me at the hospital. Sitting by my side, she eagerly shared all the news and updates from her school, giving me a glimpse into her world. Since she was a baby, she had developed a habit of confessing her mistakes to me without fear of reprimand. This foundation of trust had flourished between us, allowing her to feel comfortable sharing every aspect of her life with me.

In the midst of our conversation, the intense pain I was enduring caused me to fidget and squirm. Witnessing my suffering, Shona, unable to contain her emotions, burst into tears. It dawned on her in that moment that she hadn't seen the extent of my struggles, as she had only seen me after my discharge, and we hadn't shared many details about my illness. Overwhelmed, she left the room, and I sent our niece Namrata after her to provide comfort.

Despite the challenges, I was eventually discharged and on the road to recovery once more. However, on the second day post-discharge, I woke up in the morning to find the sheet, mattress, and my dress soaked in blood. The stitches had been disturbed, leading to bleeding during sleep, adding another layer to the journey of recuperation.

Raj promptly contacted the doctor, who advised us to bring me in without delay. With Karuna's assistance, as she had volunteered to help me out this time, the three of us hurriedly dressed and made our way to the hospital. Upon arrival, we found that the doctor was still occupied in the operating theater. The nurse directed me to the post-surgery care room. When the doctor finally joined us, the sheet in that room was also soaked in blood. He reprimanded the nurse for the delay in bringing me for a check-up or dressing change. After thoroughly cleaning and re-dressing my wounds, this time with a different and more secure bandage, he permitted me to return home.

Raj had to depart for his duties, so he arranged for a cab to take us home. However, during the journey, halfway through, I couldn't control my nausea and requested the driver to pull over. There, I promptly vomited. After feeling a bit better, we resumed our journey, and I remained extremely tired and weak until we reached home.

The following afternoon, with Karuna asleep, I didn't want to disturb her. Despite having a craving for cookies, I couldn't reach the higher shelf. I had to wait for a couple of hours until I could satisfy that craving. During those moments, I felt overwhelmed by helplessness and fury. However, I never surrendered to despair. Most of the time, I would strategize and find ways to manage, determined to move forward.

The recurrent surgeries became not just physical battles but a profound exploration of the human spirit's endurance and the ceaseless pursuit of normalcy in the face of adversity. Life, much like a challenging puzzle, demanded a constant rearrangement of pieces, and in that puzzle, cancer became a formidable opponent. Through it all, the unspoken pact with destiny echoed—a silent understanding that life, with its dual sides like a coin, is a precious, unpredictable gift. It taught me to savour each day as a blessing, appreciating the simple joys amid the complex symphony of existence.

CHAPTER TWENTY-ONE

Through Loss and Healing

Despite my general optimism, occasional bouts of despair would overtake my mind. What if everything fails? What if I fail? The fear of losing everyone I loved lingered in my thoughts. I'm uncertain about an afterlife; for me, once the last breath leaves the body, it's a closed chapter. There's nothing more to it. Nothing beyond. I wasn't ready for it. Life, no matter how feeble, I wanted to fight for it. What I didn't realize is that suffering could come in different forms, sometimes in the form of losing loved ones.

Around 2011, Amma's health began to decline, and she was diagnosed with Dementia. Often, she lost track of past and present. Sunanda and I started visiting Aurangabad more frequently, hoping to spend as much time with her as possible.

During one of my visits to Aurangabad, Shona accompanied me. She walked into Amma's room with a tray of food, where Amma sat on the bed, staring blankly at the wall. Shona, placing the tray on the table, approached her gently. "Amma, I brought you some food. It's your favourite, fish and rice," she said softly. Amma turned her head and looked at her with confusion. "Who are you?" she asked in a frail voice. Shona, aware of Amma's Alzheimer's, said she was Rekha's daughter, hoping to jog her memory. Amma burst into laughter. "Rekha is not married yet... How can she have a daughter?" she said incredulously. Shona felt a pang of sadness but also a smile. She hugged Amma and sat with her for a long time, and Amma responded with a smile.

While Amma never forgot her children, the later years of our lives gradually dimmed in her recollection. During one visit from my cousin Ajay and his wife, Amma kept staring at Ajay's wife, later asking my sister if our uncle knew that Ajay was going out with a girl.

In the last few months of Amma's life, many people from distant places traveled to visit her. Through their kind and philanthropic hearts, Amma and Anna had earned love and affection from people beyond blood ties. Many prayed for her and shared stories of how Anna and Amma helped them in times of need. Occasionally, she would recognize someone, her eyes lighting up at their presence, though still not fully comprehending why they might have come to see her out of the blue. It was frustrating at times.

In the formative years of our lives, we naturally look up to our parents as our guardians, the steadfast protectors who shield us from the perils of the world. This initial perception shapes our earliest memories of them, creating an indelible image of caregivers always ready to prevent us from stumbling, mend our wounds, and envelop us in a comforting embrace when no other solace suffices. Our parents, in essence, become the bedrock of our support system, the source from which we draw the resilience to confront life's most arduous challenges. Witnessing them in a state of vulnerability, frail and delicate, is an experience that tugs at the very core of our emotions, evoking a profound sense of heartache.

Regrettably, Amma eventually slipped into a coma, an irreversible state from which she never emerged. My visits to her bedside became more frequent, each moment carrying the weight of impending farewell. During my final visit to Aurangabad, while she still clung to life, the difficulty of parting became almost unbearable. I stood by her bedside, observing her pale and frail form, breathing ever so faintly.

As I was leaving, I had a feeling, will I be able to see her alive next time. I gazed into her eyes, the windows to a lifetime of shared joys and sorrows, a torrent of love and pain surged within me. Grasping her hand, a hand that had always offered unwavering support, I kissed it gently. My lips traced the contours of her forehead and cheeks, a desperate attempt to imprint every inch of her being onto my soul. In hushed tones, I whispered declarations of love, the depth of my longing, and the futile desire to prolong our time together. Fate, however, unfolded a different script, cruelly tearing us apart. Shortly after my departure, she breathed her last,in about a month, leaving me with nothing but a shattered heart and a treasure trove of memories etched indelibly in my soul.

Amma's final moments in a coma were tragic, yet her last words remain a cherished beacon of wisdom. She expressed contentment that I didn't engage in elaborate prayers in front of God, recognizing my inclination towards practical deeds, particularly in aiding the less fortunate. Proudly, she acknowledged my commitment to charity for those in need, urging me to persist in these altruistic endeavours. According to her, the blessings of the poor and needy held unparalleled value, ensuring my well-being and happiness. In those parting words, she bestowed upon me a legacy of compassion and a profound understanding of the genuine impact of benevolence.

Amma's wisdom illuminated the path to honouring her memory, revealing that genuine tribute lies not in mourning and lamentation, but in extending a helping hand and serving others selflessly. Through her guidance, I learned that the pursuit of material wealth and fame pales in comparison to the enrichment found in spiritual peace and joy. In her teachings, she bestowed upon me a timeless truth, a testament to the enduring power of love, compassion, and service to others.

Amidst the somber passage of time, on the 8th of September 2014, after enduring five months ensconced in a coma, she peacefully departed. The weight of her absence left me reeling, enveloped in a tempest of grief and loss.

Amma epitomized selflessness, a beacon of unwavering devotion to others, placing their needs above her own. Her life was a testament to the boundless capacity for love and care, even amidst the most daunting trials. Following her example, I pledged to devote the remainder of my days to the well-being of Raj and Shona, the very essence of my world. Despite grappling with the relentless onslaught of cancer and other afflictions, I refused to succumb to despair.

Throughout the arduous journey, I clung to the enduring legacy of my Amma's words and spirit, drawing sustenance from her unwavering belief in resilience and hope.

The journey to Aurangabad was marked by the somber occasion of bidding farewell to Amma. The prospect of witnessing her lifeless form proved to be an overwhelming challenge, prompting a realization that life inexorably moves forward.

In that moment, I recognized the pressing need to shift my focus to Anna, acknowledging his heightened need for attention and care in the wake of Amma's departure.

After the completion of the intricate rituals surrounding Amma's farewell, the weight of grief became insurmountable. It was then that I found solace in confiding about the escalating pain caused by a sizable fibroid in my left breast to Sunanda and Jagdish Kaka. The fibroid, conspicuous and causing excruciating pain even with the slightest touch or jolt, demanded urgent attention. Driven by the urgency to comprehend my condition, I resolved to undergo a mammogram immediately, preempting the scheduled one.

Upon my uncle's recommendation, I proceeded with a needle biopsy at Kamalnayan Bajaj Hospital in Aurangabad. The sampled tissue underwent scrutiny in the pathology lab, and after a span of four days, the report arrived, delivering the relieving news that the biopsy results were benign. My uncle, relying on this assessment, reassured me that surgery was unnecessary.

However, despite the benign report, the persisting pain left me uncertain about the best course of action. Hoping for a natural resolution over time, I returned to Mumbai. By the end of September, a disconcerting realization dawned as the fibroid exhibited growth, accompanied by an escalation in the intensity of the pain.

Despite patiently enduring for a few months, the persistent discomfort propelled me to seek medical advice once again. The need for consultation became imperative as the pain persisted, prompting a quest for a clearer understanding of the situation and a more comprehensive approach to addressing the escalating health concern.

Upon consulting with the doctor, a thorough examination of the fibroid was conducted, leading to the recommendation for a mammography to ascertain its size. The procedure, albeit excruciating, became imperative for a comprehensive understanding, involving an examination of both breasts.

Subsequent to the mammography, we reconvened with the doctor to discuss the findings. To our concern, it became apparent that the fibroids were not only persisting but were actively growing, necessitating prompt intervention. The doctor conveyed that the size of one particular fibroid had reached three centimeters, underscoring the urgency for their removal.

During that time, Shona was attending college. As per our routine, Raj and I opted to arrive at the hospital a day before the scheduled surgery for the admission process. The day of the surgery arrived, and plans were made for Shona, Kunal, and Varun (Sujata's sons) from Mumbai to join us at the hospital during the procedure.

Anticipating the upcoming surgery, the day before the scheduled date found me rising early to prepare meals for the day and the following one. These were carefully packed and stored in the refrigerator, ensuring everything was in order for the surgery day. Following this, I made my way to the hospital to complete the admission process. As was customary, I took charge of setting up the room while Raj attended to the necessary admission formalities. The following morning, the kids, including Shona, arrived early at the hospital with the lunch I had meticulously packed for them the day before.

In October, I underwent my sixth surgery. Reflecting on the events of 2015, I find myself in awe of the resilience that allowed me to endure the pain throughout the year. By then, the hospital had become a familiar setting, almost like a zoo visit for a child—marked by the routine of surgeries. Despite the myriad challenges, I persisted and emerged from each ordeal stronger than ever before.

As I regained consciousness after the surgery, Shona, displaying her unique sense of humour, teased me about the fibroid or mammary glands, describing it as "huge in size." Amusingly, she referred to it as a "breast mouse" due to its remarkable mobility. In that lighthearted moment, I was struck by the realization that my baby, Shona, had grown into a strong and mature individual.

The routine of hospital trips continued, with Shailaja dutifully bringing lunch for our post-surgery recoveries. Following my discharge, the next day saw me heading to Aurangabad for the recuperation period, opting to stay with Sujata. Anna, too, was at her place, displaying a newfound contentment, likely influenced by the delightful company of Sujata's entertaining granddaughter.

The atmosphere brightened further that evening when Seema and Swati joined us. The occasion took on a special significance as we celebrated Seema's birthday with friends and a cake, fostering a sense of joy and camaraderie amid the challenges.

Reflecting on this journey, it becomes evident that infusing elements of entertainment and celebration has been instrumental in uplifting my spirits. Despite the physical toll these experiences have occasionally imposed, prioritizing a stress-free mindset has been paramount. These moments of joy have not only served as a source of resilience but have also played a crucial role in sustaining my adventurous journey through life.

Little did I anticipate that this particular stay with Anna would be our final one together. The time spent with him was marked by shared enjoyment, and I seized the opportunity to engage in extended conversations with him. This was a stark departure from my childhood expectations, given that he was a disciplinarian who spoke sparingly. Discovering this newfound avenue for heartfelt communication allowed me to realize that perhaps, I inherited my never-give-up attitude and strong willpower from both him and Amma.

Despite my ongoing battle with cancer, numerous surgeries, and various ailments, Anna steadfastly refrained from revealing or expressing his concerns in my presence. Instead, he sought updates from Amma and Sunanda, maintaining a stoic and supportive demeanour.

The dynamics with Anna underwent a noticeable shift as time advanced, especially in the realm of his authority. Old age brought about a transformation, and he embraced a more relaxed approach, participating in our conversations, sharing jokes, and indulging in the delectable dishes prepared by Sujata and Priyanka. Although he had become a small eater in recent times, a daily array of tempting dishes was presented with the hope of pleasing his taste buds. Thankfully, his appetite showed signs of improvement, a positive turn undoubtedly facilitated by the attentive care provided by Mr. Subhash, Sujata's husband.

This period of shared moments allowed me to collect a treasure trove of cherished memories with Anna that would last a lifetime. One particular instance stands out when he expressed pride upon discovering my involvement in Nutrition and diet planning. During my stay, he came across a diet plan I had created for a family friend, shedding light on a facet of my life that had remained unknown to him until then.

Merely two months following that memorable stay, on December 22nd, I found myself in the hospital caring for my neighbour Ritika when I received the distressing call about Anna's fall. He had taken a tumble while standing in the front yard, attempting to bask in the winter sunlight. Unfortunately, he lost his balance and collided with a large stone, resulting in a severe impact to his head. Moin, his business manager, who worked from an office adjacent to the front yard, witnessed the fall and swiftly responded. He immediately called for Shivnath and Supriya, my younger brother and sister-in-law, who promptly rushed to his aid. Together, they managed to lift him up and bring him indoors. Despite the quick response, Anna's condition necessitated a shift to the hospital. To our profound sorrow, we learned that his skull was fractured, and within a couple of hours, he slipped into a coma.

Upon receiving the distressing news of Anna's fall while caring for Ritika in the hospital, I promptly informed Ritika and her husband Sandeep before hastily leaving the hospital. The urgency of the situation compelled a swift departure, and I had already communicated the situation to Shona and Raj. Shona, who had returned home from college, had efficiently packed my bags, and Raj, in turn, arranged for my flight ticket.

As soon as I reached home, I collected the packed bags, and with Raj and Shona following later, we made our way to the airport. Arriving in Aurangabad, I was picked up by Shrishail,

Shivnath's elder son, and headed directly to the hospital. However, the heartbreaking reality awaited me as I found Anna heavily bandaged, connected to various medical gadgets, and in a coma. The moment turned into an overwhelming tragedy as he passed away on December 26th, 2015. Within the span of a year, I had lost both Amma and Anna, a profound and significant loss. May God grant them eternal peace. I am very thankful to God that I had ample opportunities to serve both Anna and Amma. Through their guidance and presence in my life, I have learned the true meaning of devotion and the importance of serving others with sincerity and dedication.

Returning from Aurangabad and attempting to navigate the tumult of emotions following Anna's passing, I took a significant step in my healing journey. Joining a general counseling class, the focus was on acquiring the skills to understand various mentalities and guide individuals towards leading better lives. In the midst of this therapeutic process, a particular session required us to recount our life stories.

As I began narrating the chapters of my life, the weight of emotions overwhelmed me, and I found myself breaking down into tears. In those vulnerable moments, the struggle to contain one's tears often proves futile, as the emotions fight against restraint, flowing freely.

It was later, as my batchmates learned about the multitude of health issues I had been silently grappling with, that their shock was palpable. Despite being in constant touch, the depth of my struggles had remained concealed. Shehnaz, an ex-principal of many reputed schools in Mumbai, one of my friends, moved by the realization, remarked, "You are your own product!" In essence, she conveyed that despite enduring a considerable amount in life, I had spared no effort to make the most of it. Her gesture of hugging, kissing, and treating me to ice cream on the way home spoke volumes of the camaraderie and support that blossomed in that moment.

Another friend, perhaps reflecting on the metaphorical nature of life, commented, "Aaina bhi kuch chupata hain" (Even the mirror hides some things). This observation encapsulated the profound truth that beneath the surface of daily interactions, there are often hidden struggles and triumphs that shape the fabric of one's existence.

Attending the counseling session provided me with the courage to open up and share my struggles. When I visited Aurangabad and reunited with my school friends, I decided to confide in them about the challenges I was facing. The revelation left them shocked; the depth of my issues had remained hidden from them until that moment. In our previous meetings, we would reminisce about the good old days, share stories, and erupt in laughter. However, as the time came to bid farewell, they would return to their lives, and I would return to the routine of managing my pillbox.

It appears there was an incident that deeply affected me, shedding light on the prevalent misinformation and taboo surrounding both mental and physical health issues. That incident occurred within the first two years following my cancer diagnosis. During that challenging period, I found myself spending a considerable amount of time alone at home, while Raj, occupied with his duties, often returned late into the night from his posting at the Mahim police station. To alleviate the solitude, I sought solace in the company of my next-door neighbour, a young Maharashtrian lady blessed with two charming daughters.

It was during one of our regular hangouts when, as usual, we shared life stories. At that time, her elder daughter had just returned home from school. I was discussing my health and insomnia issues when, innocently, her daughter asked her mother, "What happened to Aunty?"

To my surprise and dismay, my neighbour promptly replied in Marathi, "Aunty vedi zhali" ("Aunty has gone crazy"). This statement caught me completely off guard, and I excused myself, leaving immediately. Following that incident, I chose not to engage in further conversations with her.

While the incident was hurtful initially, I later realized that the burden I carried was mine to bear. I chose to distance myself from negative influences, especially those who lacked empathy for others' struggles. Thankfully, I was surrounded by people who genuinely cared for me, so I decided to share my challenges only with those who showed genuine concern.

Whether it was the impact of the high dosage of thyroid medicine or the overall strain of my health issues, I had become irritable by nature. That was undoubtedly a challenging time for me and those around me, particularly my parents and siblings. Despite their own challenges, they were willing to bear my occasional outbursts. It became clear to me that I needed to prioritize sharing my concerns with those who truly cared for me.

From that incident onwards, I limited my sharing to my close-knit family and my fellow warriors in various hospitals who understood each other's struggles. We shared therapies, home remedies, and provided mutual support that comes from a shared journey through the trials of health challenges.

Despite being an ideal patient who diligently followed the doctor's instructions from A to Z, I found myself grappling with irritability. Perplexed by these mood-changing episodes, I sought clarity during one of my visits to the doctor. I questioned why, despite maintaining a fitness regime, adhering to a healthy diet, and making lifestyle changes, I continued to experience various health issues and irritability. I yearned to understand the root causes and find ways to overcome them. He replied,I would have been bedridden by now,if I had not followed a healthy lifestyle.

The doctor's insights resonated deeply with me, serving as a reminder of the multitude of reasons to be grateful to God. Determined to delve further into the issue of irritability, I turned to Sunanda for guidance. She consulted with an endocrinologist in the US, and the response shed light on the underlying factors—specifically, the high dosage of my medication and the insomnia it induced.

Taking matters into my own hands, I decided to focus on meditation, dedicating more time to meditation. Additionally, I explored various home remedies and incorporated yoga asanas into my routine, all aimed at finding peace within myself. The commitment to these holistic approaches began to yield positive results.

I vividly recall an encounter with my grocer during a visit to the hospital for a regular appointment with my endocrinologist. Surprised to see me, he inquired if I was facing any issues. I calmly explained that I was there for my routine check-up with my endocrinologist. When he learned about my health challenges, he expressed astonishment at my composed demeanour. He shared that his wife also had thyroid hyperthyroidism and was constantly irritable. In response, I suggested introducing yoga and meditation into her routine, as these practices had proven beneficial for me in achieving a sense of calm and composure.

I found comfort when, a few months later, he approached me with profuse gratitude, acknowledging that my counseling had played a pivotal role in bringing peace to his life. He shared that his partner had transformed into a serene soul, alleviating him from the burden of incessant complaints and irritations. Receiving such feedback brings me a sense of contentment, and I willingly offer counsel to those in need. Contributing positively to others' well-being is a gratifying endeavour for me, drawing from my own experiences during the challenging initial years. I recall an amusing incident shared by my sister Sujata; during a health issue, she informed a doctor familiar to us that she would seek my advice, prompting the doctor to humourously inquire about the identity of this "doctor" she was referring to.

CHAPTER TWENTY-TWO

Triumphs Amidst Trials

The aftermath of my thyroid cancer surgery brought along several other ailments, but it also presented new challenges. Besides grappling with insomnia, I discovered that my ability to absorb calcium had been severely compromised. That revelation marked the beginning of a lifelong battle against calcium deficiency.

To address the ongoing health concern, I committed to a dedicated fitness routine focused on muscle toning and bone strengthening. It involved incorporating various exercises, including yoga asanas, stretching, and aerobics, into my daily life. For an impressive span of thirty-three years, I remained steadfast in adhering to this fitness regimen. The consistency in my efforts aimed at maintaining overall health and countering the effects of calcium deficiency became an integral part of my journey towards my well-being.

In January 2016, I made the decision to incorporate weight training into my fitness routine. Initially, it went well, and I found enjoyment in the challenge. However, after just 20 days of training, my body sent me a clear and alarming message—a sharp, searing pain radiated from my right knee, compelling me to halt my workout.

In an effort to promptly address the issue, Shona and I took to Google to investigate my symptoms. The findings pointed to a potential synovial sac burst. The synovial sac, a thin tissue that lines the joint and is filled with fluid, serves to lubricate the joint and facilitate smooth movement. Continuous strain or being overweight over an extended period can lead to the rupture or destruction of this sac, resulting in stiffness and the potential development of arthritis.

Facing the challenge of a potentially ruptured synovial sac, I sought the expertise of one of Mumbai's finest orthopedists. The journey to the doctor involved a five-hour wait, but finally, I was called in for examination. After observing my walk, the orthopedist confirmed the diagnosis—my synovial sac had indeed ruptured, causing the excruciating pain. He prescribed two types of tablets, including a painkiller, instructing me to take them regularly for the rest of my life to manage the relentless pain.

Being diligent about my health, I began taking the prescribed tablets that very night. However, after about four days, a new issue surfaced—palpitations. This alarming sensation prompted me to call out for Raj urgently. Sensing my panic, he immediately summoned Sunanda for guidance. Describing the frightening palpitations, Sunanda swiftly recognized the potential danger and asked about any new medications. Upon receiving the name of the painkiller, she advised me to discontinue it immediately, as the palpitations were perilous side effects of the medication.

During a period of relaxation suggested by Supriya in Aurangabad, I found a welcome change that helped refresh my spirits. Sujata's caring hospitality further contributed to my comfort during this break. Upon my return to Mumbai, I resumed my routine, adjusting to a new normal that included some restrictions due to my knee pain. It was during this time that Berry, our pet Labrador, entered our lives. Just a couple of months old, Berry's arrival coincided with my knee issues, creating a simultaneous challenge of raising a lively and mischievous puppy.

Given my limitations, Raj and Shona took on a significant portion of Berry's care. However, as the demands of caring for a young and energetic pet became apparent, tensions arose. In the midst of frustration, a heated argument ensued, leaving all of us upset. Reflecting on the situation, Shona expressed regret over her decision to insist on having a pet. In a collective decision, we decided to hire a caretaker for Berry until she grew up and settled down. Though the caretaker was not trained for the role, we chose to be patient and committed to training her despite the initial challenges.

During the same period, I had a follow-up appointment with my endocrinologist, Dr. Archna Juneja. Having been her patient for many years, I continued seeking her expertise when she shifted to Kokilaben Ambani Hospital from Seven Hills Hospital. Dr. Juneja, well-versed in my medical history, inquired about my age during the appointment. Before I could respond, she swiftly checked my file and complimented me, saying, "Kudos to you. You look so young, not your age at all." Her words filled me with joy and pride, serving as a testament to the power of discipline and perseverance in maintaining good health and well-being.

Given that an endocrinologist typically addresses various hormonal and health issues, when I discussed my knee problem with Dr. Archna Juneja, she recommended consulting a physiotherapist, Dr. Parag Paluskar.

Initially, I harboured skepticism about physiotherapists, influenced by stories of cases worsening due to inexperienced specialists. Despite my reservations, Dr. Juneja assured me that Dr. Parag Paluskar was the perfect person to handle my case. Trusting her judgment, I decided to visit the physiotherapist at least once, hopeful that it would contribute positively to addressing my knee issue.

Dr. Parag Paluskar, also from Seven Hills Hospital, left a lasting impression on me with his incredible simplicity and humility. His kind and respectful tone immediately put me at ease. Unlike rushing into a quick diagnosis, he approached my case with patience and thoroughness. He conducted a detailed investigation, asking a series of questions and meticulously noting down the information.

Much like my previous diagnosis, Dr. Paluskar arrived at the conclusion that my synovial sac had ruptured, leading to permanent damage to my knees. However, his treatment approach differed. In the first session, he instructed me to lift my leg, place it on the bench, and then stretched and flexed it. While the process was painful at the moment, it remarkably alleviated half of my excruciating pain.

Dr. Parag Paluskar provided a realistic assessment of my knee condition, explaining that there was permanent damage. However, he offered a ray of hope, assuring us that with proper management through diet, exercises, and supplements, the situation could be improved. In addition to prescribing some SOS painkillers and a course of medicine, he demonstrated basic exercises that could contribute to the well-being of my knees.

With an international trip to the US planned for July, I inquired if I could visit him a fortnight before my departure. To my surprise, he responded with genuine concern, advising me not to waste money and to come only when absolutely necessary. His pragmatic treatment, counseling, and assurance acted as a tremendous relief. The initial dread of a life spent limping transformed into a hopeful outlook on leading a fit and manageable life.

Being a disciplined individual, I incorporated Dr. Parag Paluskar's exercises, medicines, and supplements into my daily routine. With unwavering commitment, I adhered to these practices until one fine day, it struck me— "Voila!" I realized I was walking normally without any signs of limping.

Up to this day, I haven't discontinued the exercises recommended by Dr. Paluskar. The realization that I could reverse some of my ailments through hard work, discipline, and the guidance of compassionate individuals like Dr. Parag has been empowering. Grateful for the support of Dr. Archna, Dr. Parikh, and a series of doctors in my life journey, along with my family doctors, I express my gratitude to God for guiding me through hurdles.

Dr. Parag Paluskar's intervention not only alleviated half of my excruciating pain in just four days to five days but also introduced a series of daily exercises that I diligently continue to follow.

Over the years, Dr. Paluskar became more than a medical professional; he became a valued member of our extended family. Raj, Shona, and I sought his expertise on various health issues, and we also recommended him to numerous friends and relatives. Those who diligently followed his exercise routines not only found relief but were completely cured of their ailments. Dr. Parag Paluskar, through his dedication and expertise, had worked wonders for us, emphasizing the crucial role of trust in the healing process.

With the knee issue resolved, I began contemplating what could be the next item on my agenda. As I diligently followed my fitness regime and physiotherapy to prepare for my upcoming US trip, an exciting development unfolded in Shona's life. She received the wonderful news that she had been chosen as an Assistant Chair for the Harvard World Model United Nations (WorldMUN), scheduled to take place in Rome for eight days.

World MUN is an annual traveling model United Nations conference organized by Harvard University and a local university team from the host city. It is considered one of the most prestigious international MUN conferences globally, and Shona had participated twice before, winning awards on both occasions. This time, being selected as an Assistant Chair was a prestigious position for her. Raj and I were overjoyed for her, recognizing what a fantastic opportunity this was.

As she began preparations for the trip, Shona wanted us to = accompany her for the second half of the trip, primarily for sightseeing. Considering the rich cultural offerings of Italy, renowned for literature, design, fashion, opera, art, and cuisine, we eagerly agreed to join her for this memorable experience.

While I was still contending with knee pain, making my travel plans uncertain, I chose not to express my concerns to Shona, determined to fulfill her wish for us to accompany her. Despite the persisting knee pain, Dr. Parag Paluskar's expertise and care had enabled me to manage it miraculously. His guidance played a crucial role in my decision to join Shona in Italy.

In March 2016, Shona left for Italy a week ahead of me, where she had a remarkable experience chairing for delegates from around the world. A week later, I joined her, and she warmly greeted me at the airport. We embarked on a train journey to Sorrento, which surprisingly turned out to be trouble-free and uneventful. Exhausted, we reached Sorrento late in the evening and went straight to bed.

However, in the middle of the night, I was abruptly awakened by excruciating leg cramps. Shona tried to assist, but fortunately, the discomfort gradually subsided on its own. Recognizing that Shona was battling a severe cough and cold, I insisted that she prioritize rest. Subsequently, we both commenced medication for our respective health issues – she for her throat infection and I for my leg problem.

After a delightful view of the Amalfi Coast, our journey continued to Siena via train, and we relied on trains for transportation throughout our trip. The Italian countryside unfolded its beauty from every train window. Upon our late-afternoon arrival in Siena, our stomachs were eagerly anticipating a satisfying meal.

Due to cab entry restrictions, we were dropped off in the town center. As recommended by Sunanda and Kunal, we opted for lunch at the recommended Trattoria La Torre, a quaint restaurant, which turned out to be a fantastic choice. The owner himself prepared an authentic meal, delighted by our praises and glowing recommendations.

Post our filling supper, we began the ascent to our hostel villa. Siena's hilly terrain featured steep cobbled streets throughout the town. Following Google Maps' instructions, we kept climbing, but the path seemed endless. My knee began hurting, exacerbated by the increased asthma due to elevated climbs. Despite the strain, I decided to spare Shona the stress. Finally reaching the top, we discovered it was the back entrance.

Upon turning around, we found the front door locked, surprising us both. Exhausted and laden with luggage, Shona grew concerned for me. Dialing the supplied number, she reached the caretaker, who arrived shortly after with the keys.

Following a nap, we revisited the same place for supper. Shona, not feeling well, opted for juice. The remainder of the journey wasn't devoid of challenges, yet it was undeniably unforgettable.

Exploring places like Venice, Murano and Burano Islands, and of course, Rome, proved to be a delightful adventure. Abiding by the adage "When in Rome, do as the Romans do," we savoured authentic pizzas, quattro formaggi pastas, and the iconic gelato! Those shared experiences during our mother-daughter trip with Shona crafted enduring memories that still evoke nostalgia today.

Jokingly dubbed an international traveler after Italy, I soon had another trip lined up for the US, embracing my inherent globetrotter spirit.

Come July, Sunanda prepared to welcome her beloved daughter through surrogacy. She requested my assistance in the US for the significant moment and to care for her baby afterward. However, a cloud of worry loomed over me - "What if my knee problem decided to act up again during the trip?"

My consistent physiotherapy substantially alleviated the issue, becoming a constant companion in my life. Adhering to my exercise routine proved to be a straightforward equation: it kept discomfort at bay, while any slacking off brought back those pesky pains and aches.

I had initially traveled to the US in 2001 as a tourist. After 15 long years, the prospect of going to the US again loomed. I had grown accustomed to my new lifelong companions, Asthma and Diabetes Mellitus. Meanwhile, Shona had transformed from a little kid into an adult.

The idea of leaving Shona and Raj to travel to the US for three months posed a considerable challenge. Previously, I had never been away from Shona for more than ten days, and even then, it was for my radiation treatment. This time, mental preparation was essential as Sunanda needed me to take charge of the baby while she managed her hospital duties. Balancing work and childcare in the US are demanding, and Sunanda had to provide for the baby, scheduled for delivery in July.

Sunanda facilitated the travel arrangements, and I began planning for the trip. Consistent knee exercises, pranayama, and yoga for asthma management as earlier was part of my routine. Gathering regular and emergency medicines, I secured a travel health insurance, recognizing the potential challenges and costs of obtaining medical aid in the US. Packing for a three-month stay proved to be a meticulous task, yet my planning and experience ensured its timely completion.

Coincidentally, Raj and I departed together as he was also scheduled to travel to the US for a work conference. Both of us carried a certain level of anxiety, having never left Shona alone for an extended period. To ease Shona's time alone, Sujata and Varun stayed with her initially. When they departed for Aurangabad, Shona found comfort in Berry's company, during the moments when she missed us. The anxiety lingered for both Raj and me, as this was the first time we had left Shona alone for an extended duration.

Nonetheless, we arrived in San Francisco, where Satyam, Raj's nephew, graciously picked us up. Satyam's beautiful bungalow became our residence, and we were warmly welcomed by his family, including his wife Laxmi and two sons, Parth and Shiva.

After a restful period to overcome jet lag, we sat down with Satyam to plan our sightseeing trip, being first-timers in San Francisco. However, our plans were disrupted by a sudden asthma attack I experienced. Taking the basic medicines I had brought along, I attempted to rest, but by morning, a high fever had set in, an unusual occurrence for me, given my usual resilience with rest.

Homesickness and a deep yearning for Shona became evident. Raj and Satyam provided me with some medication, yet my experience indicated the need for an antacid. Before long, a severe bout of acidity added to my discomfort, making it seem like everything was working against me.

Despite not having much opportunity to explore San Francisco, it was time for me to travel to Orange County to stay with Sunanda's friend and his partner, a gay couple. Despite not feeling well, the prospect of visiting a new place and meeting new people excited me. I had never had the chance to gain insights into the spectrum of sexualities and gender preferences. This lack of understanding made me somewhat apprehensive about staying with them, fearing I might unintentionally offend them. Despite this initial uncertainty, I chose to be mindful and embraced the experience.

CHAPTER TWENTY-THREE

Celebrations and Crises

Upon landing in Orange County, I opted for a wheelchair at the luggage hold, as walking long distances continuously wasn't comfortable for me. While waiting for my bags, a voice called out, "Hi Rekha!" Turning around, I saw a couple smiling at me. One of them remarked, "You look so similar to Sunanda! It's difficult to miss you." We shared a good laugh, and that's how I was introduced to this gentle and caring couple. Upon reaching their home, the mother of one of them, who resided with them, warmly embraced me. This memory is etched in my mind forever.

Excitement filled me as I began on my stay with them, determined to start on a positive note. It became evident that my preconceived notions about same-sex relationships were completely unfounded. In the evening, they promptly began preparing dinner. One of them, Sunanda's ex-colleague deeply involved in fitness, surprised me by announcing that dinner would be at 5 pm. This took me aback, as 5 pm is tea time in India, and having dinner so early meant potential midnight hunger. I shared this concern, leading to shared laughter. They assured me not to worry, mentioning the well-stocked refrigerator, and encouraged me to take whatever I wanted to my room. I relished a delightful meal with them and then carried some food to my room.

During my stay with them, their love and care overwhelmed me. Battling homesickness, one of them took me for a ride to the beach and even brought us something special from Starbucks, knowing that I had lost my appetite. His thoughtful gesture truly touched my heart. However, halfway through the ride, I started feeling unwell and communicated my discomfort. Without hesitation, he promptly took me back home. Remarkably, despite the inconvenience, I witnessed no frustration or anger on his face. This experience profoundly made me realize that love and compassion know no boundaries.

Once, while in the washroom, I suddenly felt faint. Panic gripped me, and thoughts raced, "How will I manage to go out?" Determined to reach the doctor on the other side of the door, I fumbled with the lock and rushed out, struggling to breathe. I called out to Sunanda's friend one of the gay couple, who was a doctor. Sensing the urgency, He responded promptly and rushed to my aid. He made me lie down on the bed and administered medicine immediately.

I had been nervous about flying to a new place, fearing it might be isolating and lonely. However, I encountered strangers who shattered my misconception. These individuals went out of their way to make me feel at home, with one of them even having roots in India. His forefathers had migrated to Trinidad and settled there permanently a few generations ago. This experience taught me never to judge people based on articles or hearsay. Their hospitality remains etched in my memory.

Sunanda arrived a day later, and the following day, we went to the hospital to meet her baby's surrogate mother, Laura. Witnessing our family baby growing in someone else's womb was a unique and emotional experience. The doctor informed us that the baby could be delivered at any moment. We waited in anticipation, and soon, Laura started experiencing contractions. However, signs indicated that the baby wasn't getting enough oxygen. Sunanda, being a Neonatologist, recognized the seriousness and promptly called the Gynecologist. Laura was urged to push, and after a tense moment, the baby was born. Initially appearing blue, like a baby monkey, which startled me, she started breathing normally with immediate care. It turned out she had become hypoxemic.

During this intense time, my illness faded into the background as I became engrossed in the birth of the baby. Health concerns took a backseat to the joyous occasion. The child was later named Roma, synonymous with Lakshmi, the Hindu Goddess of Wealth.

The following day, we returned to Sunanda's friend's place, where we stayed for about a week before heading to New York. Though my health remained fragile, and my appetite hadn't fully returned, I pushed through. Sunanda stayed home for a couple of days but soon had to return to work.

That's when my real task began. Sunanda had demanding hours of duty, often lasting 16 or 24 hours, and I assumed the responsibility of caring for Roma and managing household chores. Additionally, I had to handle calls from India to mediate Shona and Raj's arguments, often revolving around ordering groceries, and coordinating with domestic help. Despite ongoing knee pain and intermittent knee locking, managed through regular physiotherapy exercises, I remained motivated.

When out, I refrained from carrying Roma due to a lack of confidence in my ability to handle her with my knee issue, wanting to avoid any potential accidents. However, I did carry the heavy baby bag whenever necessary.

Sherisha, Raj's niece, and her two kids, Laya and Bhargav, residing on the outskirts of New York, provided invaluable moral support. Meanwhile, my friends in India were celebrating their 50th birthdays with great enthusiasm. My own 50th birthday, according to the Hindu calendar, arrived in September. A school friend, now residing in Chicago, Tauqeer, sent me a lovely fruit bouquet—a thoughtful gesture that I genuinely appreciated. Thankfully, the trip unfolded smoothly without any major health issues, despite it being just a year since my last surgery.

The US trip with Roma came to an end as Sunanda and I brought her to India in the first week of October 2016.

As I flew back to India, lost in thought, Seema's approaching golden jubilee or fiftieth birthday lingered in my mind. Knowing she had no plans to celebrate it, an idea struck me - why not throw her a surprise party? Immediately, I began jotting down ideas on my phone, and soon enough, we had landed in Mumbai. Shona and Raj were there to receive us, both captivated by Roma's sweet and naughty smile.

Sunanda spent a couple of days in Mumbai. After she left for Aurangabad, I discussed my idea of celebrating Seema's birthday with Raj and Shona. They both loved it, and I couldn't wait to get started on the planning!

Bubbling with excitement, I commenced on planning Seema's surprise birthday party. I called Jawahar, Seema's husband, and enthusiastically shared my idea with him. He was thrilled and offered his full support. Working in secret, I made all the arrangements, ensuring Seema had no inkling about the preparations happening behind her back. The anticipation of seeing the look on her face when she walked into the party was almost too much to bear!

I was thrilled at the prospect of making Seema's birthday a truly memorable one. The night before the party, I traveled to Aurangabad and visited the venue during the day to ensure everything was perfect. Fortunately, Rajesh, Raj's cousin, had assisted me with the arrangements, and Swati was there to support me during the daytime.

By evening, we were all at the venue, eagerly awaiting for Jawahar and his parents to bring Seema to the party. When they arrived, we lined up and dimmed the lights. As soon as Seema entered, we surprised her with a loud cheer and started singing and dancing. The look of surprise and happiness on her face was priceless, making all the effort worthwhile. We had a great time together, and it's a memory that I will cherish forever.

Thrilled with the success of the party, I didn't want to leave Shona and Raj for long. Having already been in the US for three months, I felt the need to ensure they didn't stay alone. Early the next day, I left for Mumbai with Vandana, one of the childhood friends who had come down from Navi Mumbai for the party. The six-hours journey was filled with good company, as we chatted and discussed on variety of topics.

As I traveled back to Mumbai, I started experiencing heavy bleeding, a concern that had intermittently occurred during my US trip but was now excessive. Initially attributing it to hormonal imbalance, reaching home became my immediate worry. Despite my concerns, I somehow managed to reach home safely.

However, the frequency of my bleeding increased day by day, causing and escalating to worry. Unfortunately, there was no time to get it checked as we soon had to leave for a family wedding, and this problem seemed like a routine thing for me at home. I tried to manage it as best as I could, but it continued to cause pain and discomfort.

In December, we went to Nanded for Shailaja's daughter Parinita's wedding. During the visit, I faced a lot of problems, and not being in the comfort of my own home heightened my worries and discomfort. Eventually, I decided to seek advice from my gynecologist friend, who promptly prescribed some tablets. It was a great relief as the bleeding stopped completely. With this issue resolved, I was able to fully enjoy the wedding rituals without any hindrance.

I returned to Mumbai by the end of the month after spending nearly a month in Nanded. After settling everything at home, I returned to Aurangabad for our school's golden jubilee celebrations in January. The joy of reuniting with our teachers and classmates after about 34 years was immeasurable. We reminisced about old times and actively participated in all the activities we used to enjoy during our school days. The sports day, in particular, brought back the fun and excitement of my youth, and I had a blast!

After the sports session, our batch mates decided to go for lunch. We all enjoyed making fun of each other, recalling past incidents in the classroom and the assembly ground. It was a gala time. As we dispersed, knowing we had to be back in the school for the evening's DJ night, the spirit of celebration continued.

As most of our batch mates had already left, only about six of us remained when I suddenly started experiencing cramps in my legs. Although this was a usual occurrence for me, the pain intensified minute by minute. After about 10 minutes, the cramps became unbearable, spreading throughout my body from top to toe. My friends had never seen me in such a state before, understandably becoming tense and trying to help me in every possible way. They gave me massages and even practiced Reiki to ease the pain.

Feeling embarrassed that they had to go through all this trouble for me, I kept apologizing for causing them so much inconvenience. It took about thirty minutes for the cramps to subside, and I don't know how I would have managed if I had been alone. I am more than thankful to all six of them for their support.

By then, I was mentally exhausted, and all these issues were extremely draining. I felt upset that all this had to happen in front of my friends, and tears welled up in my eyes. One of them expressed their surprise, mentioning they never knew I had to endure so much, reassuring me that it wasn't my mistake. They commended me for being brave in facing both physical pain and mental agony, expressing that I should be proud of myself.

Upon reaching home, I took some rest, and it occurred to me that the cramps may have been due to dehydration caused by the sports events. I immediately increased my fluid intake and started taking an extra dose of calcium for some days.

I was back in school for the DJ night, surprising everyone who never expected me to return after the afternoon episode. The news had spread like wildfire, and everyone was inquiring about my health. It was a pleasant surprise to see how much everyone cared about me.

As I've mentioned before, I never stopped myself from anything. I knew that if I had stayed at home, it would have occupied my thoughts throughout. It was such a relief to be able to enjoy the DJ night with my friends. Taking proper care of myself, I was back to normal in just a few days.

Upon returning to Mumbai, I underwent my routine yearly Sonography tests, which had become a standard procedure for me. During the test, the doctor inquired about any history of lymph nodes, and I shared information about my multiple breast lymph nodes. After hearing the details, she suggested consulting my doctor, expressing concerns about a cyst that needed further examination.

Surprised by this information, I decided to consult my regular doctor soon. During our discussion about my bleeding problem, he mentioned that it was a separate issue and advised consulting a gynecologist. He recommended a skilled gynecologist from his hospital, and we were fortunate to secure an immediate appointment with him.

The gynecologist, being polite and soft-spoken, recommended some tests after hearing about my problem and instructed us to return soon with the reports. Not wanting to waste any time, given my increasing weakness, we promptly returned within a few days.

The gynecologist immediately took us in, providing what felt like VIP treatment. After reviewing the reports, he conveyed that he had a preliminary idea about my issue but wanted to reconfirm it through further tests. To my surprise, after a year and a half since my previous surgery, I learned that I had a sizable polyp in my uterus. This polyp was the cause of the profuse bleeding, a shocking revelation. Despite initially thinking the bleeding was due to menopause, I was relieved that we had finally identified the root cause of my problem.

This marked a new chapter in my medical journey. Having undergone cancer surgery and dealt with multiple breast fibroids, facing a polyp was an unexpected development. Concerned, I asked the doctor if taking tablets was the only solution and whether the size would reduce with medication. To my surprise, he replied, "I am afraid it is not so simple. While polyps usually shrink with menopause, considering my cancer history, they can't take a chance lest it becomes malignant with time."

I felt a sinking sensation but then he added, "Do not worry. I will perform a laparoscopic treatment, minimizing incisions." I went numb, feeling like I was playing an adventurous medical game. What I initially thought to be a menopausal problem turned out to be an ongoing process that persisted year after year. Despite the shock, I consoled myself, thinking, "Maybe this is the end of my problems. It will probably be the last surgery of my life, and I will be a free bird afterwards."

Raj inquired about the critical aspect: the hospital, surgery charges, etc. The doctor mentioned that as it is laparoscopic, the charges would be around INR ten lakhs. Both Raj and I were dumbstruck, looking at each other in disbelief. The doctor explained that he would be performing a robotic surgery. Composing ourselves, we told him we needed to discuss this with Jagdish kaka and would get back to him.

That night, we spoke to Kaka. He dismissed the entire situation, saying, "This is all rubbish!" He advised us to come straight to Aurangabad and get the surgery done there. After giving it some thought, considering Raj's entitlement to a significant amount from his office's health plan, we decided not to waste anybody's money unnecessarily. Finally, we made the decision to undergo the surgery in Aurangabad.

CHAPTER TWENTY-FOUR

Sacrifices and Silver Linings

My initiation into writing wasn't fueled by inspiration; instead, it was born out of necessity. Once Cancer designates someone as its target, one is never truly out of the risk zone. It's akin to a lifelong race, being pursued by an unrelenting storm that shows no signs of relenting. The only option left for me was to keep running as far as I could, attempting to evade the inevitable. Thus, I reasoned with myself—if this looming shadow of death was to be an unwavering and undefeated companion, I might as well spend my time getting acquainted with my scourge. As I embarked on this expedition, the written word became my compass, guiding me through the labyrinth of emotions and uncertainties. Each sentence penned was a stride, a purposeful step in comprehending the intricacies of an adversary that defied conventional understanding.

Gradually, this journal evolved into a holy grail, documenting everything from the inception of Cancer. Like any sacred text worth its religion, the journal held every pertinent piece of medical information concerning my case. From MRI films and scan reports to prescriptions, it encompassed the entirety of my medical journey. I affectionately dubbed it "Chikitsa Granth," translating to "The Medical Bible." This sacred tome was not merely a record; it was a source of solace, a talisman of knowledge that became the first item to find its place in my travel bag whenever a new journey called for me.

In the latter part of 2017, Shona, my daughter, was preparing to commence on her journey to pursue a Master's degree in the United States. A sense of impending change lingered in the air, prompting us to organize a family getaway to the captivating Andaman & Nicobar Islands. This wasn't just a leisurely escape; it carried the weight of a farewell before Shona's departure.

Simultaneously, a family wedding was on the horizon, demanding our presence. The joyous occasion added a celebratory note to our already eventful plans. In the midst of these arrangements, the news of my cousin's husband passing away reached me. Compassion called for a visit, and I intended to make the journey to offer solace and support.

The prospect of extensive travel loomed large over my schedule for that year. However, In April, my meticulously planned calendar faced a disruption when my surgery was scheduled. The destination changed to Aurangabad, and I found myself preparing for a different kind of journey—one not of leisure but of recovery.

The decision was made; I would undergo my surgery at Kamalnayan Bajaj Hospital (KBH) in Aurangabad. Jagdish Kaka, ever the meticulous planner, intended to personally oversee every aspect of the medical procedures. As the date approached, I found myself in Aurangabad, days ahead of the scheduled surgery.

Anticipating the arrival of Raj and Shona, who were due to arrive a day later—coinciding with the surgery day—I took charge of the administrative aspects. With paperwork neatly completed, I checked myself into the hospital. Accompanying me for moral support and company was Aditya, the son of my brother Shivnath. He graciously stayed overnight at the hospital, a reassuring presence by my side.

In the quiet corridors of Kamalnayan Bajaj Hospital, preparations unfolded as I faced the imminent medical intervention. The atmosphere carried a blend of determination and vulnerability, a juxtaposition of emotions that only a hospital setting can evoke.

On the first day, the hospital routine commenced with a battery of tests and vigilant monitoring of my vital signs. A representative from the blood bank reached out, seeking confirmation regarding potential blood requirements for the upcoming surgery. The intricacies of medical preparation unfolded methodically.

As dawn broke on the following day, Aditya and I were up early, gearing up for the day ahead. Aditya, with his commitments to classes, had to bid farewell, leaving me momentarily. However, the day took a brighter turn as Raj and Shona arrived just in time for the preoperative rituals. They had chosen the early train, prioritizing being by my side.

Surrounded by the warmth of my family's support, a surprising calmness enveloped me instead of the expected nervousness. Turning to Raj, I shared a moment of lightness, saying, "No matter what the doctors do, I have every intention of coming out of that operating room just fine. After all, I haven't finished troubling you yet." Raj, meeting my attempt at humour with a smile, responded, "Well, I guess I'll have to start preparing for the worst then!" Laughter echoed in the room, a therapeutic release of tension.

As the moment approached, I found myself being ushered into the preparatory phase before the surgery. A reassuring presence awaited me in the form of Jagdish Kaka, my uncle and the head of the Anesthesia Department. True to his commitment, he stood vigilant in the operating theater room, overseeing every detail.

In a twist of fate, Kaka's watchful eye caught a momentary misunderstanding between a nurse and his instructions regarding the Cannula (IV Needle). Preferring not to leave anything to chance, he swiftly intervened. Requesting the nurse to step aside, Kaka took charge, ensuring the delicate insertion of the cannula into my veins. His expertise spared me any unnecessary discomforts. The memory of a previous encounter with a less considerate doctor lingered in my mind. A stark contrast to Kaka's gentle approach, this experience involved a rough insertion of the needle, causing an unpleasant sensation as it hit my bone. With the administration of anesthesia, the journey into the main surgery room began. Amidst the flurry of activity, I couldn't catch a glimpse of the surgeon who would be operating on me.

As consciousness gradually reclaimed its hold, I found myself being wheeled back to my room. To my pleasant surprise, a welcome committee awaited my return. The pride and joy radiating from their faces gave the impression that I was a war hero returning home. At that moment, I half-expected them to break into cheers, chanting my name and perhaps even contemplating hoisting me up on their shoulders.

Raj took on the role of explaining the intricacies of the procedure to the gathering of family members and relatives. With a touch of humour, he remarked, "I'm surprised you didn't ask for a frequent flier card after spending so much time under the knife!" Laughter filled the room as we acknowledged the tension that had built up among the well-wishers.

The atmosphere shifted from a sense of relief to one of comradeship. As we shared anecdotes and exchanged banter, the room became a hub of warmth and connection. The journey through a major surgery had not only left its mark on me but had also woven a collective narrative of resilience and shared laughter among those who had stood by my side. In that moment, the welcome committee transformed into a fellowship celebrating the triumph of overcoming a significant chapter in the ongoing saga of life.

Later in the day, Jagdish Kaka summoned Raj to his cabin, and when Raj returned, he carried five boxes with him. Settling beside me, Raj unveiled the contents, revealing my uterus, ovaries, appendix, lymph nodes, and a liquid extracted from my body—all neatly packed and displayed. The only unsettling aspect was that they were no longer inside me but rather housed in those boxes.

The impact of this sight was immediate and profound. Rajesh, Raj's cousin, caught a glimpse of the boxes and was so disturbed that he couldn't contain his emotions. Uncontrollable tears welled up, and he hastily left the room. Sensing the need for support, Raj rushed outside to comfort him, leaving me alone with my thoughts.

Meanwhile, attached to a catheter and a drain, all I could do was wait. When Raj returned, he briefed me on the emotional scene that had transpired outside my room. The surreal display of my internal organs, now preserved in boxes, had inadvertently created a ripple effect of emotions among those who cared about me.

Rajesh's concerns echoed the sentiments of many, questioning the extent of resilience that my spirit and body could endure. He pondered on the mysteries of my mental state, marveling at how I managed to exude energy and positivity despite the challenges. The absence of any visible signs of depression or sadness in me, puzzled him. In response, Raj conveyed that the wellspring of positivity within me couldn't be overshadowed by even the darkest hours of our lives.

In the midst of the serious reflections, a member of the family injected a touch of teasing humour, asking, "So how is the vehicle functioning with the spare parts missing?" Raj, ever quick-witted, laughed in response, "The ride won't be interesting without a few bumps along the road."

The inquiry about whether I felt empty inside, coming from a family member, was a discomforting moment that struck at the heart. It was a question that stirred a whirlwind of emotions, for how does one articulate the complex array of sentiments when a part of oneself is being chipped away while still breathing?

The disquieting realization that a piece of me was being sacrificed for the sake of the whole was difficult to grapple with. Yet, amidst the turmoil, I reminded myself that perhaps, these sacrifices were the very essence of my survival. Everything that is part of nature has its place in the universe. If human anatomy was meant to have these organs for a full life, then not having them inside me, meant in some way I was broken. The question then was whether it was the body that made up for all thing I was or that one spark the doctors were trying to keep aflame. Perhaps that spark is what the world refers to as the soul.

As I continued to contemplate, a reassuring thought echoed within me – that, with a good lifestyle, the potential side effects could be managed. This, I thought, marks the conclusion of my problems, and with God by my side, I felt an overwhelming sense of reassurance. I found myself expressing genuine thanks to a higher power for granting me a level of healthiness that surpassed many others.

The revelation of a benign report later amplified my belief in the divine guidance that I felt throughout this ordeal. In the face of adversity, this acknowledgment became a cornerstone, an enduring source of comfort and fortitude.

"Every Dark Cloud Has a Silver Lining" – a philosophy that has not merely been a saying for me, but a guiding principle that has illuminated the path through the darkest corners of my life.

Life's journey is rife with storms and shadows, yet this philosophy has been a constant companion, urging me to seek the silver lining even when clouds loom overhead. It is a mindset that not only sustains me but also empowers me to face whatever may come with courage, resilience, and an unwavering belief in the brighter possibilities that await beyond the shadows.

CHAPTER TWENTY-FIVE

Mother's Journey of Resilience

The nursing staff's unwavering commitment to the patient care during my hospital stay left me in awe. Their tireless efforts to assist us, patients, throughout the day prompted me to wonder if the level of hospitality at the hospital matched that of a 7-star hotel. The facilities were truly impressive. From spacious and well-maintained rooms to a hygienic environment, everything spoke of a commitment to excellence. The disciplined and well-trained staff further contributed to the sense of professionalism that permeated the hospital.

While I can only imagine the quality of the food provided by the hospital, in my case, my family, along with Raj's cousins Rajesh and Shailesh, and my friends, went above and beyond. They coordinated among themselves, ensuring that I received homemade food during my stay. Even when I was in Mumbai, Shailja and Sankalp took the initiative to bring nourishing meals to the hospital. Their dedication to providing me with familiar and comforting homemade food added a personal touch to my recovery journey, turning the hospital stay into a space where care extended beyond medical procedures and into the realm of genuine human connection.

When it was time for the discharge, The revelation of the hospital bill, a mere 1.25 lakhs compared to the estimated 10 lakhs in Mumbai, left us utterly shocked. The stark comparison highlighted the preposterous overpricing of the surgery in Mumbai, made us question the disparities in health care costs across different regions.

Raj, unfortunately, had to return to Mumbai just a day before my scheduled discharge. Shona, my daughter, took on the responsibility of staying with me in Aurangabad, providing the support and care needed during the post-surgery period.

Following my discharge, instead of heading back to Mumbai, I went to stay with my brother Shivnath and his wife Supriya. Their warm invitation to come directly from the hospital was heart-warming. It was a sanctuary of care and comfort, a space where recovery continued under the nurturing embrace of family support.

Shona's decision to stay back in Aurangabad led to a great time of bonding between a mother and daughter. Her caring and attentive nature provided not just emotional support but also an opportunity for joyous moments with cousins, uncle, and aunt. It became a cherished period of time, creating a bouquet of memories that would be treasured, especially with her impending departure to the US later that year.

After a few days in Aurangabad, Shona bid farewell while I extended my stay for over a month, surrounded by the warmth of my maternal family. The connection, laughter, and shared moments served as a healing balm during the recovery phase.

Returning to Mumbai felt somewhat ironic, considering that essential "spare parts" had been taken out of the machine that was my body. Yet, as long as the engine continued to work, a sense of contentment enveloped me. Missing a few nuts and bolts no longer bothered me. It was the smooth drive on the road that mattered more than the intricacies of the machinery.

Back on my feet and renewed, it was time to shift my focus back to home priorities. The impending US trip for Shona's 16-month-long Masters course became the central point of attention. With plans to accompany her and ensure a smooth settling-in process, we decided to begin on a crucial pre-travel ritual - shopping.

Shopping, between Shona and me, was not just a necessity but a cherished pastime. While Raj occasionally joined us, Shona and I shared a particular fondness for the activity. It became our little joy ride as we ventured out to purchase essentials – clothes, bedding, toiletries, and, notably, preventive and emergency medications.

The aisles became our ramp and as we strode through the racks and shelves, the shared laughter and conversations turned a seemingly routine task into a bonding experience. The act of shopping became a way to prepare, not just materially but emotionally, for the upcoming adventure. It was more than just shopping; it was a shared exploration of anticipation and readiness for the adventures that lay ahead.

Next on the checklist were Doctor's appointments and vaccinations. Raj's work trip came in perfectly timed. He had to leave early for an Ernst & Young conference. Shona and I followed a few days later. Just two months after my surgery, Raj, Shona, and I left for the US to kickstart Shona's Master's degree journey.

In the weeks leading up to the trip and during the trip, it felt like nothing had changed for me. Life was going as usual, with making plans, experiencing adventures and returning to the Hospital for my routine regimen.

Post-surgery, a peculiar habit crept in; every now and then, I found myself jiggling my body, almost as if to check if any other parts were threatening to come loose. The absence of five organs, including the thyroid glands removed in 1991 due to malignancy, left me contemplating if I was facing a shortage in my troops battling against the rival—cancer. Five soldiers had been shot down in this ongoing battle, and the war was far from over.

The recurring question that echoed in my mind was profound: "What is the nature of our identity? Is it our body, our mind, or something else entirely?" It was a contemplation that delved into the core of existence, particularly in the face of physical alterations brought about by surgeries and ailments.

The journey had been long and arduous, yet the determination to keep moving forward remained unwavering. The recognition of strength and resilience became a guiding light, reassuring me that I could overcome any obstacles that lay ahead. The ordeal didn't conclude with the surgery, but the confidence in emerging from this experience stronger and more resilient fueled my optimism.

Gratitude filled my heart for the unwavering support of loved ones, knowing they would stand by me in every step of the way. The anticipation of the next chapter in life carried excitement, and I looked forward to discovering what the future holds.

Embarking on a journey spanning approximately 12,530 kilometers for Shona, I endured around 26 hours of travel time. The vast distance and shifting time zones presented unique challenges, particularly in maintaining my medication routine. The grueling effects of jet lag took hold, persisting for about 8 to 10 days and leaving a tangible impact on my body.

Our initial stay in New York, hosted by Sunanda, provided a brief respite before the next leg of our journey. Joined by Sunanda and Roma, we ventured to Miami, where Raj joined us after his conference. The ensuing five days became delightful memories of our trip, filled with shared experiences and cherished moments in the vibrant city of Miami.

In moments of idle contemplation, my mind naturally gravitated towards thoughts of my recent major surgery and the lingering physical pain. Yet, I was resolute in my determination not to let these shadows cast a pall over my trip. Instead, I chose to redirect my focus beyond the dark clouds, fixating my gaze on the beautiful horizon that lay ahead—a trait that Raj consistently admired.

His observations often reflected on my resilience, emphasizing the lesson that everyone could glean from my ability to stay steadfastly focused on the positive. It became a conscious choice to navigate beyond the realm of discomfort and uncertainty, steering towards the brighter aspects of the journey. In doing so, each moment unfolded as an opportunity to embrace joy, gratitude, and the profound beauty that life continued to offer.

After Sunanda and Roma returned to New York, we set our course for Pittsburgh. Upon arrival, we checked into a motel, and the following day, we embarked on a significant visit to Heinz College at Carnegie Mellon University—an institution poised to become Shona's future educational haven. The three of us were captivated by the impressive architecture and the lush green surroundings that enveloped the campus. While natural beauty was abundant throughout the United States, this particular campus held a uniquely soothing appeal.

Our exploration extended to Shona's off-campus apartment, a place she had meticulously searched for and rented after a virtual tour. To our delight, it turned out to be a charming residence in close proximity to her college. It marked the beginning of a significant chapter as our daughter, Shona, secured admission to this prestigious institution, ultimately graduating with accomplishments that filled us and our family with immense pride.

As Raj departed for India a few days later, the responsibility of helping Shona settle in Pittsburgh rested on my shoulders. The journey, both physically and metaphorically, continued to unfold, carrying with it a sense of accomplishment and anticipation for the promising academic years that awaited Shona in this new and enriching environment.

The task of setting up Shona's room, kitchen, and apartment for her incoming roommates became a collaborative effort. Despite my asthma, I actively participated in the cleaning process, using a cloth to cover my mouth since face masks were not as prevalent until 2020 when COVID-19 emerged. The determination to contribute and create a welcoming space overcame the physical challenges, emphasizing the importance of those moments for both Shona and me.

Shopping became a shared adventure as we sought out items that we couldn't bring from home, ensuring that Shona's living space would be equipped with everything she needed.

Additionally, I took the initiative to prepare some of her favourite dishes in advance, freezing them so she could enjoy them after my departure.

The following day, I had to undertake the journey back to New York on a night bus. Throughout the day, a reluctance to leave Shona alone lingered, and we engaged in continuous conversation. While she likely sensed my hesitation, she did not reveal her own feelings. As I settled into my seat on the bus, tears welled up in my eyes. It marked the first time Shona would be on her own for an extended period, an emotional moment that tugged at my heart.

In an attempt to find solace, I spoke to Raghav, our future son-in-law, who was also in the US pursuing his Masters at Syracuse University. His assurances that they would manage everything provided some relief, yet the difficulty of the moment lingered. The separation, coupled with the emotions of a mother watching her daughter begin on a journey of independence, prompted a few tears to escape.

As Raj had departed for India earlier, I found myself alone on a flight back, leaving behind my daughter in the United States. The distance between us gradually increased, and as I soared through the skies, I felt like a feather lost in the wind. The two anchors of my life were oceans away from me, creating an unsettling turbulence within me.

Returning home to Mumbai, I found myself instinctively entering Shona's room—a space filled with her toys, medals, and belongings. The room served as a tangible reminder that she was now away, and it took me a while to fully accept that I had let her go for the sake of her future. The room became a sanctuary of memories, a repository of moments frozen in time, and reminiscing with Raj about the times spent with her became a source of solace, keeping me grounded.

Oddly, throughout this journey, I hadn't shed a tear for my own illness. The emotional release that typically accompanies such moments had been reserved for the act of letting go, for the bittersweet realization that my daughter was oceans away from me.

Life, in its practicality, often obscures the emotional nuances that underscore such separations. I reflected on the challenge of realizing that my little baby had grown into a capable young woman, ready to navigate the complexities of life independently. Despite the worries that clouded my thoughts, I reminded myself that she deserved the opportunity to write her own story, just as I had done in my journey.

CHAPTER TWENTY-SIX

Rhythms of Life

December held a special place in my heart as, after months since my return from the US, it marked the much-anticipated homecoming of my Shona. The end of the year ironically became the beginning of my joys.

Throughout her Master's degree, Shona and I adhered to a rule that became a comforting ritual — calling each other once a day. This routine, noted by one of her mentors, highlighted a unique and cherished connection. It was observed that only a few of them spoke to their parents daily, and Shona took pride in maintaining this steadfast link.

Come December the plan was made for her to return home for a short vacation. To celebrate this reunion, I had planned a family vacation to Udaipur. This trip held a unique significance, especially since our earlier plans for the Andaman and Nicobar Islands had been canceled due to my surgery. Shona's arrival was a moment of pure joy, and even Berry, our dog, couldn't contain her excitement. She joyfully jumped all over Shona, showering her with affection.

After Shona had a well-deserved rest, we began our journey to Udaipur eight days later. Rajasthan, with its rich history and stunning architecture, had always held a magnetic pull for travelers like us. Udaipur, known for its rich cultural heritage and vibrant colours, stood out as one of the gems of Rajasthan. The trip unfolded as enchanting as we had hoped, weaving together moments of exploration, cultural immersion, and the warmth of family bonds against the backdrop of Udaipur's captivating beauty.

In mid-January, Shona left for the US again. Towards the end of the month, I received a call from her that left us shocked – she was in the hospital, having collapsed due to some infection. Raj and I discussed the situation and promptly decided that I should leave for the US immediately. We booked a ticket to ensure a swift departure.

The following day, Shona called again, asking if I could come to the US. Assuring her that the ticket was already booked seemed to provide some relief. The process of packing for this trip was a whirlwind, especially considering that my usual preparation time spans 8 to 10 days. This time, urgency prevailed. I needed to gather a substantial amount of groceries, eatables, medicines, and more, both for Shona and for my own needs, turning the packing process into a crucial and swift endeavour.

Setting up everything in Mumbai for Raj and the maids' convenience proved to be a tough task. Managing multiple responsibilities simultaneously was indeed challenging. However, driven by determination, I pressed on, resolved to get everything in order within such a short span of time. Despite the exhaustion, I knew I would manage it.

Sunanda was in India during that time, but upon reaching her place in the US early in the morning, I took a brief 8-hour break and then boarded a bus to Pittsburgh that night. Shona had thoughtfully arranged for a cab to pick me up. Witnessing her when I arrived home brought a profound sense of relief.

She appeared weak and exhausted, prompting an immediate inquiry into her infection and overall health. In that moment, my own health issues and the usual jet lag took a back seat – Shona needed my support, and that became my immediate priority.

From day one until my departure for India in mid-March, my sole priority was taking care of Shona. As her schedule became increasingly occupied with school commitments, my role evolved into a caregiver, managing tasks such as cooking healthy and delicious meals, cleaning, grocery shopping, and more. To alleviate moments of loneliness during the afternoons, I embarked on solo explorations, venturing out to discover new places.

By the time I left for India, Shona was on the path to recovery, and although relieved by her progress, parting from her always carried a tinge of disheartenment. The bond forged through care and support, as well as the shared moments during her healing process, made leaving a difficult experience.

In September 2018, I made my third trip to the US, once again to be with Shona. The last visit occurred in May 2019, coinciding with Shona's Masters convocation in Pittsburgh. By then, she had already started working in Austin, Texas. Following the convocation, we began on a trip to Austin, and I seized the opportunity to visit NASA's Johnson Space Center in Houston, which was nearby. Our exploration extended to San Antonio during our time there.

What struck me during the trip was Shona's growing financial independence. She had taken charge of all our travel arrangements for San Antonio, showcasing not only her independence but also her resourcefulness. The meticulous planning reflected her care and dedication, emphasizing her desire to spend quality time with us. Witnessing her financial independence and career commencement filled us with immense pride. Shona's achievements stand as a testament to her hard work and dedication, and we consider ourselves fortunate to have her in our lives.

Throughout those trips, a recurring issue marred my travel experiences at various security checkpoints. Security personnel frequently stopped me, inspecting and removing my medicines from my bag during security checks. I consistently had to present my prescriptions and documents detailing my ailments, emphasizing that I carried only a 100 ml bottle in my hand baggage, with the rest securely stowed in the checked baggage. On occasion, the weight would exceed the 7 kg allowance, but after explaining the necessity, authorities usually allowed me to carry them. Based on my experience, airlines and law enforcement authorities generally exhibit understanding and sympathy towards patients in such situations.

In June, during one of our trips to the US, we celebrated our wedding anniversary and Shona's birthday together. A couple of days later, we left for India.

In less than two years, I found myself embarking on four trips to the US, spanning from July 2017 to May 2019. Those visits evolved into a somewhat half-yearly routine, a series of journeys shuttling back and forth between India and the US. As my friends kept abreast of my travel stories, their comments often reflected a certain nonchalance, saying, "Tu to US aaise jati hai, jaise ke Churchgate" (You visit the US as casually as you'd visit

Churchgate, a nearby neighborhood in Mumbai). The frequency of those transcontinental journeys became a testament to the intricacies of life, marked by the ebb and flow of responsibilities, health concerns, and the unwavering bonds shared across borders.

Gratitude fills my heart for these past couple of years, during which I remained problem-free. Consistent adherence to my regular medications allowed life to become not just bearable but enjoyable and relaxing. It felt like the end of my medical history, opening up the possibility for new activities, such as engaging in work or social initiatives.

It was within this period of newfound serenity that the idea of writing this memoir began to take shape. Numerous incidents had become intertwined with the journey of life, prompting a desire to make my experiences a guiding spirit for people at large. The aim was to convey that life can be a joyride if approached with an intent to savour every moment, contrasting with the potential of a doomsday scenario if one succumbs to the adversities and accepts them as destiny.

My newfound confidence faced an unexpected setback when, just a few days later, I experienced a bad fall in the bathroom. The incident was quite a scare as I ended up with a deep cut on my head that was bleeding profusely. Fears of a permanent patch of missing hair crossed my mind. However, after a visit to the local hospital, they assured me that there was no serious damage and proceeded to stitch the wound. Despite the reassurance, the hospital's responsiveness to my inquiries was not always satisfactory. Nonetheless, the cut healed within a couple of weeks, and I even jokingly referred to the bandage they provided as my new "hairband."

Between 2018-2019, I embraced another new adventure — singing. Despite Raj's initial skepticism about its potential impact on my asthma, I was determined to give it a shot. I signed up for singing classes. From the very first session, I proved to be an eager and diligent student, practicing tirelessly throughout the day.

As Republic Day approached, Raj accompanied me to an event organized by the Singing Institute. The event kicked off with the presence of a Bollywood celebrity as the chief guest, turning the affair into a star-studded spectacle.

After a couple of students, it was my turn to grace the stage. Raj, taking the stage before me, introduced me to the audience and shared the poignant story of my life's struggles, marked by multiple surgeries and various ailments. His heartfelt introduction brought tears to my eyes. Despite Raj's concerns that my emotional outburst might hinder my performance, as soon as I began to sing, everything else faded into the background. I found myself immersed in the song, thoroughly enjoying the experience.

However, a sense of helplessness crept in when my dedication to extra practice clashed with the mentors' consistent tardiness. Hours of waiting proved fruitless, and the frustration of striving for a goal while encountering a lack of support mounted. It's disheartening when those meant to guide you in your pursuit are consistently absent. Despite attempts to practice with fellow singers in the mentor's absence, the sessions yielded little progress. Eventually, I ceased attending these sessions altogether. The melody that briefly enriched my life started to fade away after the disappointing incident with the disinterested mentors.

Through life's teachings, I've cultivated the ability to embrace each moment, whether it be a long-awaited reunion or an unexpected setback. My determination to savour new experiences has opened exciting chapters, from exploring new places to finding a creative outlet in singing, keeping me motivated. However, this journey hasn't been devoid of frustrations.

In the midst of it all, I focus on the gems — the pride in my daughter's achievements, the thrill of adventure, the comfort of enduring bonds. These glistening moments serve as a reminder that life's beauty lies not in perfection but in our willingness to fully engage with it, navigating through all its unpredictable rhythms.

CHAPTER TWENTY-SEVEN

Strictures and Stents

As the year 2019 unfolded, medical tests and reports had become the new routine in my life. Every one of those routine appointments, my Endocrinologist would provide instructions for the necessary tests. The reports from those tests found a meticulous place in my "Chikitsa Granth," ready to be discussed during our next visit scheduled for September 2019.

During the consultation, my Endocrinologist thoroughly examined each report, but her expression changed as she delved into a specific section – protein leakage in my urine. This unexpected anomaly left both of us puzzled. After my last surgery two years ago, my life had regained a sense of normalcy without any major ailments, though my previous conditions remained as constant companions.

Initially, I dismissed the protein leakage as a minor issue, thinking it could be easily resolved. However, my Endocrinologist stressed the importance of consulting a specialist, a Urologist.

Dr. Anita Gite, Jagdish kaka's daughter, is also a renowned surgeon and head of the surgery department, she has advised and assisted me throughout these years. And her husband, Dr. Venkat Gite, is a renowned urologist who was serving as the head of the Urology department at Mumbai's prestigious JJ Hospital.

Following my Endocrinologist's advice, we promptly sought Dr. Venkat's consultation. He recommended a CT scan and KUB X-ray, emphasizing the need for immediate action. I booked an appointment for these medical tests the next day.

That night, as we drifted into slumber, a sudden jolt shook us from our peace. At 4 AM, Raj was writhing in agony due to severe abdominal pain. At first, we suspected it might be an acute case of acidity, so he took an antacid. However, the pain relentlessly surged, and it was evident that this was no ordinary discomfort. Raj asked for painkillers to ease his suffering.

In a panic, I searched through my "SOS pouch", only to find it devoid of any painkiller. I swiftly ordered one from a nearby 24-hour pharmacy. While waiting for the medication to arrive, I tried to ease Raj's pain with hot compresses and any remedy I could think of, but nothing provided relief.

Finally, the chemist arrived with the painkiller, and Raj took it immediately. We waited for some time, but the pain persisted. We waited until 7 AM, and then I made a call to a doctor well-known in our locality who was familiar to us. He advised us to bring Raj to the hospital where he practiced. Raj was scheduled to conduct an important training session at one of India's leading banks. However, he had to postpone it.

At the hospital, they admitted Raj and began administering treatment and conducting tests. The pain, fortunately, subsided somewhat and became more bearable. Upon reviewing the test results, the doctor recommended a CT scan and MRI. As we awaited the test reports, the doctor summoned us to his office with grave news – Raj was suffering from appendicitis, and an urgent appendectomy was imperative to avert a potential rupture.

I immediately contacted Kaka, to discuss the situation. Kaka insisted that we come to Aurangabad immediately for the surgery. We informed the doctor that we would be having the procedure in Aurangabad.

It's often said that we can't multitask effectively. But then, there comes situations in life, where you just manage to surprise yourself by doing the impossible. It was a time when I needed to be everywhere at once. After leaving the hospital, my responsibilities were far from over. I called the travel agent to book our tickets for the flight to Aurangabad on the way home. Order medicines from the chemist and also jot down further line of action. Upon reaching home, I had to pack our bags, as we were scheduled for an early morning flight the next day. Despite my exhaustion, I was driven by the urgency of the situation, and there was no time to spare.

After arriving in Aurangabad, we wasted no time and immediately headed to the renowned Kamalnayan Bajaj Hospital for Raj's routine checkups. His surgery was scheduled for a day later, and thankfully, everything went smoothly. He needed to stay in the hospital for about four to five days to recover fully.

While I was tending to Raj's needs in the hospital, his cousin Shailesh was sitting with him and chatting. I seized the opportunity to get my CT scan and KUB X-ray done since I had a morning appointment. Rushing down to the radiology department, I aimed to return quickly to be there for Raj if he required anything. Fortunately, I completed the tests and made it back to the room promptly, arranging for someone to collect the reports later.

Upon our discharge from the hospital, we temporarily stayed with Shivnath. We were with them for about a week for Raj to recuperate and were back to our Mumbai.

I felt it was time to visit Dr. Venkat with my reports in hand. However, when Dr. Venkat examined both the CT scan and X-ray reports, he expressed his dissatisfaction, claiming they didn't provide a clear picture of the situation. Consequently, he suggested that we proceed with an MRI immediately. Though I had undergone numerous brain MRIs due to a benign cyst in the brain related to hormonal imbalance, this one was different—it was a ureter MRI, and like all the previous MRIs, it left me feeling utterly drained. The MRI process can be mentally taxing, and I kept praying throughout the procedure every time I had to get it done.

After reviewing the MRI report, Dr. Venkat delivered the news that there was an 80% stricture in my ureter. He went on to explain that there could be various causes for this condition and that if left untreated, it could potentially damage the kidney. I felt overwhelmed and helpless, and it took some time to process the information. Seeing the worry on our faces, he assured us not to be overly concerned. He proposed a solution – a stent placed in the ureter for three months to alleviate the stricture and return the ureter to normal.

The procedure was scheduled for a fortnight later, in November 2019. I promptly got to work the following day, arranging various tests and paperwork for medical claims. As the day of the procedure approached, I also prepared our bags, knowing we would be in the hospital for about five days.

I got admitted, arranged our things in the room, and Raj took charge of paperwork. The day went in the battery of doctors from different departments coming throughout the day for various checkups and consultations and to understand my other ailments, in addition to the tests conducted at intervals.

The next day, I was wheeled into a massive operating theater, and as the technicians were attaching the medical gadgets to my body to monitor my vitals, a nurse wanted to put a band over my eyes. I refused, telling her I will be fine without it.

This was a lower body procedure, so I was given spinal anesthesia. This was the scariest part of the whole procedure. I could watch the whole procedure and also listen to the interesting conversation between the surgery team regarding my procedure. Everything was different. I was brought back to the room after some monitoring.

I was advised not to eat anything until evening. Furthermore, I was instructed not to elevate my head to prevent nausea and the risk of vomiting due to spinal anesthesia.

Experiencing numbness in my legs for nearly five hours after the procedure was a terrifying ordeal. Thoughts about whether my legs would return to normal were ever-present, adding to the anxiety. However, as the numbness gradually subsided, I felt better, and by evening, I was back to a more comfortable state. A relaxed sleep that night alleviated the stress surrounding the new procedure. Fortunately, I felt better as the night progressed, and the next day, I underwent continuous monitoring to track my progress. On the fifth day, I was discharged from the hospital, eagerly anticipating the hope that the stent would be removed after three months.

As usual, Raj took charge of completing the formalities while I packed our personal belongings.

The decision to have my surgery at JJ Hospital surprised many acquaintances, as we had never opted for a government hospital before. However, the experience turned out to be remarkably positive. I received the best treatment. The nursing staff displayed professionalism on par with private hospitals, maintaining clean and hygienic rooms. The medical facilities were top-notch, with experienced doctors attending to me throughout the day.

After the surgery, I felt a mix of nervousness and apprehension. Following Dr. Venkat's advice, I understood the importance of post-surgery care, especially with a foreign object now in my body. Restrictions on certain activities reminded me to prioritize my health and recovery.

Dr. Venkat's specific instructions about maintaining hygiene while using public washrooms left me cautious, and the fear of severe infection lingered. In my quest for additional precautions, I discovered a solution – a toilet seat sanitizing spray. Since then, I made it a habit to carry it whenever I ventured outside my home.

As time passed, the stent became integrated into my daily routine, almost like another organ rather than a foreign object. However, occasional reminders, in the form of pain, prompted me to "take it slow" and not "fly too high."

In February 2020, as the three-month period recommended by Dr. Venkat approached its end, I followed his advice and got admitted to JJ Hospital. Our routine remained consistent – Raj took care of the admission formalities while I settled into the room. Once there, I commenced drinking water to meet my daily target of around 4 liters, crucial for ensuring unrestricted urine flow.

The following day, Dr. Venkat assessed the improvement of the ureter stricture by removing the stent and passing some dark liquid through the ureter. After his evaluation, a new stent was inserted for another three months. Dr. Venkat shared the positive news that the ureter was showing promising progress, hinting that the next time, the stent might be removed permanently.

CHAPTER TWENTY-EIGHT

Unpredictable Journey and Unseen Challenges

The arrival of Covid by the end of December 2019 had a profound impact on the country, causing havoc throughout India. The situation escalated to a total lockdown and numerous restrictions by March 2020. The alarming news of a high number of daily deaths instilled fear in everyone.

Dr. Venkat had emphasized the importance of avoiding any outings for me, especially considering the susceptibility of ureteral stents to infections and the added risk of Covid. I became meticulous in my hygiene practices, sanitizing everything from small door knobs to larger household items. My daily routine began with consuming Kada and ensuring the entire house was sanitized.

As Berry's dog walker couldn't come, Raj took on the responsibility of taking her for a walk three times a day, each time spending about half an hour outside. To minimize the risk, he would take a bath upon returning home, and I was meticulous about hygiene whenever he went downstairs for any household items.

My concern extended to Shona and Raghav, who were in Austin and Syracuse, respectively. I constantly prayed for their well-being during those uncertain times. The fear and uncertainty brought about by the pandemic were palpable in every aspect of our lives.

The approaching date for the change of my stent amid the Covid pandemic had heightened my anxiety. Dr. Venkat, understanding the circumstances, assured me that this time, he would only perform the stent change and not assess the ureter's opening extensively. He explained that the detailed evaluation would take a considerable amount of time, and he wanted to minimize my stay in the hospital due to the ongoing pandemic.

Despite his reassurance, the fear of the unknown persisted. I tried to maintain a positive outlook, reminding myself that hospitals were implementing necessary precautions for patient's safety. However, concerns about my health and safety were a constant companion, contributing to a sense of unease during that challenging period.

In May 2020, as the world grappled with the challenges posed by COVID-19, I was scheduled for the reexamination and removal of the stents. In this unusual year, someone suggested that I wear a PPE kit for added protection. After considering it, I opted against the PPE kit due to concerns about breathing difficulties in such restrictive gear. Known for my commitment to sustainability, I chose to wear old clothes that I could easily discard.

On the way to the hospital, we encountered police checkpoints twice. Raj had to explain our hospital visit to the authorities. Dr. Venkat had advised us to purchase the stent from a medical store en route to the hospital. I felt uneasy about approaching the medical shop, but I asked Raj to maintain a safe distance from other customers. The pandemic had added a layer of complexity to even routine hospital visits, heightening the sense of caution and apprehension.

Upon our arrival at the hospital, the atmosphere was eerily deserted, with only a few scattered patients visible. The COVID-19 section appeared to be in a distant part of the building.

It marked the first time we witnessed the hospital with an unsettling, ghostly feeling—fewer patients, and an empty elevator. Raj efficiently completed the payment procedure, benefitting from the lack of queues at the counter.

With no delay, Dr. Venkat directed me to change into the hospital uniform. The stent change itself was a quick 15-minute process, abbreviated due to COVID restrictions. Following the procedure, he allowed me to change back into my clothes. Surprisingly, we were in and out of the hospital within half an hour, a smooth experience that exceeded my expectations, all thanks to Dr. Venkat's meticulous planning. This time, he had inserted a 6-month stent to minimize the need for frequent hospital visits.

It was a source of regret that I couldn't determine the extent to which the stricture had opened up since Dr. Venkat couldn't perform the entire procedure due to COVID restrictions. The disappointment stemmed from the fact that the stent was not permanently removed. However, considering the unprecedented times and the critical importance of minimizing hospital visits, it was a decision that prioritized safety and efficiency.

Upon returning home, I hurriedly took a shower and promptly discarded my clothes. I soaked Raj's clothes in a disinfecting chemical solution, as advised by someone, but it ended up discoloring the shirt in patches. It was a shirt his cousin had sent all the way from the UK and happened to be one of his favourites. Raj still wears the shirt and hides the discoloured part by rolling up the sleeves.

Gradually, a change occurred within me. I became more composed and less finicky about the Covid situation. Eventually, I regained my positivity and motivation. Our days began with a cup of Kadha, an herbal immunity-boosting concoction, and a variety of songs. We'd switch between devotional bhajans and the latest Bollywood tunes.

To add a semblance of normalcy to my life during those challenging times, we submitted a request to the society office seeking special permission to walk on the terrace. However, one member of the society committee, who happened to be a doctor, suggested that due to my multiple health issues, I shouldn't walk alone and should be accompanied. I didn't react to it, given that I had been walking in the garden since I moved to the society back in 2001.

Like everyone else, we had to manage household chores ourselves since it was risky for maids to come out of their dwellings. After completing our daily household routine, I found myself making phone calls. These weren't just any calls; they were like lifelines to relatives and friends who were overwhelmed and depressed by the challenges posed by the COVID-19 pandemic.

I reached out to people not just in Mumbai but across the globe, trying to- bring some comfort and cheer to their lives. They were grateful for a friendly voice amidst the chaos and uncertainty.

The pandemic had taken a toll on everyone's mental health, and it was important to stay connected with our loved ones.

I realized that a simple phone call could make a huge difference in someone's life. It was heartwarming to hear their voices and know that I could bring a smile to their faces.

By November 2020, the situation with COVID had significantly improved, and the number of cases had decreased. However, the need for precautions in public spaces remained critical. Armed with bottles of sanitizers and masks, we ventured to the hospital, reassured by the sight of others also taking necessary precautions. The usual admission procedure was completed, and I ensured I had all my pre-procedure reports, including the mandatory RT-PCR (COVID test) report. The emphasis on safety measures reflected the collective commitment to maintaining a secure environment within the hospital premises.

On the day of the procedure, Dr. Venkat assured us that everything would proceed as before when they inserted the stent in my ureter. The only difference being that they had inserted the stent in November of the previous year and changed it twice, once in February and once in May.

In February 2020, they had observed improvement, and the plan was to remove the stent during the May 2020 procedure. Unfortunately, by May 2020, the Covid-19 pandemic had disrupted everything, and Dr. Venkat couldn't check the progress properly. Instead, they had simply changed the stent and sent us home.

In November 2020, six months since the last stent change procedure, I found myself back at JJ Hospital. I tried to stay positive and reminded myself that hospitals are taking all necessary precautions to ensure the safety of their patients. But the fear of the unknown kept creeping in. I was constantly worried about my health and safety.

The stent removal surgery began as usual, with Dr. Venkat and his team carefully monitoring everything. Since a full recovery was expected by then, we were not asked to get the stent while getting admitted to the hospital. However, during the procedure, Dr. Venkat realized that the stricture had not improved as expected.

Unaware of this, I lay on the operating table. Dr. Venkat sent a message to Raj, urgently instructing him to obtain a stent from the medical store in the hospital premises. Raj hurriedly headed to the elevator, but the lift operator denied him access, as it was reserved for doctors, and the patient lift was out of order. Raj rushed down the stairs from the sixth floor. In the meantime, Dr. Venkat had already informed the storekeepers to keep the stent ready and advised them not to request immediate payment due to the emergency.

Raj brought the stent and raced back up all six floors. He arrived just in time, and the stent was successfully inserted. All of this unfolded while I remained unaware, lying on the operating table. The professionalism of Dr. Venkat and his team was truly remarkable. They had kept their composure, not letting any hint of urgency show during the procedure. I couldn't help but think that had I known what was happening, I might have become quite anxious on the operating table.

Thankfully, everything went well after the procedure too. My only grievance was that the stricture had not completely cured. As I was mentally assured of the stent removal and being free of everything, I was a bit upset. But as it usually is, I was back to my normal self and hopeful that the stent would be removed next time. My life is a roller coaster ride of emotions with these intermittent surgeries and ailments—some I enjoy, some I try to keep up my spirits. Whatever it is, the universe is always trying to help me, thankfully.

One thing to cheer me up was that Shona and Raghav managed to come back to India in December. I was glad Shona was back with us after those harrowing Covid times, which she and Raghav had to face alone in their homes in the US. I bounced back to my normal self again.

It was again time for a stent change. On April 24, 2021, amidst the harrowing grip of the second phase of the COVID-19 pandemic, we embarked on a journey to JJ Hospital. The virus was at its zenith, casting a long shadow of fear and uncertainty over the city. We arrived at the hospital promptly at 8:45 AM.

As the team geared up to initiate the procedure, a sudden hurdle emerged just as we were on the brink of commencing. My blood sugar levels took an alarming plunge to a mere 55 mg/dL. It was a precarious situation that demanded swift action. The necessary treatment was administered promptly, but it inevitably led to a temporary postponement of the procedure. In those moments of uncertainty, I found myself hanging on a thread, tethered to hope.

Amidst the backdrop of checking my vitals, my vigilant anesthetist detected an irregularity in my ECG. Turning to me with a subtle hint of concern, she inquired about any prior cardiac issues. I reassured her, responding in the negative. Despite the unexpected twist, she recommended consulting a cardiac specialist post my discharge. Her voice, though carrying an undercurrent of concern, also held a reassuring tone as she probed about my emotional state.

I admitted to not feeling particularly tense, though a subtle realization dawned that perhaps I hadn't fully grasped the anxiety that had silently gripped me. In response, she offered a comforting smile, assuring me that everything would be alright.

Dr. Venkat, with skilled hands and a focused demeanour, undertook the surgery and meticulously examined the strictures. Unfortunately, the outcome didn't align with the optimism I had clung to; there was no improvement. In a sobering discussion, he indicated that the likely next step would be ureter reconstruction surgery, urging me to mentally prepare for what lay ahead.

In the backdrop of the persistent second wave of the COVID-19 pandemic, I found myself promptly sent home after the procedure. The aftermath was marked by an unusual amalgamation of sensations – weakness and an unsettling strangeness seemed to have taken residence within me. The journey back was a subdued experience, as I reclined in the car, both physically and mentally drained. Upon reaching home, I sought solace in a shower before settling into a period of rest.

Ordinarily, I would have expected to bounce back to my usual self within a few days, but this time, the script of recovery seemed to deviate from the familiar narrative.

As the pain intensified, a sensation unfamiliar to my usual experiences, concern etched across my face. Discussing this unsettling development with Dr. Venkat became imperative. In response, he advised undergoing tests to unravel the mystery behind the heightened discomfort. The results, when they arrived, confirmed his suspicions – I was grappling with a urinary tract infection (UTI). Memories of a prior unpleasant encounter with UTI during my time in the US added an extra layer of apprehension.

What escalated the gravity of the situation was the revelation that, for the first time in my life, I was confronted with the concept of antibiotic resistance. The test results laid bare the fact that I had developed resistance to many antibiotics commonly employed to address UTIs at that time. The weight of this realization settled heavily; the prospect of being resistant to antibiotics felt like an unwelcome companion, a potential health complication threatening to persist throughout my life. The landscape of my health journey had taken an unexpected and worrisome turn.

Confronted with the complexities of managing the UTI and the specter of antibiotic resistance, I started on a personal research project, delving into home remedies to navigate this challenging situation. Those were not easy days; a palpable weight of depression gripped me, causing a diminishing interest in almost everything.

In a heartening turn of events, my sisters, Sujata, Sunanda, and my sister-in-law Supriya, emerged as beacons of support, offering sound advice to navigate through the storm. Their suggestion to channel my energy into artistic activities became a turning point. Many years had passed since I had last explored my artistic talents, and to my surprise, I found solace in painting. It was a rediscovery of a long-forgotten skill that brought a glimmer of joy. While my foray into other art forms was less successful, the act of creation became a therapeutic outlet during those challenging times.

Guided by Dr. Venkat, we tweaked my antibiotic routine, and after a tough two weeks of ups and downs, I finally found my way back to normalcy.

In the intricate dance of life, it seemed as though I was constantly flipping a coin – heads for the aspects I could control and tails for those moments where unpredictability reigned supreme. Each passing moment presented another flip, and with each flip, I yearned for the reassuring sight of heads. However, reality often unfolded as tails, where the reins of control slipped away. In those moments, I took a deep breath, composed myself, and prepared for the next toss of the coin.

I recall an insightful anecdote about Mike Tyson when he was asked about the importance of skill versus will. Tyson, a formidable boxer, leaned towards will, elucidating that his skill alone couldn't keep him on his feet against a worthy opponent. It was his indomitable will that prompted him to rise every time he fell, ready to face the challenge anew. In the realm of cancer, I found my formidable adversary. Yet, with every tumble, I echo Tyson's sentiment to myself – get up and face it once more.

CHAPTER TWENTY-NINE

A Surgical Wedding Planner

As the final months of 2021 unfolded, I found myself hesitating to proceed with a surgery that Dr. Venkat had strongly recommended for immediate attention. The significance of this surgery lay in the need for ureter reconstruction, a crucial step following the previous procedures. Although Dr. Venkat insisted on prioritizing the surgery without delay, he ultimately respected my decision to postpone.

Somehow, I couldn't bring myself to opt in for this particular surgery. Perhaps it was my own reservation or perhaps it was because I didn't want my surgery to eclipse one of the joyous moments of my life.

In December, my beloved daughter, Sonika Shriwastav, was to be wed to Raghav Raheja, a classmate from her undergraduate days in computer engineering. Raghav embodies a graceful blend of composure, maturity, refined manners, humility, and a grounded authenticity deeply rooted in his distinguished Punjabi heritage. His demeanour, characterized by a poised coolness, resonates with a sophisticated character.

Raj and I were naturally elated for our daughter as she embarked on this new chapter of her life. She had found her life partner in Raghav. Consequently, by September, we were already halfway through the meticulous planning of Shona's wedding.

Sonika and Raghav - Wedding Mehendi Ceremony

Sonika and Raghav - Wedding Mehendi Ceremony

Sonika and Raghav - Wedding Sangeet Ceremony

Sonika and Raghav - Wedding
Engagement Ceremony

Sonika and Raghav - Wedding Reception

Sonika and Raghav - Wedding

Sonika and Raghav - Wedding

Sonika's MBA Convocation in 2023 at the Smith
School of Business, Queen's University, Canada

In September, Raj and I made a significant decision regarding the return gifts for the wedding guests. We opted for dinner sets made of Kasa, a unique alloy. To procure these gifts, we set our sights on Bhuleshwar, the largest wholesale utensils market in Mumbai. Given the distance from our home in Andheri, a western suburb of Mumbai, a day trip was in order. However, with numerous wedding preparations on our plate and time constraints, I saw an opportunity to multitask.

During that visit to Bhuleshwar, we connected with a shop owner who was acquainted with us. In a gracious gesture, he offered us an aerated drink. While Raj accepted the offer, I declined. The owner, insistent on my partaking, was met with my explanation that I was on my way to J.J. Hospital for surgery. Understandably, the shock registered on his face. He was astonished that I was considering shopping at such a critical juncture, given the imminent hospital admission. Raj clarified that it was my insistence, driven by the desire to leave no stone unturned for Shona's wedding. We successfully placed an order for the Kasa dinner sets and then proceeded to the hospital for my surgery.

During this period, my fervent prayers were directed towards the hope that the stricture in my ureter would exhibit signs of improvement before Shona's wedding. Understanding the significance of the upcoming event, Dr. Venkat made a considerate decision not to conduct an extensive procedure during the stent change. As a result, he refrained from checking for any improvement in the urethral stricture. This decision was based on the understanding that a major surgery with potential complications required mental and physical preparation, especially considering the wedding was scheduled to take place in Aurangabad, not in Mumbai.

In the hospital, I found myself so immersed in wedding planning that I nearly forgot about the impending surgery. Raj and I were deeply involved in planning every detail of the wedding, from the menu to the guest list. This heartfelt discussion, held within the hospital confines, brought a touch of amusement to the hospital staff witnessing our devoted wedding planning.

After the surgery, I rested for a couple of days and was ready to jump back into the wedding planning, which incidentally, had been going on for a year. We had meticulously planned every tiny aspect. Couple of times, amidst overseeing renovations at home, having meetings with the caterer, I got extremely tired. So, during the car rides, while Raj was driving, I would recline in the seat, seek some desperately needed rest before we reached our destination and I had to bounce back up for the next task. I was enjoying every moment and didn't want to miss out on anything. I also didn't want to leave any task unfinished.

Shona approached her wedding plans with a clear vision, aligning with her values of veganism and minimalism. For certain rituals, she chose cotton and vegan silk saris, even upcycling my old sari for the Haldi ceremony. What struck me was her decision to wear my wedding sari from 31 years ago for the reception. Initially hesitant due to the challenging health journey that began with my own wedding, I expressed concern about casting any shadow on Shona's life. However, she remained resolute in her decision, and just like Raghav and his family, I honoured her choice.

In Indian weddings, the Haldi ceremony embodies a beautiful tradition, one that resonates deeply with the essence of celebration and blessing. The bride and groom are surrounded by loved ones, adorned with a paste crafted from turmeric powder, oil, and water. It's not just a ritual; it's a moment of connection, anticipating the journey ahead.

Sonika recycled my old sari to create a beautiful outfit and requested each one of us to do the same. By encouraging the recycling of existing outfits, she tapped into a deeper current of sustainability. It wasn't just about the colour; it was about reimagining the tradition in a way that honored both the past and the future. And in doing so, she not only fostered connection but also helped everyone save a penny or two.

As the Haldi ceremony unfolded, it wasn't just about the turmeric paste or the radiant glow it bestowed upon the skin. It was about the bonds forged, the laughter shared, and the stories woven into the fabric of the day.

On the 13th of December 2021, just two months after my stenting procedure, Shona and Raghav were united in matrimony. Their wedding was a celebration of feminism and inclusivity, marked by unique choices. Shona intentionally assembled an all-women team of wedding vendors, including the photographer, wedding designer, and event manager. Even the wedding rituals were led by a priestess, breaking away from traditional norms. Shona's choices reflected her open-mindedness and liberal thinking, challenging stereotypes and advocating for a more inclusive society. The wedding stood as a beautiful reminder that small steps can collectively lead to a more equal and diverse world.

Shona's commitment to social impact extended beyond the wedding itself. Instead of accepting traditional presents, she directed guests to two social organizations mentioned in the E-invite. The first organization focused on supporting an orphanage for deaf and mute children in Goa, while the second contributed to the well-being of abandoned, ill, and sick animals in Mumbai. Shona's gesture exemplified her genuine belief in giving back to the society and making a positive impact on the world.

During the wedding, my younger brother-in-law, Anil, shared his observations with Raj. He expressed amazement at witnessing my ability to manage everything, despite grappling with multiple health issues and having a stent in my body for many years. Anil marveled at how I found the energy to run around, organize events, dance, and fully enjoy the celebration with everyone. When Raj communicated this to me, I replied, "The Almighty is there for me." Given my discipline with the medicines, everyone around me was so reassured that nobody even asked if I had taken my medication. Knowing me, they were sure I wouldn't skip my doses. During those days, I hardly slept, managing only about two hours of sleep each night for three consecutive nights.

The day after the wedding, I returned to Mumbai. I immediately started to prepare for welcoming Raghav's family, assisted by my neighbor Ritika. Despite the late hours, I remained active and engaged. The following morning, we conducted a small puja, and in the evening, we hosted a wedding reception. The event drew a diverse group of attendees, including Shona and Raghav's friends, the doctors who played a crucial role in my thirty-three years health journey, my friends, and senior police officers, ex colleagues of Raj from Police and the Corporate who came to bless the newlyweds.

As Shona's wedding day approached, a surge of elation overcame me. Witnessing Shona and Raghav embark on their journey together, surrounded by love and unique choices, I feel blessed to be a part of one of the greatest milestones of my daughter's journey.

The successful orchestration of a wedding, even in the face of adversity, has time and again provided me solace. On that special day, the radiance of love and celebration triumphed over the shadows, allowing the luminosity of life to cast its enchanting spell.

After the wedding, Shona embarked on her next adventure, moving to Canada for her MBA. Having graduated with a Master of Information Systems Management from Carnegie Mellon University in Pittsburgh, USA, she pursued her second master's degree in Business Administration at Queen's University in Kingston, Ontario.

Today when I look back, I realize that I was at the crossroads of my personal journey and the radiant celebration of my daughter's union. As I navigated the tumultuous waters of my own health battles, an unspoken fear lingered – the apprehension that the shadows of my illness might inadvertently cast a dark cloud over Shona's brightest day, a day that deserved to be bathed in the purest hues of joy.

CHAPTER THIRTY

Renewing Life Journey

In March 2022, it was time again for my stent change. Everything went according to the routine. Last time, the status of the stricture was not checked, and I was hopeful this time. I prayed to God for positive results.

Dr. Venkat performed the surgery and also checked the strictures, but sadly, there was no improvement. He inserted a six-month stent to provide some time. He made it clear that the ureter reconstruction surgery could no longer be further delayed, emphasizing the need for me to be mentally prepared for the upcoming procedure.

For the first time since my stenting procedure started, I was extremely agitated with the outcome and found myself in tears. When Shona called from Canada and inquired about the result of the surgery, I was unresponsive. This unusual behaviour puzzled her as it was the first time I had reacted in such a manner. Raj stepped in and shared the disappointing outcome with her. Shona, understanding the gravity of the situation, didn't attempt to console me immediately. Instead, she skillfully changed the topic, diverting my thoughts and helping me regain my fighting spirit.

Six months later in August 2022, the time for the surgery had arrived. However, there was a significant change by then – Dr. Venkat had been transferred to Aurangabad. Since I was planning to visit Aurangabad, I decided to take the opportunity to meet him and discuss my concerns, seeking potential solutions.

Dr. Venkat, a distinguished doctor and multiple award winner, had a hectic schedule. I had to check his availability and finally visited him at his residence one evening after his duty hours. During our meeting, I expressed my doubts about the upcoming ureter reconstruction surgery and inquired if there were any alternative options. Dr. Venkat explained that it had been three years of attempting to bring improvement with the stent. Typically, stents show positive results in many patients within the first few months, but unfortunately, it hadn't been the case for me. He emphasized that he didn't want me to endure further pain, countless precautions, and additional medications without substantial improvement.

I refrained from disclosing my underlying hope of a full recovery with a stent to Dr. Venkat or anyone else during our conversation. Instead, I inquired about potential alternatives. Dr. Venkat mentioned that he had recently inserted a one-year stent for an older female patient, suggesting it as an option for me. Intrigued by the possibility, I promptly agreed to it but sought more information regarding the precautions I should undertake, given the extended duration of the stent. Dr. Venkat assured me that maintaining the same precautions I had been following until then should help manage the situation.

Deciding to discuss this with Raj, who was in Mumbai at the time, I called him and provided a detailed account of the conversation with Dr. Venkat. I informed him of my decision to opt for a one-year stent and sought his input on the matter.

The decision now revolved around where to undergo the stent change procedure. Dr. Venkat had moved to Aurangabad, and his new hospital lacked the necessary facilities for this specific procedure. Despite my concerns, Dr. Venkat reassured me, emphasizing the efficiency of his Mumbai team in handling the procedure. While initially considering waiting for Dr. Venkat's visit to Mumbai for the stent change, practical constraints emerged as the scheduled date approached rapidly. Exceeding this timeframe could pose infection risks. Faced with a challenging decision, I opted to trust Dr. Venkat's expertise and judgment, gearing up to confront the forthcoming challenges with resilience.

In Dr. Venkat's absence, his Mumbai team delivered the same level of care and attention that I had become accustomed to. The procedure unfolded smoothly, with Dr. Venkat maintaining constant communication with both his team and me. Within five days, I was back home, profoundly grateful for the exceptional care I had received during that period.

In mid-April 2023, I encountered shooting pain in the lower part of my body, a discomfort that would temporarily subside. Initially occurring at weekly intervals, the persistence of this pain raised concerns about the condition of the ureteral stent.

Without delay, I contacted Dr. Venkat, sharing the details of my discomfort. Dr. Venkat suspected that it might be time for an early stent change. This caught me by surprise, as the scheduled procedure was still a couple of months away in July. However, he explained that sometimes stents need to be replaced prematurely. Concerned about the possibility of stent dislocation, I inquired about the likelihood of this scenario. Dr. Venkat recommended a KUB X-Ray to assess the situation.

Acting promptly, I visited Seven Hills Hospital the following day to undergo the X-Ray and forwarded the images to Dr. Venkat. In his prompt response, he confirmed that it was indeed time for a stent change, as it had shifted slightly from its original position.

The procedure was scheduled to be carried out promptly, and this time, it was planned at Jivdaya Hospital in Ghatkopar, Mumbai.

On the morning of May 24, 2023, I admitted myself, placing my trust in the capable hands of Dr. Gaurang Shah, an ex-senior colleague of Dr. Venkat. Dr. Shah and his team took exceptional care, surpassing my expectations. The hospital room was compact, with everything within arm's reach. A foldable bench, reminiscent of a train berth, served as a resting place for Raj. Given his tall stature, the arrangement was a bit cramped for him. However, we appreciated the coziness of the room, and the hospital staff exhibited cordiality. Fasting without water since morning had left me with a severe headache at the time of admission.

Varun, my sister Sujata's son, arrived promptly at 4 PM, right on time for the surgery. He has been a constant presence during most of my surgeries, providing invaluable support. While Raj was away handling paperwork, Varun sat with me, sharing stories about his adorable newborn daughter. Later, he went downstairs to grab a sandwich for Raj and coconut water for me to have at midnight.

The anesthetist visited my room to discuss the details of my previous surgeries and to determine the course of action for the upcoming stenting procedures. Since I was visiting this hospital for the first time, he took the time to explain everything to me.

Typically, I receive spinal anesthesia, so I requested him not to administer a very strong dose as it can be unsettling when my legs go limp for about 5 to 6 hours. He assured me that he would try his best, but he had to administer a higher dose as it was required.

My procedure was scheduled for the evening. As I've mentioned in my earlier procedures, I prefer to observe each step clearly and monitor the progress. The team of doctors was chatting and discussing among themselves, a normal occurrence for them, and by now, I have become accustomed to this atmosphere. I found myself getting involved in their conversations, learning about the medical terms and equipment used in the operating theater.

One of the nurses was checking my file and asked me which side the procedure was supposed to be done. The anesthetist and I responded at the same time, and he went on to jest, "Just ask ma'am, she will tell you." I informed them that it was the right side, and he humourously remarked that I seem to know everything.

The doctor arrived after some time, and the procedure commenced. To make me comfortable, the team engaged in casual chatter, discussing everything with me, as if it was a social gathering or dinner chat.

So, there I was in the operating theater, lying on the stretcher, with all the gadgets attached to my body. In the midst of all that, I found myself engaging in conversation with the team, despite my severe headache.

After the procedure, the doctor informed me that there was still a one-centimeter stricture in the ureter. While relieved that the procedure was over, I couldn't help but feel concern about the remaining stricture. Nevertheless, I was grateful to the team for making the experience less painful and for their support throughout the procedure.

I was brought into the room immediately, and I was parched. The desire for water was strong, but I knew it was not possible, as I had to maintain an empty stomach for about 7 to 8 hours after spinal anesthesia to avoid nausea and vomiting. Therefore, my water intake was scheduled for 1 AM. Meanwhile, the nurse came and started instructing me about the further precautions. I informed her that I was aware of the fasting and other necessary precautions, listing everything out for her. She chuckled and said, "Ma'am, this is a picnic for you now."

Despite my persistent headache, having some company was comforting. In Mumbai, my surgeries had a specific set of visitors who always came to check on me. Shailaja, her daughter Namrata, Sankalp, my brother-in-laws, Sunil's son, and his wife Sneha had come to meet me around 9 PM. Engaging in conversation with them served as a welcome distraction.

After their departure, I instructed Raj to place water and coconut water on the bedside and then retire to bed early. For me, it was going to be a long night. I had to stay awake until 1 AM and start sipping water at regular intervals. By the time I finished the coconut water, it was 2:30 AM. Just as I was about to get some sleep, the other patient, a teenage boy in the adjoining room, encountered some problems, and the nurse was attending to him, operating in hyper mode. Consequently, my hopes for a good night's sleep were dashed.

My go-to remedy for sleepless nights at that point was meditation, a practice that had sustained me for years, boosting my immunity and maintaining my positivity.

Upon discharge, we returned home, and Prakash, Karuna, and Shailaja paid a visit. In their company, somehow, my mind managed to drift away from the pain for most of the day.

Nevertheless, my recovery took longer this time around. Later, I discovered that some additional tests were conducted to assess the situation. Despite the extended recuperation, I remained optimistic that by the time of the next stent procedure, I would be back to my normal routine, moving about freely.

My current status involves awaiting my next stent change procedure, scheduled within a couple of months in April 2024. Despite the challenges, I remain hopeful and determined to continue going strong in life.

CHAPTER THIRTY-ONE

Embracing the Extraordinary

Our society is intricately designed to cater to the needs and aspirations of individuals deemed "normal" by its standards. Whether it's health, career, lifestyle, or social status, an invisible scale serves as the benchmark against which every person is measured. Those grappling with any form of illness find themselves falling short of these societal expectations, promptly labeled as "abnormal" — individuals who, in the eyes of society, deviate from the established norm.

While the warmth of compassion, support, and love emanates from those closest to us, there remains an undeniable sense of estrangement from the broader world. In this dynamic, it becomes almost natural for those deemed "abnormal" to face a dichotomy. On one hand, they find solace within the embrace of their loved ones, and on the other, a palpable disconnect from the rest of the society.

In such a scenario, the "abnormal" individuals may perceive no alternative but to distance themselves from a society that doesn't fully comprehend their struggles. In the realm of self-healing, I firmly advocate that there is no universal prescription. The path to healing is as unique as the individuals undertaking it; what works for one might not necessarily work for another. In my personal journey, meditation emerged as the beacon guiding me towards restoration. Intrinsically drawn to its calming embrace, I wholeheartedly embraced this practice.

The beauty lies in the personalized nature of self-healing. It's about discerning what resonates with your own being, acknowledging that each individual's journey is a mosaic of diverse experiences. In my case, meditation became the cornerstone of my self-healing odyssey, a practice I pursued with unwavering dedication.

For me, Vipassana became a transformative journey into the heart of ancient Indian meditation practices, dating back over 2,500 years. This meditation technique, centered on the principles of being fully present and observing thoughts and feelings without attachment, resonated profoundly with my quest for self-healing. Often referred to as insight meditation, Vipassana promised a myriad of benefits, including heightened concentration, inner calmness, clarity, and overall well-being.

Participating in the Vipassana course required a commitment to five ethical precepts during the course: refraining from causing harm to any living being, theft, engaging in sexual activity, lying, and using intoxicants. This mind-body practice involved a focused exploration of the breath and bodily sensations, aiming to cultivate awareness and understanding of the present moment. The very term "Vipassana" itself translates to "insight" or "clear seeing."

The prospect of undertaking Vipassana meditation had been a lingering contemplation for Raj and me. With the unanimous encouragement from my support system, comprised of caring loved ones, the idea gained momentum as they believed it could fortify my mental resilience.

Our initial attempts to secure admission at the Vipassana Centre in Igatpuri, founded by the revered Goenka Guruji, proved unsuccessful. Undeterred, we redirected our efforts to Dharamsala, Himachal Pradesh, only to encounter another roadblock. Persistent in our pursuit, we explored other Vipassana training centers associated with a Japanese group.

In the midst of this quest, a serendipitous turn of events occurred in mid-2022. Tshering Sherpa, a close friend of Raj, shared her profound Vipassana experience at the Buddhapada center in Kalimpong, West Bengal. Tshering, originally from Kalimpong and acquainted with Raj since the mid-nineties when he was stationed at Sahar Airport Police Station, provided invaluable insights. At that time, she was working with Air India. Intrigued by the potential of the place and the transformative process, Raj sought more information, and Tshering eagerly shared intricate details about the center and its admission process.

Raj, taking the reins of our Vipassana journey, initiated contact with the center's head, Miss Reena, expressing our keen interest in the upcoming session scheduled for November 2022. To my pleasant surprise, Raj later informed me that we had successfully secured admission for the Vipassana course. Eager to share this transformative experience, we enlisted the company of our friends Prakash and Karuna, and the preparations for our sojourn began in earnest.

Anticipating the unique challenges of the meditation course, I sought advice from Tshering, who had previously undergone the Vipassana experience at Buddhapada. Our discussions covered a spectrum of practicalities, ranging from the facilities at Buddhapada to hygiene standards and the permissible items during the course. Tshering particularly emphasized the necessity of warm clothing, given the plummeting temperatures during winter sessions. Inspired by the idea of exploring Sikkim, particularly Gangtok and Lachung, post our meditation venture, our plans took shape.

Our journey unfolded with a palpable sense of excitement. After a flight to Siliguri, we traversed by road to reach Buddhapada in Kalimpong, a scenic locale nestled on the border of Nepal and Sikkim. Arriving late at night, the morning unveiled the breathtaking beauty of our surroundings, setting the stage for a memorable stay.

Tshering, our gracious host, took us on a captivating sightseeing tour of Kalimpong. We indulged in an authentic local lunch, relishing mouthwatering momos and curry. Later, we paid a visit to her aging parents, fostering a deeper connection with the place and its warm-hearted inhabitants.

The meditation course officially commenced that evening with an orientation, guidelines, and a brief guided meditation. From the second day onwards, our daily routine was well-defined.

We had an early wake-up call at 5AM, and their attendant, who was 70 years old, would come with a bell ringing in his hands and walk up to all the floors and buildings where we all resided. This was followed by guided meditation until 7 A.M., a breakfast break, and back to meditation until 11 A.M. We had lunch at 11 A.M. and rested till 1.30 P.M. The next meditation session commenced and continued till 6.30 P.M.

For dinner, only patients like me partook; healthy participants enjoyed evening tea, coffee, or juice. Meditation continued until 9 P.M., followed by a well-deserved night's rest. It was a refreshing change from our usual routines and helped us focus on our well-being. The bell ringing was a unique way to wake us up and set the tone for the day. The guided meditation sessions helped us stay calm and centered throughout the day. Overall, it was a great experience that we will cherish forever.

The initial days of the Vipassana meditation proved to be a struggle for me, with concentration eluding my efforts. However, a pivotal transformation awaited on the third day, an experience that defied easy articulation. During a guided meditation led by the Buddhist monk (Bante), a remarkable occurrence unfolded. As Bante concluded his sermon and departed, an extraordinary sensation enveloped me—an overwhelming sense of lightness and profound happiness. To my astonishment, this feeling lingered, even extending into the lunch break. Tears of pure happiness streamed down my face, a manifestation of a long-sought and deeply desired emotional state.

Despite my initial skepticism about my ability to meditate effectively, a profound shift occurred. Soon, I found myself meditating for hours on end, often up to five hours at a stretch. As the emotions welled up, I occasionally teetered on the brink of tears during meditation. The extended sitting periods, however, started causing backaches. Seeking a remedy, I obtained permission to meditate in my room, leading to two instances where tears of deep emotion flowed during my practice.

Forgiveness meditation became an integral part of the session. During one such session, as I sought forgiveness from Brainy, my emotions overwhelmed me, and I found myself crying profusely, emotionally drained by the thoughts of sending Brainy away. Yet, in a surprising turn of events, the image of Shona replaced that of Brainy in my meditation. The unexpected appearance left me puzzled, navigating a complex web of emotions and introspection.

On the ninth day of the Vipassana course, we were tasked with providing feedback about our transformative journey. This feedback session was a crucial culmination of our experiences, and each participant's reflections were recorded and later uploaded to YouTube. It served as a collective expression of our individual odysseys on the path of self-discovery.

Regrettably, our friends Prakash and Karuna faced an unexpected twist of fate. Unable to attend the final session the next morning, they were compelled to depart urgently due to Prakash's father's hospitalization, their journey redirected towards Nanded. The abrupt change added a somber note to the conclusion of the course, emphasizing the unpredictable nature of life and the importance of adapting to unforeseen circumstances.

This transformative odyssey through meditation, marked by moments of struggle, tears, and unexpected revelations, has served as a vessel for profound self-discovery and healing. The intricate dance of emotions, the newfound resilience, and the overwhelming sense of happiness attest to the transformative power inherent in this ancient practice. To those courageous enough to venture on this spiritual sojourn, I wholeheartedly advocate the experience, for it transcends the ordinary and opens pathways to the extraordinary.

In a world often dictated by societal norms and expectations, Vipassana emerged as a gurukul, a revered teacher imparting lessons of self-reliance. It urged me to place my bets on my own strength and inner wisdom. Whether one chooses the path of meditation or not, the essence lies in choosing oneself over the cacophony of societal judgments and naysayers. It is my sincere hope that the echoes of my journey resonate with those seeking solace and self-discovery, encouraging them to embrace the path that leads to the core of their being. May all those who have sought healing just like me, embark on their own journeys of healing and self-realization, for within each one of us lies the potential of profound transformation.

CHAPTER THIRTY-TWO

Crises in the Mountains

Following the conclusion of our Vipassana course, our journey extended to Gangtok, and we were fortunate to have Tshering as our companion.

Arriving in Gangtok late in the evening, our first priority was to drop off our friend Tshering at her friend's place before retiring to our hotel for an early night. The following day, with Tshering by our side, we set out on an expedition to Lachen. Prioritizing our health in the challenging high-altitude terrain, I wisely purchased oxygen cans from a local medical store, cognizant of the risk of an asthma attack due to the elevation and low temperatures.

Lachen, nestled at a lofty altitude of 9000 feet above sea level, often necessitates supplemental oxygen owing to its high elevation. The journey to Lachen proved to be demanding, winding through mountainous terrain that induced considerable nausea. Fatigue set in as we finally arrived in Lachen, but the exhaustion was momentarily eclipsed by the breathtaking view from our hotel room window.

The hotel manager's valuable advice for our early morning trip to Gurudongmar Lake, perched at a staggering 17,000 feet above sea level, emphasized the need for acclimatization. Having already ascended to 9,000 feet, we were gearing up to climb another 8,000 feet. Following the recommendation, we decided to take a walk to acclimate to the altitude. While climbing a small hill on our way back, Raj remarked to Tshering, "If no one else was feeling breathless, or is it just me?" It caught me by surprise, as it's typically me who grapples with breathlessness due to my asthma. Despite my concerns, I kept them to myself, not wanting to discourage him.

After an early dinner, we retired to bed, bundled up between electric blankets to combat the chilly 4-degree Celsius temperature. In the middle of the night, around 2:30 a.m., I woke up for a restroom visit. Upon returning, I found myself unable to sleep, tossing and turning. At 4 a.m., Raj woke up to use the washroom, and within a minute, I heard a thud. Alarmed, I rushed to the washroom to find him on the floor. Feebly explaining that he had fallen, I helped him back to bed, but he collapsed backward.

Alarm bells began ringing loudly in my mind. I hurried to my SOS pouch, retrieving a tablet and giving it to him. Despite growing anxiety, I didn't relent. I checked his oxygen levels, finding them dangerously low. Offering him a piece of chocolate to suck on, I swiftly opened the oxygen can, placing it in the right position on his mouth and nose and started pumping oxygen. The surreal realization that the oxygen cans, intended for my asthma, were now crucial for Raj, added a layer of urgency. Administering a puff of my inhaler, my mind raced as I was determined to do everything within my power. Continually instructing him to inhale deeply from the oxygen can, I navigated through a surreal moment, grappling with the unexpected turn of events.

In the midst of the unfolding crisis, I promptly called Tshering, who was in the next room, and alerted the hotel manager. Initially, both of them thought that I was the one facing a health issue. As I remained on the phone with Sunanda, who advised us to seek immediate medical attention, I inquired about the availability of a doctor from the hotel manager. Regretfully, he informed us that there was no doctor on-site. However, he mentioned an army field hospital, the 327 Field Hospital in Mangan, approximately 3.5 kilometers away.

Amidst this urgency, Tshering utilized her Apple Watch to take Raj's ECG, revealing a spike in his blood pressure. Adhering to Sunanda's advice, we wasted no time and set out for the army field hospital. Upon contacting our driver, his initial question was whether I was the one facing health issues. Clarifying that it was Raj, even he was taken aback, as nobody had anticipated any health problems given Raj's fitness.

The driver arrived promptly, and with the assistance of the room boy, we carefully navigated the descent down two steep and challenging flights of stairs. Raj reclined on the back seat, and throughout the journey, I consistently provided him with oxygen, hoping for a swift resolution to this unexpected health crisis.

Upon reaching the Army Field Hospital in Mangan Taluka without delay, the medical Army officer, a Captain, promptly attended to Raj despite the early hours. Conducting another ECG, she delivered the diagnosis: Raj had experienced syncope, a sudden temporary loss of consciousness. She explained that such incidents often occurred due to low oxygen levels at high altitudes. Administering a blood thinner for Raj, she reassured us that he would begin to feel better once we descended to a lower altitude.

Expressing heartfelt gratitude for their assistance, I couldn't help but admire their dedication and unwavering commitment to serving their country. After our brief stop, we resumed our journey as advised by the medical officer. She recommended that we proceed to the Mangan Government Hospital, where Raj could receive further medical attention and care. With a renewed sense of hope and determination, we began on the next leg of our journey, guided by the invaluable assistance of the compassionate medical team.

Tshering's friend, despite being in the United States, had a connection at the Mangan Government Hospital, having worked there previously. Tshering maintained constant contact with her during this critical time. Following her friend's advice, we aimed to meet a cardiologist acquaintance at the hospital. After a 1 ½ hour drive, we arrived, and the cardiologist conducted a comprehensive examination, including another ECG. She provided assurance that Raj was showing signs of improvement but recommended a return to Gangtok for a 2D Echo test to rule out any potential complications.

Back in the vehicle, I offered Raj some juice while consistently providing him with oxygen throughout the journey. Our destination was Manipal Hospital in Gangtok. Upon arrival, Tshering and I assisted Raj in settling in the hospital's reception area, where one of her friends joined us. We swiftly completed the necessary payments and hurried upstairs to consult with the cardiologist, seeking further insights and guidance on Raj's health.

The cardiologist conducted a thorough examination, considering Raj's detailed medical history and reviewing reports from our previous stops. She instructed a technician to perform a 2D Echo and ECG for Raj. Patiently waiting in the cardiologist's office, our anticipation was accompanied by a slight delay due to another patient's presence.

In the evening, the cardiologist delivered a reassuring verdict – Raj was now in good health and deemed fit to travel. A palpable wave of relief washed over us. In gratitude, I first thanked God profusely and then expressed my gratitude to Tshering for her unwavering support. It was then that the realization dawned on us – we hadn't eaten anything since morning, and by now, it was 5:30 p.m. Despite the late hour, we decided to finally have a meal. After our long-delayed lunch, I asked Tshering and Raj to wait in the vehicle while I set out in search of the SOS tablets prescribed by the cardiologist. Scouring nearly five to six pharmacies, navigating the hilly terrain of Gangtok proved to be a challenging task. I could barely manage to walk back to the vehicle, exhausted, and also realized that my stent was causing discomfort, perhaps exacerbated by the exertion. Throughout this ordeal, I had kept Raj's head on my laps, providing comfort throughout the journey. Amidst all this, I discovered that I had forgotten my day's medicine in the restaurant, intended to be taken after food. It dawned on me that I had missed my morning dose as well.

After dropping off Tshering, we returned to our hotel. Seeking help, I approached the hotel manager to assist in procuring the prescribed medicine, but our efforts were in vain. Exhausted, I could hardly muster the energy for a bath. That night, despite the day's events, I found myself sleeping soundly—a rare feat for me.

Within two days, we were back in Mumbai. I promptly scheduled appointments with two renowned cardiologists for second and third opinions. Both affirmed that there was no major problem, diagnosing Raj with Benign Arrhythmia. They reassured us that there was no need for excessive worry, providing much-needed comfort and validation to counter the uncertainties we had faced during our journey.

As I recounted this experience to my relatives and friends later, some marveled at how I handled the situation. They expressed that they might have panicked, potentially making the patient more tense. Acknowledging my health history, they suggested that my ability to handle such situations alone had given me the courage to act meticulously and calmly in stressful circumstances. I explained that when it comes to the health of a loved one, I had been driven to act like a machine, leaving no stone unturned.

I sometimes reflect on the mental switch inside me. Ever since my tryst with cancer, I've learned to rely on the support of my loved ones. I understood it wasn't a lonely fight, and I needed all the love and care my family could offer. Yet, occasionally, the situation would reverse. Whether it was Shona's life and career or Raj's health, if I sensed any risk at any point, the switch inside me would flip on. For that brief moment, I would no longer associate myself as a cancer patient; instead, I became an individual with one goal – to fix whatever problem lay in front of me. Raj's recent health scares had taught me about the power of mental strength, particularly when dealing with unexpected situations, especially involving loved ones. When it comes to the health of a loved one, there are no limits to what we can do.

CHAPTER THIRTY-THREE

Adventures in the Face of Cancer

The general perception of an ill patient is someone resting and recuperating either in the comfort of home or at the hospital, being attended to by doctors and loved ones. I myself perhaps would have thought the same if I were on the other side of the table. Unfortunately, I had been struck by cancer. And when the doom finally stares at you, you realize there's no going back. You are heading straight towards your end. Every moment of life that has passed, is a moment lost forever. And once you see the end, you somehow absolutely and obsessively fall in love with the remainder of moments that is keeping you from your last breath. In my case, that was exactly what had happened.

It was only after cancer, I realized, that I missed out on so many opportunities thinking I would get to it someday. But eventually, we all run out of our somedays. So, I made up my mind to cherish every moment that came my way. The plan was simple: If I am going to hit the dead-end, I might as well take as many detours as possible, before it happens.

I believe that's how travel became its own chapter in my life. From family engagements, to family outings, to bucket lists, for one reason or another, I kept traveling. And before I knew it, my husband realized I had become a wanderlust. Raj even remarked that I might have traversed more miles than the average person, himself included. His insight wasn't off the mark.

Over the past thirty-three years, despite being a patient, I steadfastly refused to let my medical condition impede my pursuit of adventure and various activities. While well-meaning loved ones might have urged caution, I held firm in my belief that my adventurous spirit bolstered my willpower and mental resilience, allowing me to savour life's richness to the fullest.

I vividly remember the extraordinary journey that followed after my first cancer surgery. Accompanied by Raj, our ten-month-old daughter Shona, Mummy, her elder sister, Raj's uncle, and his daughter, I commenced on the pilgrimage to the Vaishno Devi Shrine. This 13-kilometer trek from Katra to Vaishno Devi served as a resilience test post-surgery. Despite the recent operation, Raj had considered the option of a pony ride for me, but I was resolute about walking; I didn't want to miss this spiritual journey.

Commencing our ascent around 5:00 PM, Shona, our little bundle of joy, became the focal point of our attention. Passing her between us, we shared moments of laughter and bonding as we continued the journey. However, as the night progressed, it became apparent that Shona needed rest and attention. Breastfeeding had become uncomfortable and needed short intervals, prompting Raj to arrange a pony for me. I climbed uphill on the pony, and the porter (referred to as Pithu in the Vaishno Devi pilgrimage region) tied Sonika to my abdomen with my dupatta (long scarf). On my request, he intermittently freed Sonika for feeding.

Securing Shona to my abdomen with my dupatta, we continued our ascent. As we reached Vaishno Devi at 3:00 AM, the weather took an unexpected turn, with heavy rain and a sharp drop in temperature greeting us. Undeterred by the adversity, we pressed on in separate groups for our darshan. After paying our respects, we sought refuge in the warmth of the Langar at 6:00 AM.

Langar, a communal meal offered at religious places, is made with donations from devotees and is either free or highly subsidized. The steaming hot Rajma (kidney beans) and rice filled our famished bodies, and the taste remains etched in our memories.

Following this nourishing meal, my determination to walk back down the hill persisted, and this time Raj offered no resistance. I practically ran downhill, covering the return journey to Katra in a mere two and a half hours.

Our adventures didn't end there. The trip continued for the next nine days, taking us from Vaishno Devi to Jammu, Haridwar, Mathura, Delhi, Agra, Jaipur, and back to Mumbai.

After exploring the North, I set my eyes on South India. In the late nineties, my quest for self-improvement led me to the Sri Aurobindo Ashram, a renowned meditation center on the Malabar Coast in Puducherry, India. Here, I delved into the art of meditation, a practice that has since become an integral part of my daily routine, fortifying my mind and spirit.

Then, in 2001, soon after my second surgery, I ventured into the hills of Mhaismal, a hill station in Maharashtra, India, perched at an altitude of 1067 meters. This marked the beginning of my trekking journey. Despite facing multiple breaks and surgeries over the years, I continued to trek the hills of Mhaismal, Ellora, and Ajanta several times.

Following my third surgery, in 2003, I embarked on yet another adventurous journey to Harsil, a tranquil hill station in Uttarkashi. This time with my maternal family as Raj couldn't join me. Shona was with me, given that she had her vacation going on. Excited at the rare opportunity, I decided to participate in a challenging trek from Gangotri to Gomukh, spanning a daunting 18 kilometers, at a high altitude of 13,200 feet, I suffered an asthma attack due to low oxygen levels. Regrettably, I couldn't complete the trek, but I made the most of my time by sitting by the Bhagirathi River, meditating, and observing pilgrims. By the time my family returned, I was collecting pine cones. During this trip, I had my first taste of river rafting on the Ganges. The exhilaration of navigating different levels of rapids left an indelible mark.

Another travel plan of ours took us to South Asia to celebrate the completion of Shona's Grade X ICSE Board examinations in 2010, just a year after my 2009 surgery. During our trip to Southeast Asia, in Pattaya, I expressed my desire to go paragliding to Raj. Initially, Raj was hesitant, but Shona and I convinced him to join us. Together, we soared through the skies and began on underwater sea walks, creating unforgettable memories of shared adventures.

Years later, even after my fourth surgery in 2012, I revisited the thrilling experience, embarking on another rafting expedition in Kolad, Konkan, India.

In 2013, we started on an unforgettable trip to Shimla, thanks to Citibank's Annual Leave Travel Concession program. Namrata joined us on this adventure, and our stay at Club

Mahindra Resort offered breathtaking views of the valley. We savoured Himachali cuisine, and strolling down the Mall Road gave us a taste of Western countries. The highlight of this trip was my first encounter with skiing. While I couldn't conquer great distances, the sheer joy of trying it was immensely satisfying. I also braved the ropeway, suspended above the snowy terrain. It was a nerve-wracking experience, but I didn't dare to look down. Shona managed to do quite well in both of them.

Unfortunately, I fell ill on the last day due to the cold and snow, suffering an asthma attack. This episode prompted me to become better prepared, both physically and materially, to carry more SOS medication for future trips.

In 2015, I fulfilled a long-standing dream of learning to drive just a few months after my surgery. Obtaining my driver's license filled me with excitement, envisioning newfound independence. However, my dream hit a roadblock when Raj put a stop to my driving aspirations after I fumbled a couple of times behind the wheel.

My travel streak came to an abrupt stop during the pandemic. In 2021, when the pandemic was at its peak, I had not stepped out of our apartment for over three months, except for a visit to JJ Hospital to change my stent.

Given that Mumbai had become a Covid hotspot, our family members urged us to temporarily relocate to Nanded. My elder brother-in-law, Sunil, informed us of a vacant bungalow near his house in Nanded. Raj saw it as a breath of fresh air for me, a welcome break from confinement. We arranged for transportation and embarked on the journey to Nanded, a refreshing escape.

Along the way, we shared a meal at Sujata's place in Aurangabad and had a chance to catch up with Shivnath's family. The prevailing safety measures meant that everyone maintained a safe distance from each other.

Our stay on the outskirts of Nanded was idyllic. Morning walks among the fields, observing peacocks dancing, and the playful antics *Jugalbandi* (face-off) of monkeys and our dog, Berry, made our days enjoyable. Raj could now breathe easy, knowing that I was content.

Then, one morning, about two weeks into our stay, I woke up to an unexpected challenge. Swelling had gripped my legs from knee to foot and my wrists down to my palms This was unlike anything I had experienced before. Along with the swelling came excruciating pain and limited movement. I continued to move sideways throughout the day, albeit with a noticeable limp and a weakened grip due to hand stiffness. Holding objects became a challenge, and I was grateful for the support of my co- sister Purnima.

Five days later, during my consultation with a Rheumatologist, there was uncertainty about the cause. The doctor believed it could either be Rheumatoid Arthritis or a result of the stent. I couldn't help but wonder if it could be Covid-related, but the doctor assured me that wasn't the case. Prescriptions were given, and a series of blood tests were scheduled after a ten-day course of medication. By the time we departed from Nanded, my ten-day course had concluded.

Before leaving Nanded, we celebrated the Ganesh festival with Sunil and Anil's families, cherishing the wonderful memories of our stay and the warmth of family.

On our way back, we spent about a week in Aurangabad with Shivnath. During that period, I underwent the recommended blood tests alongside an antigen test. Along with me, Raj, Shivnath's family, and Sujata also got their tests done. Everyone's test results arrived promptly except for mine, which raised concerns. Upon reaching out to the technician, I received startling news. He inquired if I had been unwell recently, and to my surprise, he revealed that I had contracted Covid during that period and it had already passed. The revelation left me stunned; I had experienced severe pain but hadn't realized it was Covid. Back then, the situation was so dire that hospitalization was the only option. Ignorance was bliss in this case, sparing me from unnecessary panic.

Following this episode, I noticed some changes in my health, including persistent weakness. I don't know the reason but in these many years my weight was constant, but in spite of my healthy lifestyle I have gained weight post Covid. Nevertheless, I continued to follow my daily routine and persevere through each day's challenges.

In November 2019, I had my first stent inserted in the ureter, an experience that required careful precautions and constant vigilance. As a result, I hesitated to participate in water sports or play in the sea, even during a family trip to Sindudurg while Prakash was stationed there as a Block Development Officer. Although my family enjoyed the water sports and beaches, I refrained due to the risk of infection posed by the stent.

However, my wish finally came true during our Goa trip in 2022. Brimming with courage and determination, I indulged in adventure sports like the Banana ride, water scooter, and even horse riding, all the while my trusty stent remained in place, reminding me that no obstacle was insurmountable.

In my journey through life, cancer and other serious ailments, as discussed earlier, were never going to be the victor, and I refused to let them dictate the terms of my existence. Even with the medical battles I've faced over the last thirty-three years, my adventurous spirit has remained unbroken. It's been the driving force behind my relentless pursuit of exploration and new experiences.

Another travel adventure appeared on the horizon, slated for June 2023, this time taking me to the vibrant city of Toronto in Canada.

Shona had triumphantly wrapped up her second Masters in Business Administration at Queen's University in Kingston, Ontario, before seamlessly transitioning into the role of an Associate at the Canadian Imperial Bank of Commerce (CIBC) in Toronto. With her convocation scheduled for June 23rd, 2023, I was resolute in my decision to be present and partake in the celebration of this significant milestone.

However, unlike my previous journeys, this one came with its own set of complications, as I currently had a ureteral stent in place. Navigating international travel with this added medical consideration required a thoughtful approach. Consulting with Dr. Venkat, we conscientiously considered and implemented all necessary precautions. Understanding the potential challenges of medical emergencies, particularly in countries like Canada and the US, as it can be exorbitant. I was keenly aware of the importance of avoiding any health-related concerns that could burden Shona and Raghav as they navigated their busy lives.

To add a layer of complexity, I had recently undergone an unexpected stent change in May, leaving minimal breathing room between these two medical occurrences. Despite this, my determination to not miss Shona's special day remained unwavering. Mindful of the potential risk of urinary tract infections (UTIs), I took extra precautions, particularly in terms of hygiene. The restroom stops during our journey became strategic, with the frequent use of toilet seat sanitizing spray - a necessity stemming from my high water intake aimed at infection prevention.

After enduring a six-hour layover at Munich Airport, lying down on the seats provided for a while. we proceeded to board the Air Canada flight destined for Toronto, a journey of approximately nine hours. Upon touchdown at Toronto Pearson Airport, Shona promptly messaged us, notifying that she and Raghav were on their way via the Pearson Express train and expected to arrive in about 20 minutes.

With nearly 28 hours of travel under our belts, fatigue had firmly settled in. Expressing my concerns to Raj about navigating the Immigration and Customs area on foot, I proposed an alternative plan: taking advantage of the buggy car service specifically designed for senior citizens, expectant mothers, and individuals with special needs. Fortunately, we found two available buggies, expertly operated by courteous Indian Punjabi women, who graciously chauffeured us to the Immigration and Customs area.

Shona and Raghav's warm welcome awaited as we claimed our luggage, the two embracing us tightly. Back home, they had crafted a thoughtful itinerary tailored to our interests - throughout our stay, Shona insisted on handling all expenses, gifting us this trip as an expression of her devotion.

Among the highlights was attending Shona's school graduation ceremony, a proud moment. I treasured visiting her workplace too - observing my dedicated daughter efficiently conducting her bank duties reminded me how far she had come.

Over the month-long journey, I almost forgot that I had undergone a stent procedure just a month prior. The demanding trip involved nearly an hour of walking to each destination, with breaks for me to catch my breath. Despite physical exhaustion, the pride in exploring meticulously planned places by our children outweighed weariness.

While these travels are etched in my memory, some viewed them as an uncalled-for indulgence. Despite suggestions to rest at home, the irony is that working rigorously raised fewer concerns. People who haven't experienced health issues are quick to pass judgment on what we should or should not do.

I have faced different types of adventures, and in these incidents, I had to be very alert. One such instance occurred when Raj had gone for a conference to the US in 2015. Shona and I made a trip to Aurangabad as it was her vacation during her undergraduate program in engineering college. After a good stay, when we were returning back to Mumbai, we alighted at Dadar station in Mumbai and were looking out for a cab. It was before dawn, so it was still dark outside. A young, decent-looking cab driver approached us. I thought that he spoke politely and practiced charging as per the meter reading, so we could go with him. He guided us to his cab, but as soon as we boarded the taxi and closed the door, a large, too bulky middle-aged man came and sat in the front seat beside the driver.

He showed me an Indian currency note of Rs. 1000 and asked me if I had change. I told him that I did have change and opened my wallet to retrieve it. However, during this short duration, he kept the note in my lap. My mental alarm bells started ringing because a decent person would wait for me to hand the change to him.

In response, I coolly asked him whether he knew Inspector Shriwastav (my husband, Raj). Immediately, he picked up the note and inquired about my identity. I calmly replied that I am Mrs. Shriwastav. He was taken aback and urged me to leave the cab, suggesting that they were involved in some illicit activities. Sensing something amiss, I decided to follow his advice and hailed another cab. I had heard many stories about such modus operandi from Raj's discussions with his team members and victims, which helped me handle this incident safely and efficiently.

When I narrated this incident to Raj, he informed me that this is a gang of taxi drivers who operate illegally, bypassing the proper queue and charging exorbitant fares. Another tactic involves distracting the passenger under the pretext of getting change for currency. They swiftly drop down a few notes while counting the money, claiming that the passenger didn't provide the exact amount. The passenger, in confusion, ends up handing them more money. This gang, known as the "Tha Gang," has been involved in several criminal cases, including a rape case. Some members of the gang had committed a gang rape against a lady passenger who alighted at Dadar station in the early hours. Under the guise of dropping her off at a hotel, they took her to a different location and sexually assaulted her until she went unconscious.

Another incident occurred when two men with intimidating physiques approached my neighbour for water. Unable to deny them due to her religious beliefs, she invited them into her home. They exited the elevator with a lot of noise, prompting me to peek out to see what was happening. I asked her if there was any issue, and she shook her head in negative, so I returned to my cooking.

Peering through my safety door every five minutes, I checked if she needed any help. After about twenty minutes, her cook came running to me and exclaimed, "God knows what has happened to ma'am; she has given a seven-tola gold chain to these two men. They put it in a glass from which they drank water and were holding it."

By now, I had come to the stark realization that my neighbours had fallen under the spell of these two imposing figures. Towering at almost six feet tall, their sturdy build exuded an air of intimidation that made me acutely aware of my own limitations. Physically confronting them, even with the aid of a maid, seemed futile.

Without a moment's hesitation, I swiftly pressed the intercom button, alerting the security personnel to the unfolding situation. Describing the gravity of the matter, I urged them to dispatch assistance, emphasizing the need for someone robust enough to assist in evicting the intruders.

In the midst of the chaos, the neighbour's cook rushed back to me, breathless, bearing news of my neighbour's peculiar behaviour and gave me the chain. My quick thinking and timely advice to the maid had proved instrumental in salvaging the situation and the recovery of the chain.

Amidst the commotion, the men's voices reverberated with obscenities, their thwarted attempt at looting the chain met with resolute defiance. As soon as the chain was back in my possession, I safeguarded it in the confines of my home, securing it away from their grasp.

Within a mere ten minutes, the security team materialized, their swift response a testament to the urgency of the situation. Led by the Chief Security Guard, they brought with them a formidable team, ready to take decisive action. With remarkable efficiency, they forcibly expelled the intruders, yet their resilience was palpable as they persisted, persistently ringing the doorbell in a desperate attempt to regain entry.

Refusing to yield to their menacing advances, I remained steadfast behind the safety of the door, unwavering in my resolve. Their vulgar tirades, aimed squarely at me, painted me as the villain of their failed scheme, but I remained resolute, unwilling to succumb to their intimidation tactics.

Indeed, the adage "all's well that ends well" echoed in the aftermath of this unsettling incident. It reiterated a valuable lesson — that in moments of crisis, maintaining composure and employing logical thinking can be the linchpin to deftly managing adversity. A steadfast belief in a higher power, an unwavering source of ideas and strength, further fortified my resolve during these trying situations.

My journey has been an unrelenting pursuit of pushing against the boundaries imposed by my own physical limitations. Each escapade, every instance of defying the odds, has shaped me into a voyager of life, charting a course guided by the whims of my heart.

Reflecting on these escapades, I do so with a sense of pride. Whether it was grappling with cancer, enduring the presence of a ureteral stent, undergoing multiple surgeries, managing diabetes, asthma, severe acidity, or battling low blood pressure, none of these adversities could confine me to a hospital bed or suppress my indomitable spirit. On the contrary, they became catalysts propelling me to embrace life in its entirety, proving that with unwavering determination, a penchant for adventure, and a sprinkle of courage, one can ascend above even the most formidable challenges.

CHAPTER THIRTY-FOUR

A Journey of Giving Back

When we look at various cultures of the world, it's easy to appreciate the beauty in the diversity. Among Asians the culture of being with your family and parents is not absurd. Among westerners the culture of becoming independent and moving out of your parents' home is equally commendable. Every culture is rooted in the practical wisdom of the ancestors who had laid out the norms for generations to follow.

Likewise, the Kandis and Shriwastavs may have been influenced by the norms established by their ancestors. These traditions, customs, and cultural practices have shaped our parents' outlook on life, which they, in turn, have passed down to us. As we carry these legacies forward and impart them to our children, the cycle of life perpetuates, preserving the rich heritage and wisdom of our ancestors.

I recall a time when I used to observe my parents, Amma and Anna, with a sense of wonder. Their kindness and compassion were qualities that I deeply admired. Today, alongside my husband Raj, I can't help but feel incredibly blessed. It seems that over time, we've imbibed the same spirit of kindness and compassion that radiated from Amma and Anna. For me, there's no greater source of joy than this realization.

Shona and Raghav have taken it a step further by adopting veganism and vegetarianism, respectively. They also actively work to reduce carbon emissions. Their commitment to philanthropy is also evident.

The instincts of being kind to one another, respecting individuals, and caring for those in need were ingrained in our psyche since childhood. We witnessed our parents embody these values, and now we see our children doing the same. So, the fact that kindness and compassion are family traits doesn't surprise me. It's something that seems to run in our blood, passed down through generations.

In my formative years, my role models extended beyond my immediate family, and among them stood the indomitable Mother Teresa.

So, during my time in ninth grade, when I had the opportunity to meet the indomitable Mother, I seized it. Mother Teresa was scheduled to visit our school. As a member of the girl guides, we were privileged to assist her in distributing clothes to orphans. Mother Teresa's soft-spoken and kind demeanour made a profound impact on me. During a group photograph with the orphans, she noticed my hesitation to join. In her gentle way, she encouraged me to step forward. Though the developed photograph didn't turn out as planned, her act of inclusivity remained etched in my memory. Her presence left an indelible mark on my heart. Mother Teresa became one of my most significant inspirations, alongside my parents, sparking a desire within me to contribute to the society.

The lessons learned at an early age can indeed have a profound impact on one's life, even decades later. After 33 years of battling Cancer, I found myself pondering if there was anything meaningful I could contribute to the society. I had never been one to withdraw and grieve in solitude. Throughout my journey, I remained an active part of the society, eager to contribute in every possible way.

In a way, Raj and I share a similar approach to life. We don't believe in succumbing to grief; instead, we choose to pick ourselves up and move forward, even in the face of pain and sorrow. Raj, in particular, has a habit of humming his favourite Bollywood song from time to time - "Duniya mein kitna gam hain, mera gham kitna kam hain. Logon ka gham dekha to, main apna gham bhool gaya," which loosely translates to - "There is so much sorrow in the world, how little is my sorrow. When I saw the sorrow of people, I forgot my own sorrow." This reflects our shared philosophy of embracing life with resilience and a focus on the broader challenges faced by humanity. The song truly encapsulates a universal truth — that amidst life's trials, our own burdens often pale in comparison to those endured by others.

I consider myself fortunate to have had the resources and opportunities that enabled me to overcome my health issues so far. Unfortunately, millions around the world lack access to proper treatment due to poverty and a lack of family support, resulting in preventable suffering and loss of life. Having personally gone through the ordeal, I feel a deep sense of responsibility to give back to the society in any ways that I can. It's a commitment rooted in empathy and the shared belief that collectively, we can make a difference in the lives of those facing adversities.

When Shona was a school-going kid, I came across an organization in the newspaper that focused on procuring kidneys for transplantation. Eager to be of assistance, I contacted them and expressed my willingness to contribute.

They invited me to attend a meeting, organized in a hospital reception area.

At the meeting, I encountered a diverse group of individuals from various walks of life – corporate employees, school teachers, and homemakers, all united by a common purpose. Despite my own health issues, they appreciated my commitment to helping. It was humbling to witness so many people united for such a noble cause.

During the meeting, I learned about the extensive waiting list of patients in India, some waiting for years to find a matching blood group for transplantation. Tragically, some had even passed away while waiting. The organization prioritized patients based on the severity of their condition and the recipient's situation.

We were briefed on ways to contribute, given brochures and booklets to spread awareness about kidney donation. Our task was to distribute these materials among people, attend awareness campaigns, and continue participating in their sessions.

I wholeheartedly attended various exhibitions and events where awareness campaigns were held, even though some were quite distant. Balancing this with Shona's schedule was challenging, but I persisted until the toll on my asthma became evident. Taking a necessary pause, The experience was fulfilling, knowing that I had made a positive impact on the lives of others.

I am also deeply passionate about supporting children with Type 1 diabetes, and I channel my commitment through regular donations to Udaan, a non-profit organization in Aurangabad.

While I acknowledge that I cannot cure diabetes, I strive to contribute by offering financial assistance to those in need. Another cause that holds a special place in my heart is caring for HIV-positive children. I actively contribute both financially and emotionally to an individual in Aurangabad who wholeheartedly provides medical care, education, and a loving home to these children.

The COVID-19 pandemic unleashed havoc worldwide, particularly affecting daily wage earners and the less fortunate. In response, we took it upon ourselves to provide essential food supplies to housemaids, security guards, sweepers, and dog walkers in our society. Additionally, we collaborated with Devesh Vajani, a friend renowned for his philanthropic work, to extend this assistance further to the needy in our area. Devesh, the father of popular TV actress Aneri Vajani, deserves a special mention, along with his wife Urmila and children—Aneri, Priya (currently in London for higher studies), and Rohan. Their tireless efforts in organizing various charitable activities throughout the year serve as an inspiration to all of us. This family's selfless acts of kindness have touched many lives, showcasing the power of unity in making a positive impact on the world. Hats off to the Vajani family for their unwavering commitment of serving others!

As the challenges of navigating the pandemic intensified, managing daily chores became increasingly difficult. Aware of my ailments, my dedicated maids expressed eagerness to come and help, having been with me for many years. Understanding their predicament and the importance of vaccinations, I made it a priority to ensure our domestic help received their COVID-19 vaccinations. Despite facing challenges in the vaccination process, we engaged with the authorities, and due to my health concerns, they were granted access to the vaccine. The gratitude and relief expressed by our domestic help upon receiving the vaccines were deeply fulfilling, reinforcing the significance of these efforts.

The festive spirit of Diwali brought a glimmer of hope to those who were financially struggling. In 2022, as restrictions eased, we, along with Devesh and his generous friends, distributed sarees and sweet boxes to housemaids, security guards, sweepers, drivers, dog walkers, and others in our society. The joy evident on their faces served as a clear reminder of the positive impact that small acts of kindness can have on individuals and communities alike.

In my daily life, I actively support elderly vendors, especially those with limited supplies. Purchasing vegetables from senior citizens and acquiring lamps from local artisans who produce handicrafts allows me to contribute to maintaining their dignity and livelihoods. It's my way of recognizing their skills and offering them the respect they rightfully deserve.

While recognizing the impact of significant contributions, I firmly believe that even small, responsible gestures can contribute to society's well-being. As an example, I have taken steps to minimize resource wastage. Installing a water-saving nozzle in my kitchen has reduced water consumption by an impressive 70%. Additionally, I've developed the habit of reusing water from washing vegetables and grains to nourish my plants, ensuring that not a drop goes to waste. The thriving condition of my plants is a testament to the positive impact of such mindful actions.

For nearly two decades, I've remained a steadfast donor to Help Age India, an organization dedicated to caring for and empowering disadvantaged elderly individuals in India. This commitment to charitable giving has been passed down to our daughter, who demonstrated excellence in collecting donations for HelpAge during her school years.

During her school years, Shona had a chance to consider a variety of clubs. While her peers opted for more leisurely options, Shona chose to join the Interact Club, dedicated to addressing social causes. Each week, she and her fellow members visited a construction site near the school to impart alphabet lessons to the children of construction workers at the mobile crèche. Through this club, Shona also had the opportunity to explore Baba Amte's Anandvan, a sanctuary for those affected by leprosy. There, she connected with individuals who had been rejected by their families but found refuge at Anandvan. These resilient individuals not only received treatment but were also provided with employment opportunities within the campus, transforming it into a self-sustaining ecosystem that met almost every survival need.

Shona's journey continued as she visited an old age home and orphanage managed by HelpAge India in Nagpur. She engaged in conversations with elderly individuals abandoned by their children and even taught dance to the orphanage residents. Those early encounters played a pivotal role in shaping Shona's character and contributing to her personal development.

The struggles of senior citizens seeking support at various road junctions deeply touch my heart. Their vulnerability, often stemming from abandonment by their own families, motivates me to assist them financially. I firmly believe that these individuals, reliant on the kindness of strangers, deserve our compassion and respect.

In my interactions with the world, whether it's a friend navigating a personal tragedy, a neighbour facing solitude in their twilight years, or various relatives and acquaintances, I am dedicated to providing support, even if it's just a listening ear. I make it a point to send a small encouraging message daily, even on my busy days, and intermittently call to check in on them.

Additionally, I extend my support to the Mouth and Foot Painting Artists Association of the World (MFPA) in any way I can. Although a for-profit organization, MFPA champions the artwork of specially-abled mouth and foot painting artists. I take pleasure in purchasing their paintings, appreciating the unique skills they bring to the world. By doing so, I hope to contribute to the economic well-being of these talented artisans, especially those from Adivasi communities.

During our daughter Shona's wedding, we made a conscious and meaningful choice by using a Warli painting created by a local artist as the backdrop for the stage. This decision was met with admiration from our guests, who recognized the significance of celebrating and supporting the artistry of marginalized communities and local artists.

In my life's journey, I have cultivated the belief that giving back to the society transcends mere financial contributions. It involves embracing responsibility in every facet of our lives and making mindful choices that not only enhance our own well-being but also positively impact the world around us.

When it comes to charitable donations, I adopt a discerning approach, directing my support towards temples that maintain transparency regarding the utilization of devotees' funds. This ensures that my contributions are channeled into noble endeavours benefiting society, animals, the environment, education, and healthcare.

I am particularly moved by the plight of children who aspire to receive an education but face financial constraints hindering their admission to decent schools. In an effort to assist them, I have dedicated my time to teaching the children of my local vendors and my maid for several years, without seeking any remunerations.

As a family, we share a deep love for animals and consider it a noble way to give back to the society while honouring the wonderful creations of God. Over the years, our home has been a haven for pets, from Brainy, our loyal dog in the early nineties, to Berry, our current canine companion who fills our lives with joy and affection. On special occasions like our Shona's wedding, we've opted to contribute to animal welfare NGOs and orphanages, inviting our guests to do the same rather than giving traditional gifts.

Conserving resources, particularly electricity, has been a conscientious effort in our household. The initiative taken by my daughter, Sonika, in excelling at environmental awareness significantly contributed to our reduced electricity consumption. As part of her school project, we adopted traditional methods of food preservation over refrigeration, minimized the use of electronic gadgets, and cut back on unnecessary power usage. The outcome was a remarkable 70% reduction in our electricity bill for that month, surprising even Sonika's teachers with this achievement over three consecutive months. This simple yet impactful approach aimed at reducing our carbon footprint became a meaningful way to contribute to the society.

I continue to advocate for responsible electricity usage wherever possible, emphasizing the importance of switching off unnecessary appliances like ACs, fans, and geysers when not in use. These small but essential steps reflect our ongoing commitment to building a sustainable future.

As surgery after surgery sliced into me, an epiphany took root - while necessity compelled each procedure, the choice was never mine. Yet, if fatal prognosis prevailed, healthy organs would remain within my depleted frame. Why not gift viability to others if mine expired?

In sharing this notion, my husband and I found accord. We took purposeful action, pledging our wholehearted commitment as organ donors upon any declaration of death. To the National Organ & Tissue Transplant Organisation we granted authorization over viable tissues - liver, kidneys, heart, lungs and more - so recipients might gain a second chance where ours concluded.

Statistics highlight the reach of this choice, noting each person can restore life of eight others. If my carefully preserved parts can offer someone else a real chance of survival, then the suffering of these years may yet yield sweetness in the end.

Reflecting on Sushmita Sen's words, spoken on the eve of International Women's Day, resonates deeply with me. She had once said - "Nothing in my life has been an act of charity. I say this with a hand on my heart. I don't believe in it. But I do believe, there's a responsibility that you are born with — to connect to another human being. I am very privileged that I got the platform to have such an abundant life so early in my life — I feel the more I do is less. Congratulations, ladies — the ones who have won tonight and the ones who had the courage to stand up and be who they are".

CHAPTER THIRTY-FIVE

A Bucket List Beyond Boundaries

Imagine you are standing in the middle of your room. The wall in front of you is mortality. The wall behind you is illusion. The walls around you are loneliness and perception. The floor underneath you is abyss and the roof above you is despair. And now imagine, being in the confines of a room all our lives. It just isn't fair. Perhaps, that's why I see myself as an outdoorsy person. I like the open field, the open road, the open sea and the open sky. This is why, I am still going around making my bucket list. Yes! My bucket list!!

It's not just a Wishlist; it's my rebel yell against life's constant curveballs. "This heart craves for more," it's my way of telling challenges, "Give it your best shot; I'm unstoppable," or, as we say back home, "Rok sake to rok lo" – "Stop me if you can."

These aren't whimsical daydreams on my list; they're my unwavering determination to grasp every fleeting moment, weaving a life adorned with vibrant experiences, unfazed by whatever hurdles attempt to block my way. Each item on this list? They're the chapters of my story, each one adding depth and colour to the narrative of my life.

At the summit of my bucket list stands a profound yearning – to unveil this book in May 2024, with Shona, my constant companion, by my side and her constant companion Raghav too. Picture it: not just a typical book launch, but an event etched in memories, resonating beyond the realms of a mere publication. My goal extends beyond the pages; I aspire for it to be a beacon of inspiration for countless individuals wrestling with ailments akin to mine. I want them to unearth the secrets of navigating their struggles, discovering resilience within. To amplify the impact, I dream of a renowned figure, a victor over similar tribulations, inaugurating the book, ensuring its message echoes far and wide.

Next on my list? Crafting a dream house, preferably an eco-friendly haven, in the heart of Aurangabad. This endeavour isn't merely a construction project; it's a sanctuary that promises profound benefits, especially for my health. Nestled amidst the homes of four of my siblings, it stands as a pillar of support during any crisis, a reciprocal arrangement where I can be there for them in times of need. Aurangabad, with its cluster of relatives who are seasoned doctors across diverse specialties, guarantees access to top-notch medical care whenever the need arises. The hidden gem of a smaller city lies in its unhurried pace, striking a balance between work and community, creating the perfect refuge for the golden years.

Sports, an integral part of my formative years, has been a lifeline, and my heart beats for basketball. Once a university captain and a shooter on the college courts, my dream now takes shape in the open expanse of my plot, where I envision a basketball court. Imagine the joy of playing with family and friends once again, and the added delight of passing on this love for the game to the younger generation in my family. It's not just about staying fit; it's about infusing life with the vibrant energy that basketball brings. Despite my ailments momentarily sidelining my post-marriage playing days, I'm gearing up for a triumphant comeback.

Hockey, another sport where I once excelled during my university days, holds a special place in my heart. The plan? To continue playing, using that same court. And why stop there? I intend to repurpose it for badminton as well. It's not just about scoring goals or hitting shuttlecocks; sports, in its subtle way, teaches us to tackle failures, to bounce back stronger.

To add a touch of enchantment to my plot, envision a beautiful gazebo gracing the landscape, right beside the basketball court. Picture this: an open-sided structure surrounded by a lush garden or yard, a haven where I can soak in the beauty of my surroundings. From here, I can watch the laughter and play of children from both our families in the sprawling open area. Beyond being a mere architectural addition, I see the gazebo as a venue for hosting family parties, a space destined to cradle countless cherished memories.

And if my affinity for adventure and nature hasn't shone through yet, let me make it clear – it's a deep-seated part of who I am. Aurangabad, with its hills and historic monuments, beckons me to embark on regular treks, exploring the uncharted territories that this city holds. Each step, a communion with nature; each trek, a journey into the heart of the unknown.

From Bollywood dance performances at family weddings to a burning desire to master the art of belly dancing, my journey in the world of dance takes an exotic turn. Belly dancing, with its undulating belly movements and rapid hip gyrations, calls out to me, despite the uncertainty posed by the stent in my ureter. Determination fuels my steps as I take on the challenge, ensuring all necessary precautions are in place. After all, the goal is to explore every fitness avenue available, pushing the boundaries of what's possible.

Shifting gears from dance to visual storytelling, photography becomes my next frontier. In an age where we all consider ourselves photographers with our smartphones, my aim is to elevate this skill to a technical proficiency. As my bucket list is brimming with activities linked to the environment, capturing those moments through the lens of a skillful photographer becomes paramount. The dream? To acquire an advanced camera, a tool that will breathe life into the moments I wish to preserve.

My dedication to serving society and the environment is a flame that refuses to be extinguished by age or time. It's a commitment that resonates deep within me, urging me to persist in aiding those in need and championing the cause of environmental protection.

In my pursuit of overall well-being, a new horizon emerges — the art of Tai Chi. This ancient Chinese practice, a harmonious blend of movement, breath, and mindfulness, becomes my next endeavour to nurture wellness. As the sands of time accumulate and health challenges weave through my journey, I firmly believe that embracing Tai Chi can be a beacon, guiding me towards fitness and a stress-free existence. It's not just an exercise; it's a mindful dance with time, a commitment to health that transcends the limitations posed by age and ailments.

Last on my bucket list, but certainly not least, is a journey into the world of Somatics. As I navigate through the life, discomfort often arises in various corners of my body or organs. Somatics, a field nestled within bodywork and movement studies, catches my attention. It's a discipline that places a premium on internal physical perception and experience – a profound way to unravel the mysteries of the body from within.

While my trusty Apple Watch dutifully provides valuable signals, aiding in the diagnosis of issues, it falls short in addressing the disorders themselves. Thus, my aspiration to dive into the realm of Somatics takes root, a conscious step towards understanding and nurturing my body for better health benefits. It's not just about external indicators; it's about fostering an internal dialogue with my body, a holistic approach to well-being that extends beyond mere diagnosis to the realm of active, personalized care.

To some, it might seem whimsical that I'm still penning down bucket lists, but I prefer to see life as an ongoing ode. It's my way of defiantly whispering to Cancer and the other ailments that persistently knock on my door – "I'm not done living yet." When the final curtain call beckons, I want to step into the darkness with an unwavering conviction that mine wasn't a tale of unrequited love. I want to believe that I loved life fiercely, and in return, life showered its love upon me.

My Wishlist has been the driving force that keeps me going, while accolades serve as a source of inspiration, propelling me forward to carry out the items on my Wishlist. It's a harmonious relationship that fuels my journey.

Post-Covid, I crossed paths with Raj's friend Kripa, whose admiration for my spirit and resilience echoed in her words. She lauded my participation in an event despite the myriad health issues I faced and conveyed her admiration to Raj. Her heartfelt message resonates: "She is one heck of a brave woman, and very graceful at the same time... Hugs to your wifey for holding up strong in these terrible times... Covid times." In those words, a recognition of strength and grace emerged, a testament to the indomitable spirit that strives to shine even in the midst of adversity.

A close relative, privy to the intricate details of my journey, once expressed, "You are the one who's shouldering everything with grace. If I were in your shoes, I might have gone away a long time ago."

Proudly, from time to time, I display my "medals" – the scars of surgeries and the visible imprints of my battles with various ailments. These tangible symbols, more than mere reminders of personal struggles, serve as beacons of hope for others. Many have remarked that I am a warrior who triumphed over cancer and other surgeries through sheer willpower. In those moments of acknowledgment, my journey transforms into a source of inspiration for others facing their own trials.

My unwavering priority has always been crystal clear: to lead a disciplined and healthy lifestyle that not only inspires my family and friends but also prompts the occasional scolding and teasing when they falter. This relentless pursuit of both physical and mental well-being has yielded substantial benefits, aligning with the timeless wisdom of Hippocrates: "Let food be thy medicine." My dedication to maintaining a healthy diet recently bore fruit during a routine eye check-up. Despite the onset of cataracts, my ophthalmologist confirmed that my eyes remained untouched by diabetes. The joy that surged within me was a testament to the rewards reaped from my steadfast commitment to health.

I am firmly convinced that every individual harbors the inner strength to confront their ailments. Yet, they must embark on their unique journey, seeking inspiration from fellow patients who have triumphed over similar challenges through sheer willpower. In this shared resilience lies the potential for hope and the transformative power of one's own journey towards well-being.

After my battle with cancer, I found myself experiencing a newfound innocence in many aspects of life. However, a subtle shift occurred within me, fostering a determination not to burden Raj with my health issues. This resolve was fueled by a deep-seated desire not to impede his aspirations and ambitions. Aware of the challenges he faced in his childhood due to his father's early demise, I was steadfast in my decision not to add to his burdens. To this day, Raj remains blissfully unaware of the intricate details of my medications, their dosages, the timing of each pill, my appointments, and doctors' advice. I've navigated this terrain independently.

This same sentiment extended to our daughter, Shona, when she entered our lives. I made a commitment to ensure that she received every ounce of love and care she deserved as our daughter, and I've never wavered on that front. Her upbringing has been a top priority for me, and I take immense pride in the remarkable young woman she has become – constantly pursuing her dreams with unwavering determination.

CHAPTER THIRTY-SIX

Finding Solace in Stories

Susan Sontag, born in New York City in 1933, was a prolific writer exploring literature, art, photography, politics, and illness. In 1975, diagnosed with breast cancer, she underwent a mastectomy and chemotherapy, inspiring her influential work, "Illness as Metaphor," reshaping societal perspectives on disease.

Sontag's openness about her battle became an example of vulnerability, finding solace in sharing struggles. Her wisdom inspired many, including me, to embrace openness in navigating challenges, particularly illness.

During my second pilgrimage to Vaishno Devi, a vivid incident etched itself into memory. After a taxing three-hour uphill pony ride, the pony paused for respite, and I sought solace on a bench. Beside me, two ladies were engrossed in a conversation about cancer, fraught with misconceptions and fear. Driven by the impulse to enlighten, I disclosed my status as a cancer patient, hoping to dispel their misunderstandings. To my surprise, they promptly distanced themselves, as if I bore a contagious affliction. In that moment, Susan Sontag's analogy of cancer to tuberculosis rang eerily true.

Once, Raj introduced me to a former law enforcement colleague in the final stages of cancer. Raj, sensing the need for guidance, entrusted me with the task of counseling this fellow cancer warrior. Our meeting unfolded into a two-hour conversation, filled with words of encouragement and a shared sense of understanding. As he left, a newfound hope seemed to accompany him, a belief in the potential reversal of his condition taking root.

Perhaps that is why those struggling with medical ailments seek fellow warriors, to connect with and share an unspoken understanding.

Amidst the challenging days in Mumbai, where the specter of loneliness often loomed, Aurangabad emerged as a sanctuary. Here, the warmth of family and the presence of childhood and college friends became the silver lining, offering some of the best days of my life. Treks, bike rides, picnics, and simple gatherings for the most mundane reasons created an aura of cherished moments.

Throughout my journey with cancer, I've encountered a diverse spectrum of individuals. Some, despite never walking a similar path, radiated empathy, offering unwavering support. On the flip side, I've faced a level of ruthlessness that cut deep. The journey, marked by these contrasting encounters, served as a stark reminder of the fragility of empathy and the resilience needed to navigate the maze of human relationships in the face of adversity.

The cruelty of harsh words never ceases to amaze me. I remind myself that nobody desires health problems, yet these negative comments can momentarily plunge me into a bout of depression. Remarkably, by the next day, my resilience surfaces again, and I reclaim my vigour, returning to my usual self while intensifying my commitment to health.

Adapting to my surroundings became a gradual process. Inevitably, when people meet me, the first question invariably centers around my health. With a chuckle, I share the ongoing saga of my health, emphasizing that it's an integral part of my life that I've learned not just to endure but to savour. Swiftly redirecting the conversation towards more enjoyable topics, I ensure we all relish the present moment.

I distinctly remember the conversation with a family friend named Nina, who faced a breast cancer diagnosis. Inquisitively, she would often ask, "Rekha, will I be like you, fit and fine after treatment?" The question lingered, weaving a silent thread connecting our shared experiences, bridging the gap between diagnosis and the hope for a vibrant, post-treatment life. I consistently offered an affirmative nod, assuring her that brighter days were on the horizon. My own plethora of surgeries and health challenges remained veiled, and I consciously refrained from casting a shadow of negativity in her presence or around her children. Becoming her steadfast support system during those testing times, Nina eventually passed away, leaving behind the enduring image of her hopeful and joyful face in my memory.

Two decades later, another friend found herself navigating a similar ordeal. This time, however, the landscape of cancer research and treatment had undergone significant transformations. Despite grappling with advanced-stage cancer, she reached out to me, engulfed in weakness and depression. My emphasis was on optimism, punctual medication, regular check-ups, a commitment to yoga and fitness, and the maintenance of a healthy lifestyle. Today, thanks to the advances in cancer care and, perhaps, a touch of providence, she stands tall – perfectly fit and healthy. The evolution of medical science, coupled with the resilience of the human spirit, manifested in a narrative that defied the odds and celebrated the triumph of hope and well-being.

Where I've had the privilege of counseling individuals from diverse walks of life, there's one person whom I admired profoundly – Mummy, Raj's mom. From the moment I became her daughter-in-law, a unique bond seemed to weave itself between us. She was a pragmatic, down-to-earth woman who had weathered immense struggles after becoming a widow, shouldering the responsibility of a family of six on a meager income. I vividly recall the day she declared, "Rekha, I'm retiring, and now that you all are well-settled, I'm going to enjoy life."

After her retirement she intermittently came to stay with us. Embracing her newfound freedom, she reveled in long walks through our society's garden, found joy in the simple pleasures of television, and engaged in heartfelt conversations with all of us – luxuries that had been beyond her reach until then. She witnessed Shona's dedication to her studies and extracurricular activities, encouraging us to nurture her dreams, for Shona, to become an IPS officer. Mummy's journey was a testament to resilience, the pursuit of joy, and the enduring power of familial support.

Tragically, cancer cast its shadow upon Mummy as well, and by the time we unearthed it, it had stealthily advanced to its later stages. Undeterred, she refused to surrender to the relentless adversary, fighting with every ounce of strength until the last minute. Our collective efforts to support her were exhaustive, yet the outcome lay ultimately in the hands of a higher force, beyond our control.

Throughout my 33-year battle, my family has remained my unwavering pillar of support, though the depth of support required by patients like me is truly immeasurable. Dealing with this trauma brought forth emotional and physical exhaustion, a relentless struggle that often left me feeling drained.

I recall countless moments when I found myself alone at home, grappling with my ailments as Shona and Raj were out throughout the day, returning late in the evening. Coupled with bronchial asthma, sleepless nights became a frequent companion, adding to the weight of my challenges. There was even a time when I was naive enough to believe that I would go bald after my cancer surgery, oblivious to the fact that hair loss only occurs during chemotherapy. The mere thought of losing my hair weighed heavily on my mind, causing undue stress and anxiety.

Add to it the regular undergoing of annual MRIs, necessitated by a cyst in my head that requires regular monitoring. On the operation table and during various painful tests, the initial stress was palpable.

However, I swiftly turned to meditation and prayer, immersing myself in an imaginary dream world that kept my spirits soaring. At my core, I am a dreamer and a builder of castles. The dream of being completely free from physiological and biological disorders has been my driving force, sustaining me for a significant duration. Some might label my optimism as irrational, but this radiant outlook brings a glow to my life and has undeniably aided me in not only surviving but also achieving numerous goals.

Initially, many of my distressing experiences were harboured within me, undisclosed even to my close ones. However, as

I recognized the empathy of some relatives and friends over the years, I began to share these experiences, fortifying my resolve in handling emotional, physical, or physiological challenges.

In the early post-cancer years, the chronic lack of sleep led to mood swings and irritability, challenges that Raj struggled to comprehend. Shona, unfortunately, bore the brunt of it. Recently, when I broached this topic with Shona, expressing guilt over the past, her response was incredibly reassuring: "Chill, Mom. I'm doing well in life, and you've put in so much effort in raising me." Her words filled me with pride and relief, knowing she had inherited the same resilience. May God bless her with boundless happiness in life.

Despite my physical limitations, particularly in my hands and legs, I adamantly refused to hold back. From early mornings to late nights, I diligently managed every task, often navigating through weariness during Raj's late-night returns in his police service years. Yet, no task was left undone.

In 2010, I consulted a renowned Reiki Master about my surgeries and ailments. He humorously noted," Aap ne to puri dukaan khol kar rakh de "(You've opened a whole shop) but acknowledged, "Your willpower is incredibly strong." These encounters motivated me, and I openly express myself to close ones and individuals like this Reiki Guru. Staying quiet doesn't mean I have nothing to say; it means I believe you may not be ready to hear my thoughts.

Believing in nurturing the spirit through body nourishment, I see life as an invaluable gift, offering a second chance to appreciate and enjoy it fully. Healthy habits transform life's game, and practices like yoga and an evolved herb garden contribute to proactive health measures.

Monitoring blood pressure and sugar levels, organizing medicines scrupulously, and maintaining a well-equipped travel kit are part of my routine, extended to my family. I advocate not restraining oneself due to the fear of illness, emphasizing the importance of self-care.

Never missing a dose, I view medication acceptance as a necessity for survival, choosing not to burden my family. Trusting in the power of kindness, valuing true empathy, and brushing aside negativity, I prioritize what truly matters, believing that agreements yield better results than arguments.

Many of my friends have bestowed upon me the title of a cancer warrior, but to me, I simply see myself as a believer in the beauty of life.

Life, despite its obstacles, is an extraordinary gift from a higher power. Yes, it comes with its fair share of challenges, but with unwavering persistence and a determination to overcome, we often find that God extends a helping hand. It is through the crucible of cancer's trials and tribulations that I've come to fully appreciate the present moment I had yearned for so long. This journey has gifted me the invaluable treasure of gratitude. Therefore, I choose not to denounce it but to wholeheartedly embrace life, with open arms, an open heart, and an ever-smiling face.

CHAPTER THIRTY-SEVEN

Dancing with Life

In the rollercoaster ride of my life, filled with years of challenges and stressful days, I found solace in diverse pursuits. Over 33 years, I persevered, drawing strength from the resilience instilled in me since childhood. My driving force was always the commitment to being at everything I set out to do. Even in tumultuous seasons, through pain and storm-battered days, I found within the fortitude to press onward.

Often when I look back at the milestones on my life's journey, I feel content with the realization that even in the face of adversity, life continued to be abundant with opportunities to thrive. This has led me to form a steadfast belief that regardless of obstacles, we can always strive for something meaningful in life.

Here is the list of my accomplishments:

- Basketball University Captain
- Hockey University Player
- Table Tennis Player
- School Vice President
- Yoga Practitioner
- Tridha (Teachers Training Course)
- Montessori (Teachers Training Course)
- Tutor

- Computer Institute Head
- Nutritionist
- General Counselor
- Voice Over Artist

Before stepping into the adventure of married life, I embarked on a distinct journey – the pursuit of education. My student years formed a fertile ground where achievements blossomed, and challenges sculpted my character. In this narrative, I extend an invitation for you to delve into that formative chapter, the bedrock upon which the rest of my story stands.

Sports played a pivotal role in shaping who I am today, imparting lessons of perseverance, fair play, mental fortitude, time management, respect for others, teamwork, and discipline. Grateful that I immersed myself in it early in life, as these qualities proved indispensable in later stages and continue to be an ongoing process.

My foray into basketball began in school in 1978, continuing until my marriage to Raj in 1990. It became a sanctuary for me, offering not just an outlet but also contributing to my fitness and positive energy during darker phases of life. This journey took me to places like Chennai, Bansthali in Rajasthan, and Anand in Gujarat, where I engaged with formidable teams. The wins and losses became invaluable life-skill building experiences.

Hockey was another passion where I found proficiency. As a hockey university player, I participated in intriguing matches in Aurangabad, competing against teams from neighboring divisions across Maharashtra. If circumstances allowed, I would have continued playing both games.

Table tennis, an indoor pursuit from my school days, remains an enjoyable but average skill of mine. Recognizing my all-round qualities – as a skilled player, disciplined student, inclusive and humble individual – I was elected as the School Vice President in 1981. This role provided invaluable lessons in leadership, laying the foundation for the qualities essential in life.

Yoga entered my life in 2001 as a response to developing allergies triggered by dust and pollen. Initially adopted for health reasons, it swiftly transformed into a cherished hobby. The joy I found in it deepened with time, and I immersed myself, refining my skills under various yoga acharyas. With the onset of the Covid era, I transitioned to online yoga classes, maintaining a dedicated practice for 23 years. Missing a session feels like something vital is absent. Even with a ureteral stent for five years and nine surgeries behind me, my body persists in seeking stillness and strength. Devoting two and a half hours daily to yoga and meditation, I continue to demonstrate that a resilient spirit can flourish even in the shadows of challenges.

Marriage and illness delineated two significant chapters in my journey, each leaving an indelible mark and sparking unique achievements. Now, let me unfold the triumphs that bloomed within the embrace of family and the profound self-discovery forged in the crucible of illness.

Serendipity played its role in the year 2005 when I crossed paths with a lady residing in our society. Our conversations were always enjoyable, and during one such interaction, she introduced me to a unique teacher training course offered by a school called Tridha.

Tridha follows the international Rudolf Steiner (Waldorf) Education System, emphasizing the enlivenment of not only thinking but also feeling, physical, social, artistic, and spiritual capacities. This system aims to empower individuals to imbue their lives with meaning and purpose while creatively fulfilling their unique potential.

Intrigued by this approach, I enrolled in the teacher training course and became deeply involved in the teaching method. I not only learned but also imparted some of the teachings to Shona. Despite the challenges of managing medications, household responsibilities, and Shona's schedule, I eagerly looked forward to each session. The course provided refreshing insights into a different way of thinking and developing young adults ready to face the world.

In 1992, our move to the Marol police quarters brought about a significant change. Unlike my upbringing surrounded by a large extended family, it was now just Raj and me. Loneliness began to seep in, prompting me to utilize my time qualitatively. Learning about a Distance Montessori Teachers Training course, I embarked on another educational endeavour.

Montessori education, based on self-directed activity, hands-on learning, and collaborative play, became the focus of my distance learning course. Due to health constraints, I couldn't join a school, but I incorporated these practices as a tutor for my students and for Shona's benefit as well.

Amidst Raj's long duty hours, I found myself alone at home in the police quarters. It wasn't long before the word spread in the neighbourhood about my education, and soon a lady approached me seeking private tuition for her daughter. She shared her concern about being a working mother, leaving her daughter in the care of maids, and how it had made the girl timid and introverted. I immediately connected with her, recalling my own childhood experiences.

Determined to make a positive impact, I committed to doing my best for her daughter. By the second day, my tuition began, and within a week, more students joined. In no time, I had a complete batch of students. The transformation in my first student was evident from the second month onwards. She started communicating with me openly, and her academic performance saw a remarkable improvement. The joy on her mother's face was palpable.

This endeavour blossomed into a close-knit family of students, each showing improvement in their overall performance. Unfortunately, this had to be discontinued when we moved from the police quarters.

In 2008, an opportunity arose for me to head a computer institute. Leveraging the skills I had honed over the years, I found enjoyment in this new role. However, a domestic challenge emerged when my maid had to urgently visit her hometown. Juggling household chores, office responsibilities, and late-night hours made it one of the toughest periods to handle. Yet, once again, I can proudly say that I achieved a lot from this experience.

Embarking on the journey of becoming a nutritionist opened my eyes to the myriad benefits of healthy eating. It also made me realize that many fundamental concepts of healthy living were already ingrained in our traditional Indian diet. The key, I discovered, lies in practicing portion control, understanding when to consume specific foods, and tailoring dietary needs to each individual.

Armed with this newfound knowledge, I shared interesting facts with my close ones, sparking a positive transformation in our eating and cooking habits. Beyond my immediate circle, I extended my passion for nutrition to counsel various individuals on nutrition issues and promote healthy eating habits.

My commitment to nutrition wasn't confined to my own plate; it spilled onto the plates of my family, friends, and even clients. Meticulously crafted diet charts became seeds of change, blossoming into weight loss triumphs and helping overcome health challenges for those I cared about.

Counsellors collaborate with individuals navigating a spectrum of emotional and psychological challenges, aiding them in effecting positive changes to enhance overall well-being and relationships. My decision to undergo counseling training stemmed from a general curiosity about human psychology and a desire to assist children lacking familial support. Subsequently, I enrolled in a day school operated by a Non-Profit Organization (NGO) to apply my newfound knowledge. Witnessing the incredible expressions and intelligence of these children reaffirmed my belief that, with the right opportunities, they could achieve great heights. Counseling not only allowed me to understand the intricacies of human psychology but also enabled me to make a positive impact on the lives of those in need.

My foray into voice-over artistry was serendipitous. Inspired by Raj's interest, I decided to give it a try, leading to a completely new and fascinating experience. Surprisingly, I excelled at it, lending my voice to radio programs, including one focused on cancer awareness. Delivering my thoughts on overcoming cancer, especially on my birthday, felt like a special gift. The positive reception and appreciation from listeners highlighted the impact of sharing my story and advice.

Overcoming a childhood fear of swimming lingered in the recesses of my mind, but with Shona pursuing her studies in the US, my focus shifted. I decided to face my fear, and under the guidance of my home coach, Raj, I can proudly say that I am now a swimmer. This journey, initiated later in life, serves as a testament to the idea that it's never too late to conquer fears and learn new skills.

My myriad transformations from educator to nutritionist, counselor to voice-over artist, resonate with the ever-shifting nature of reality. In the vast landscape of quantum possibilities and life's infinite avenues, every observation births a new reality, shaping us into distinct versions of ourselves. As we navigate this ever-evolving journey of self-discovery and growth, let us remember that our limitations are often defined by where we choose to draw the lines.

CHAPTER THIRTY-EIGHT

Beyond the Scars

Woven over thirty-three years are threads of survival, resilience, and triumph. Each surgery, each stitch, encapsulates my journey, where scars are not merely wounds healed but an ode to a spirit that adamantly refused to yield. Amidst the myriad surgeries, I discovered strength, resilience, and an unwavering will to thrive.

To be precise, I have consumed 84,207 tablets in my journey through ailments. As far as I remember, I never skipped the tablets, except on occasions like when I had taken Raj from the Army hospital to Mangan Hospital and eventually to Manipal Hospital in Sikkim for treatment. I am always extra cautious, but on a few occasions, in a rush or hurry, I consumed extra doses for which I experienced immediate side effects. However, with the help of doctors in my family, I could timely manage the crisis.

Likewise, I consumed innumerable homeopathy pills on this journey. As we all know, the quantum (number) of pills is quite high as compared to allopathy tablets. Hence, I have not gotten into counting the same but leave it to the readers.

In addition to this, I had also taken Ayurvedic treatment for some time. Again, I will not get into the calculation of how many liters of Kada and allopathy syrup or liquids I have consumed till date.

Here is a chronological account of the surgeries that have sculpted my path:

- 1991: A Battle Begins

    - Diagnosis: Papillary Carcinoma of thyroid, Metastatic in Lymph Node
    - Surgery: Thyroidectomy
    - Treatment: Radioactive iodine therapy (1991, 1993)

- 2001: Uncharted Territories

    - Left breast axillary surgery
    - Diagnosis: Bronchial asthma

- 2003: Confronting Adversity

    - Left sector Mastectomy

- 2004: Unexpected Challenges

    - Diagnosis: Cyst in the brain

- 2008: New Struggles Emerge

    - Diagnosis: Diabetes Mellitus

- 2009: A Twist in the Tale

    - Diagnosis: Fibroadenoma breast
    - Surgery: Lumpectomy

- 2011: Navigating Complex Paths

    - Surgery: Bilateral breast Lumpectomy

- 2015: A Chapter Closes

    - Diagnosis: Bilateral Fibronodular Ties
    - Surgery: Right breast mastectomy

- 2016: An Unexpected Hurdle

  – Diagnosis: Synovial Sac rupture

- 2017: A Multifaceted Challenge

  – Surgeries: Hysterectomy, Appendectomy, Oophorectomy, Lymphadenectomy

- 2019-2023: An Unyielding Journey

  – November 2019: Cystoscopy + Right-sided retrograde Pyelography + URS + Right DJ stenting
  – February 2020: Cystoscopy + Right-sided retrograde Pyelography + URS + Right DJ Stent change
  – May 2020: Ureteral stent change (DJ stent in Situ), no cystoscopy or other procedure due to Covid
  – November 2020: Cystoscopy + RT RGP + RT URS + Balloon Endo Dilation + RT DJ stent change
  – April 2021: Cystoscopy + RT RGP + RT DJ stent change (second phase of Covid)
  – September 2021: Cystoscopy + RT DJ stent change
  – March 2022: Cystoscopy + RT DJ stent change
  – August 2022: Cystoscopy + RT RGP + DJ stent change (silicon)
  – May 2023: Cystoscopy + RT RGP + URS + DJ stent change (silicon)

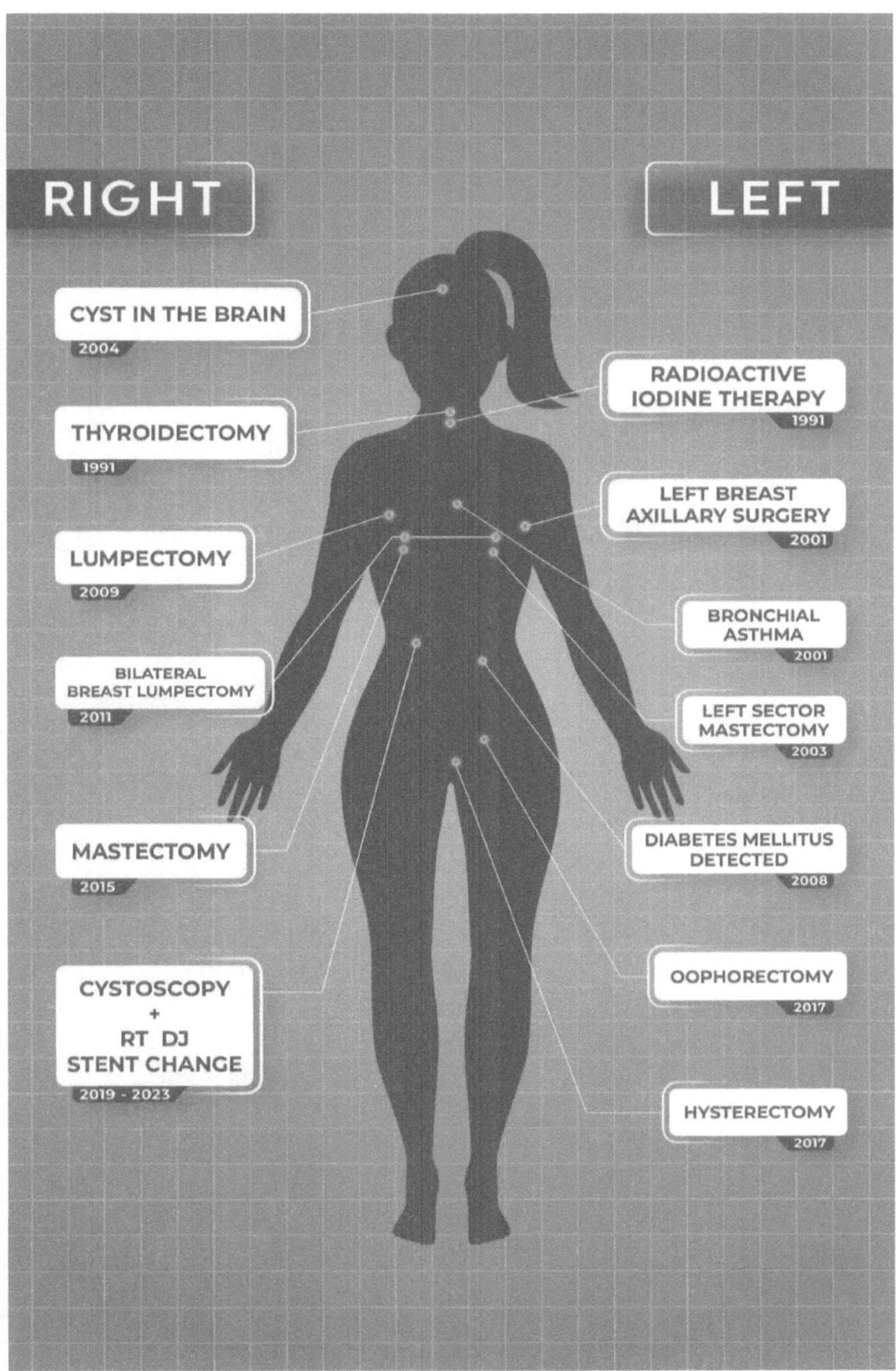

RIGHT
LEFT
CYST IN THE BRAIN
2004
RADIOACTIVE
IODINE THERAPY
1991
THYROIDECTOMY
1991
LEFT BREAST
AXILLARY SURGERY
2001
LUMPECTOMY
2009
BRONCHIAL
ASTHMA
2001
BILATERAL
BREAST LUMPECTOMY
2011
LEFT SECTOR
MASTECTOMY
2003
MASTECTOMY
2015
DIABETES MELLITUS
DETECTED
2008
CYSTOSCOPY
+
RT DJ
STENT CHANGE
2019 - 2023
OOPHORECTOMY
2017
HYSTERECTOMY
2017

Decoding the Medical Odyssey

1. Papillary Carcinoma of Thyroid: A type of thyroid cancer that originates in the follicular cells of the thyroid gland.
2. Metastatic Lymphnode: The spread of cancer from the original (primary) tumor to nearby or distant lymph nodes.
3. Thyroidectomy: Surgical removal of the thyroid gland, commonly performed in cases of thyroid cancer.
4. Radioactive Iodine Therapy: Treatment that uses radioactive iodine to destroy thyroid cells, commonly employed after thyroidectomy.
5. Left Breast Axillary Surgery: Surgical procedures involving the left breast and the axillary (armpit) region.
6. Bronchial Asthma: Chronic respiratory condition characterized by inflammation and narrowing of the airways.
7. Left Sector Mastectomy: Surgical removal of a portion (sector) of the left breast.
8. Cyst in the Brain: An abnormal sac or pocket filled with fluid within the brain.
9. Diabetes Mellitus: A group of metabolic disorders characterized by high blood sugar levels, often requiring lifelong management.
10. Fibroadenoma Breast: A non-cancerous breast tumor composed of fibrous and glandular tissue.
11. Bilateral Breast Lumpectomy: Surgical removal of abnormal tissue from both breasts while preserving breast tissue.

12. Bilateral Fibronodular Ties: Presence of fibrous and nodular tissue in both breasts.
13. Synovial Sac Rupture: The tearing or damage of the synovial sac, a fluid-filled structure that cushions joints.
14. Hysterectomy: Surgical removal of the uterus.
15. Appendectomy: Surgical removal of the appendix.
16. Oophorectomy: Surgical removal of one or both ovaries.
17. Lymphadenectomy: Surgical removal of lymph nodes, often performed to assess cancer spread.
18. Cystoscopy: A procedure using a thin tube with a camera to examine the bladder and urethra.
19. Retrograde Pyelography (RGP): A diagnostic procedure involving the injection of contrast dye into the ureters to visualize the urinary tract.
20. URS (Ureteroscopy): Endoscopic examination of the ureter, often used for stone removal.
21. DJ Stent: Double-J stent, a short tube inserted into the ureter to ensure urine drainage from the kidney.
22. Balloon Endodilation: A procedure using a balloon to widen narrowed or blocked areas in the urinary tract.
23. Silicon DJ Stent: A double-J stent made of silicone, commonly used for long-term urinary tract support.

Acknowledgements

First and foremost, I want to thank God profusely for cradling and nurturing me throughout my highs and lows.

Next up is my family

I thank my husband Raj for being my partner in crime for my hospital trotting and myriad journeys.

My daughter Shona for giving me some of the best memories in life and also my finest critic.

My son-in-law Raghav, for giving all the support and strength wherever needed

My parents Anna and Amma and Mummy (my mother-in-law), for giving me the wings to fly.

My deepest appreciation goes to my medical team.

- Dr. Deepak Parikh, my guiding light throughout my cancer recovery journey.
- Dr Archana Juneja, for guiding me through my multifarious queries in our journey of this decade.
- Dr Jagdish Kandi and Late Dr Shanta kandi for being my second parents in my existence from the time Cancer said go.
- Dr Venkat Gite and Dr Anita Kandi Gite for making me member of their fan club for the dedication they have put in my journey through these past years.
- Dr Subhash Dhawale for the holistic approach he took in curing my ailments and guiding me through these years .

- Dr Parag Paluskar for being my guiding spirit in the last decade.
- Dr Sunanda Kandi for being my Mentor and answering my inquisitive queries from the time I was sent to the Kandi family.
- Dr Anjali Vare for being available at the beck of my call and providing me prompt guidance, for taking timely action in my problems.
- Dr Supriya Kandi for her unwavering support through my health journey.

I am indebted to my sister Sujata for always being gentle and understanding me.

Mr. Rajesh Athaide, for his foreword, his words have truly captured the essence of my journey and for that, I am eternally grateful.

Sumona, for the foreword that so eloquently prefaced my story, her pen has my deepest appreciation.

Aneri, in scripting a foreword, she has lent a voice to my narrative that resonates with clarity and warmth - Thank you.

I am grateful to Parinita and Namrata for giving me inputs and guiding me through these recent times.

I am grateful to Srivinay Salian, my editor, for his invaluable suggestions and insights that have enhanced the clarity and quality of this book. I also thank Rohini Tribhuvan, my co-editor, for her meticulous editing and proofreading of my manuscript.

Finally, my thanks to the Digi-MaG team, led by Moaaz Syed, for their efforts in creating visibility and promoting this book.